LONDON'S MAYOR AT 20

LONDON'S MAYOR AT 20

GOVERNING A GLOBAL CITY IN THE 21ST CENTURY

EDITED BY
JACK BROWN, TONY TRAVERS
AND RICHARD BROWN

Biteback Publishing

First published in Great Britain in 2020 by
Biteback Publishing Ltd, London
Selection and editorial apparatus copyright © Jack Brown, Tony Travers and Richard Brown 2020

ISBN 978-1-78590-635-0

10 9 8 7 6 5 4 3 2 1

A CIP catalogue record for this book is available from the British Library.

Set in Minion Pro and Gotham

Printed and bound in Great Britain by
CPI Group (UK) Ltd, Croydon CR0 4YY

MIX
Paper from
responsible sources
FSC® C020471

Centre for London and Professor Tony Travers would like to extend our thanks to this project's sponsors, without whom this book would not have been possible: Argent LLP; Gensler; Gerald Eve LLP; Herbert Smith Freehills; Landsec; London Communications Agency; Stanhope PLC; and the project's academic partner, the School of Politics and Economics, King's College London.

CONTENTS

NOTES ON CONTRIBUTORS

Patricia Brown is director of Central, providing strategic advice to civic and business leaders on urban change. She has over twenty-five years of experience thinking about, influencing and improving London. From 1994 she was a founding director of London's first inward-investment body, helping promote London as a premier business destination. She became CEO of the Central London Partnership in 1997, leading a cross-sector partnership on maintaining the capital's position as a global world city. She has been at the heart of many of the initiatives that have been part of London's successful urban evolution, including the establishment of the Business Improvement District model in the UK, and the pedestrianisation of Trafalgar Square.

Neale Coleman CBE worked for the GLA from 2000 to 2015 advising Ken Livingstone and Boris Johnson on the bid for, delivery and legacy of the 2012 Olympic and Paralympic Games. He was a board member of the Olympic Delivery Authority throughout its life, and following the games he was deputy chair and chair of the London Legacy Development Corporation.

Isabel Dedring has been Arup's global transport leader since 2016 and a member of the group board since April 2019. Prior to Arup, she was deputy mayor for transport and deputy chair of the Transport for London board. In London government her major transport projects included creating and delivering a £1 billion cycling programme, a £4 billion progressive roads investment programme, and leading on major transport construction projects such as extensions to the underground and devolution of rail services. She also instigated and led on the London Infrastructure Plan 2050. Isabel is a native New Yorker, a qualified lawyer and a fellow of the Institute of Civil Engineers.

Michèle Dix CBE started her career at the GLC after completing her PhD in transport and land-use planning. She joined TfL in 2000 as co-director of congestion charging. Michèle led TfL's strategic thinking on the transport needs of London, testing and challenging solutions and providing clear direction on appropriate transport solutions for the future. Michèle is now responsible for developing Crossrail 2 and gaining funding and powers for it. She is a visiting professor for UCL and recently joined the Major Projects Association as a board member and became a trustee for the London Transport Museum.

Tim Donovan is BBC London's political editor. His interest in the capital's mayoralty began when he was asked to make a behind-the-scenes film about the inaugural 2000 campaign. He spent several weeks traipsing after Ken Livingstone with a small camera. Two decades of intense interest have followed.

Stephen Glaister CBE was chair of the Office of Rail and Road from 2016 to 2018 and remains on the board. He is emeritus professor of transport and infrastructure at Imperial College London and is an associate of the London School of Economics. He was director of the RAC Foundation, a member of the TfL board from 2000 to 2008 and a non-executive director of London Regional Transport from 1984 until 1993. He has published widely on transport policy and also on regulation in the telecommunications, water and gas industries.

Robert Gordon Clark is executive chairman of PR firm London Communications Agency (LCA), which he founded in 1999 just before the

GLA was created. Before that he was deputy CEO of London First and has over thirty years' experience working on the London agenda. LCA – now a 45-strong team – has advised a wide range of businesses and public sector bodies on their work in the capital, providing media relations, public affairs and design services. The company has also supported the work of organisations such as Centre for London, London Councils and New London Architecture (NLA) to help promote the capital.

Dave Hill is an experienced freelance journalist who runs the website OnLondon, which covers the capital's politics, development and culture. He was previously, for nine years, *The Guardian*'s London commentator, winning awards for his columns and work on transport issues. Dave is also a board member of the London Society and is the author of *Zac Versus Sadiq: The Fight to Become London Mayor*, an account of the 2016 London mayoral election campaign.

Leah Kreitzman is mayoral director for external and international affairs, having previously been a senior advisor to Sadiq Khan's campaign to be Mayor of London. Before this, Leah was director of public affairs for UNICEF UK. She has led advocacy campaigns for international NGOs, such as Save the Children and ONE, and worked for the UK's leading international development think tank, the Overseas Development Institute. Leah has also been a strategic communications advisor to the shadow Cabinet on criminal justice, human rights and constitutional reform. She has an MSc in international relations from the London School of Economics and a BSc in philosophy and politics from the University of Bristol.

Kit Malthouse has been the Conservative MP for beautiful North West Hampshire since 2015. In January 2018, Kit was appointed parliamentary under-secretary for family support, housing and child maintenance and was promoted to minister of state for housing and planning in July 2018. Following the election of Boris Johnson as Prime Minister in July 2019, Kit became minister of state for policing, crime and the fire service. Formerly deputy mayor of London for policing and business and enterprise, he is a chartered accountant, and founded a Midlands-based finance company twenty years ago, which he now chairs. He is married with three children.

Nick McKeogh is co-founder and chief executive of NLA, London's centre for the built environment. He is also a trustee of the London Society and a director of Pipers Model Makers. Nick studied civil and environmental engineering at UCL, before joining his father at Pipers in 1996. Nick has managed the delivery of the London stand at MIPIM since 1998 and led the transformation of the London Architecture Biennale into the annual London Festival of Architecture and its subsequent integration into the NLA in 2019. He established the London Real Estate Forum in 2013 and continues to oversee the event.

Dr Rick Muir is director of the Police Foundation, the UK's independent policing think tank. He has been a public policy researcher for most of his career, focusing on policing, criminal justice and public service reform. He was previously associate director at the Institute for Public Policy Research. Prior to that he completed a DPhil in politics at the University of Oxford. He is currently a visiting professor at Northumbria University and was previously a local councillor in both Oxford and Hackney.

Ben Rogers is an urbanist, researcher, writer and speaker, with a particular interest in urban life, citizenship, public service reform and the built environment. He founded Centre for London in 2011 and was previously an associate director of IPPR and subsequently led strategy teams at Haringey Council, the Department for Local Government and Communities and the Prime Minister's Strategy Unit. Ben is the author of several acclaimed books on philosophy, history and democracy, and is an experienced journalist and broadcaster. He has been a contributing editor to *Prospect* magazine, a visiting fellow at the Royal Society of Arts and a member of the London Finance Commission.

Bridget Rosewell was chief economist for the GLA from 2002 to 2012 and was responsible for setting up GLA Economics. In that role she worked extensively on the case for Crossrail and the role of agglomeration in the city, on the Thames Gateway Bridge and on various London Plans. She is now a commissioner on the National Infrastructure Commission.

Kath Scanlon is distinguished policy fellow at the London School of Economics. An economist and planner, she specialises in understanding the impact of housing policy at local and national level. Her first LSE research project in 1999 looked at the setting up of the Greater London Authority; she has been following London governance and policy ever since. Kath has carried out research for a range of UK and international funders including the GLA, several London boroughs, Homes for Scotland and the Council of Europe Development Bank.

Deyan Sudjic is professor of architecture and design studies at Lancaster University, and director emeritus at the design museum. He is a former director of the Venice Architecture Biennale, and of Glasgow UK City of Architecture and Design. He was part of the Urban Age team at the LSE. His books include *The 100 Mile City*, *The Endless City* (edited with Ricky Burdett) and *The Language of Cities*.

Dr Tim Williams is head of cities for Arup in Australasia. From 2011 to 2017 he was CEO of the Committee for Sydney, Australia's main cities think tank. Between 1998 and 2003 he was CEO of the Thames Gateway London Partnership and between 2005 and 2010 worked for various housing and planning ministers as a special or specialist advisor. In the run-up to the London Olympics he advised a number of host boroughs on legacy strategies and advised the CEO of Lend-lease on the building of the Athletes' Village. He lives in Sydney and regards himself as a Cambrian-Australian London intellectual.

LIST OF ABBREVIATIONS

ALA	Association of London Authorities
ALG	Association of London Government
CABE	Commission for Architecture and the Built Environment
CIL	Community Infrastructure Levy
CLRS	Central London Rail Study
DETR	Department of the Environment, Transport and the Regions
GLA	Greater London Authority
GLC	Greater London Council
GOL	Government Office for London
HS2	High Speed 2
ILEA	Inner London Education Authority
IOC	International Olympic Committee
LBA	London Boroughs Association
LCA	London Communications Agency
LCC	London County Council
LDA	London Development Agency
LEAP	London Economic Action Partnership
LFC	London Finance Commission
LFEPA	London Fire and Emergency Planning Authority
LLDC	London Legacy Development Corporation
LPAC	London Planning Advisory Committee
LRB	London Residuary Body
LRT	London Regional Transport
MBW	Metropolitan Board of Works
MDC	Mayoral Development Corporation

MIPIM	*Le Marché International des Professionnels de L'immobilier* (The International Market for Real Estate Professionals)
MOPAC	Mayor's Office for Policing and Crime
MPA	Metropolitan Police Authority
MPS	Metropolitan Police Service
OPDC	Old Oak and Park Royal Development Corporation
PCC	Police and Crime Commissioner
PCSO	Police Community Support Officer
PPP	public–private partnership
ROCOL	'Road Charging Options for London' (study)
SDS	spatial development strategy
TfL	Transport for London
ULEZ	Ultra-Low Emissions Zone
VRU	Violence Reduction Unit

FOREWORD

TONY BLAIR

Could we imagine not having a Mayor of London today? Or fighting and winning the 2005 bid for the Olympics in London without one? Or hosting it in 2012? Yet, there was no elected Mayor of London before Labour took office in 1997. We engaged as a government in the biggest constitutional reform Britain had ever seen in modern times. Scottish and Welsh devolution, together with the introduction of the Northern Ireland Assembly following the Good Friday Agreement of 1998, are often the most noticed of the reforms; but the creation of a London mayor was just as significant.

It is a great example of the change which can be made by progressive politics if it has the discipline and strategy to win power and retain it. Never forget that the position of a London mayor was at the beginning politically controversial – the 1980s had seen the abolition of the GLC – and three terms of government were important in bedding the institution down. Now its abolition would be unthinkable.

As part of the broader policy aim of putting power in the hands of local communities it was felt that there was a particularly urgent need to make change in London. As we set out in our 1997 manifesto, at that point London was the only Western capital without an elected city-wide government. Our aim was that both the elected assembly and the mayor would speak up for the city and its needs, plan for the future and take responsibility on city-wide issues, such as economic regeneration, planning, policing, transport and the environment.

Both of these reforms came into effect in 2000 after a referendum and legislation had passed in Parliament.

In the twenty years since there is much for us to look at and reflect on in terms of successes and areas for improvement.

It seems clear that the mayor has been a powerful and effective political voice and advocate for the capital, both domestically and internationally. Within the mayoral remit of powers there have also been important successes: the congestion charge, bike hire and both a broader and better offering of public transport.

With the next stage of Brexit on the horizon it is the right time to think about the next phases of devolution, both at a micro and macro level.

At a micro level, does the Mayor of London have enough powers, for instance? What can be improved in the capital and learned for other municipalities across the UK?

At a macro level we must ensure that the spirit of regional and local devolution remains undiminished. It is a critical route to bringing more people into the political process, as well as ensuring accountability and leadership on local issues.

So, twenty years on from the establishment of the Mayor of London and the London Assembly, the existence of both are almost unquestioned in reasonable political debate. They have changed the landscape of political life in the city for the better. With the benefit of all we have seen over that time, and with deep change in the UK on the horizon, now is the time to deepen devolution, creating a new political settlement across the country.

INTRODUCTION

JACK BROWN, TONY TRAVERS
AND RICHARD BROWN

On 3 July 2020, the Mayor of London turned twenty years old. Following a referendum on 7 May 1998, the introduction of legislation to establish the Greater London Authority the following year, and the first mayoral election on 4 May 2000, this was the day when the GLA formally (and finally) came into being.

This book marks twenty years of the mayoralty, a notable landmark that provided a good opportunity to review progress to date, and to consider what might, and perhaps should, happen in the next phase of London's devolved city-wide governance. But it has also been written, in large part, during a global pandemic. It is therefore also a time of great uncertainty, for the mayoralty, for London, and some would argue for cities themselves all around the world. We hope that this makes it even more interesting, but it has not necessarily made it easier to write.

We have endeavoured to include a wide range of voices in the writing of this book, blending independent expertise with first-person experience. We hope that this makes for a diverse, interesting and nuanced final product. We also made extensive efforts to engage with all three of the individuals to have held the office of Mayor of London to date. While former mayor (and current Prime Minister) Johnson was understandably unavailable, we have endeavoured to engage widely with members of his former mayoral team, and ensure that their views are also represented within the book.

This book has been written by a number of contributors and thus benefits from a number of perspectives and styles. Inevitably, individual writers have had to consider the same policies and events, albeit from different angles. As a result, there will be some repetition of elements of the history of London's mayor at twenty. Thus, for example, the analyses of housing and planning since 2000 each consider policies and developments which, rightly, affect the two related spheres of city government. Similarly, the way in which the GLA was created in the years from 1997 to 2000 (and the purposes that the new institution was intended to serve) overlaps to some extent with the way that the three mayors have operated the machinery of government. The editors decided it would be better to leave these varying perspectives in rather than to adapt them to remove all instances where the same event or policy is analysed from different points of view. We have also asked external authors to analyse their particular mayoral policy areas from the creation of the mayoralty up to the beginning of the Covid-19 pandemic, which while potentially transformative for London is also an ongoing and rapidly changing situation. Some early thoughts on the longer-term impact of the pandemic are offered in the book's conclusion.

PART ONE

DESIGN

1

THE ROAD TO REFORM

TONY TRAVERS

O ver the last two centuries the governance of London has been constantly evolving. Public health epidemics when the city was governed by mid-nineteenth-century parishes generated the impetus to create the Metropolitan Board of Works (MBW). Concerns about the lack of accountability of the MBW paved the way for the London County Council (LCC). The LCC was superseded by the Greater London Council (GLC) following years of campaigning about the lack of coherence in the government of the capital's metropolitan sprawl. The GLC was abolished by a government which felt that the council was inefficient and ineffective. Finally, the Greater London Authority (GLA) was created to re-establish city-wide government and also to introduce a new kind of leadership.[1]

The origins of the 2000 reform of London government can be found in the abolition of the GLC in 1986. Margaret Thatcher's radical centre-right administration abolished the GLC and six other metropolitan counties to 'streamline' city government. In reality, the abolition of the GLC was an overwhelmingly political reaction to the activities of Ken Livingstone's radical centre-left leadership at County Hall.[2] The GLC had only existed since 1965 and the metropolitan counties, governing six other big English cities, since 1974. As the millennium approached, a very British unwillingness to tinker with the structures of sub-national government had left London and other major cities with no city-wide authorities since 1986 apart from a series of clunky joint committees.

GLC ABOLITION AND THE LONDON OF 1986

In London, abolition initially triggered a sense of gloom about the capital's future. Not only had the GLC gone, but the thirty-two boroughs and the City of London were separated into two distinct groups, each with its own representative organisation. Thus, from 1 April 1986, not only was there no London-wide government but (for the first time since soon after the Metropolitan Boroughs Standing Joint Committee was set up in 1912) the boroughs were segregated.

Moreover, by the mid-1980s, London's population had dropped to 6.6 million from a pre-war high of 8.6 million.[3] Despite housing and commercial office building in the 1950s and 1960s, many parts of inner London were seriously deprived and showed signs indicating that this deterioration would continue. London's docks had declined dramatically by the 1970s, as had many other traditional industries. As if to emphasise the enfeebled state of the city's government, Mrs Thatcher had imposed the pro-market London Docklands Development Corporation on a number of riparian boroughs. In 1984, London Transport, which had been GLC's responsibility since 1970, was taken away from it and turned into a nationalised industry with a government-appointed board, becoming known as London Regional Transport.[4]

As it turned out, 1986 was a nadir for London both in terms of the fragmented nature of its government but also the city's resident population. Indeed, the resurgence of the capital can be dated from around this time. A third of a century on, the abolition of the GLC can be seen as an incidental, if highly political, change which had the effect of paving the way for a more modern and effective form of city government.

London's resurgence, which occurred from the late 1980s onwards, has created a contemporary 'global' city on a par with New York, Paris, Toronto, Hong Kong and Singapore. The vacuum created by the abolition of the GLC triggered a debate about London which, by the late 1990s, delivered a form of government for the city that better suited

4

the globalised political culture of the 2000s than the GLC's cumbersome leadership and huge bureaucracy. Mrs Thatcher may in the end have been right, albeit for constitutionally questionable reasons.

AFTER ABOLITION: CURIOUS CONTINUITY

In the immediate aftermath of GLC abolition, not much changed. County Hall, the council's gigantic headquarters on the South Bank, continued to run most of the services that the GLC had responsibility for at the point of its demise. The Inner London Education Authority (ILEA), which had been a special committee of the GLC, became a directly elected authority in its own right. Almost everything else the GLC controlled became the responsibility of the London Residuary Body (LRB), a government-appointed body set up to handle the winding-down of GLC services. The London Fire Brigade became the responsibility of a joint committee of the boroughs. Statistics and research were handed to another borough committee, as were grants to voluntary organisations. Thus, in the late spring and summer of 1986 the officers of the GLC continued to operate from the long corridors of County Hall, albeit answering to different political masters.[5]

With the benefit of hindsight, it is remarkable how little changed after the GLC was gone. The reason for this was that Thatcher's government, though it liked to be seen as radical, was cautious about upsetting those who benefited from the council's services. Any failures in, for example, housing, the fire service, education or the funding of voluntary organisations, would have been attributed to the political decision to get rid of the GLC. Every aspect of the former authority's key provision was carefully protected by the LRB, ILEA and a number of joint committees which were created to ensure continuity.[6]

The institutional evolution of London's government has been considered extensively in earlier studies.[7] The array of quangos and joint committees spawned by abolition effectively sustained city-wide government. Some Whitehall departments adapted by creating London divisions to deal with planning, waste disposal and transport. Between 1986 and its own demise in 1996, the LRB (which also handled the disposal of assets and responsibilities following the abolition of the ILEA in 1990) disposed of all GLC land and buildings, while negotiating the placement of a number of responsibilities with bodies such as individual boroughs and, particularly, the apparently immortal City of London Corporation.[8]

Looking back from the period during which the GLA was created, between 1997 and 2000, the decisions taken between 1985 and the early 1990s to ensure the continuity of GLC services was of significant importance. It was as if most of the GLC's valuable assets had been carefully packed away until a new owner came along to return them to their rightful place under the control of an elected and accountable institution.

When the political battle surrounding GLC abolition ended, there was a brief lull in the debate about the capital's government, and a general sense of acceptance that what had happened had happened. During this time, Labour councils attempted, with only limited success, to protect some of the initiatives and funding streams favoured by Ken Livingstone's administration during the council's final five years. This was largely done through the Association of London Authorities (ALA), which represented all the Labour boroughs, and which had John McDonnell as its chief executive (long before he became shadow Chancellor under Jeremy Corbyn's Labour leadership). All the Conservative, SDP–Liberal Alliance, and 'no overall control' councils, plus the City of London, remained within the London Boroughs Association (LBA) which had existed since the boroughs had been created in 1965. Barking and Dagenham, eccentrically, was a member of both.[9]

The Conservatives were returned with a large majority in the 1987 general election, suggesting no lasting damage to their reputation as the result of the abolition of the GLC and the six metropolitan counties. Labour's 1987 manifesto promised to 'establish a new

6

democratically elected strategic authority for London and consult widely about the most effective regional structure of government and administration in England and Wales'.[10] The SDP–Liberal Alliance manifesto also committed the party to a new London-wide authority. Although it was barely a year since the GLC's demise, opposition politicians were already, if somewhat mechanistically, arguing that the void left by abolition had to be filled.

A NEW NORMAL: TENTATIVE EVOLUTION OF LONDON'S GOVERNANCE

Elsewhere, one of the post-GLC joint committees was establishing itself in offices in Romford. The London Planning Advisory Committee (LPAC) had been statutorily established to provide planning advice to Whitehall as central government had become responsible for the capital's strategic planning after abolition. LPAC – a joint committee of the thirty-two boroughs and the City – cautiously set about creating a research base and delivering advice to central government. This task was challenging, given the politically charged nature of politics at the time and also because the relevant ministers, notably the environment secretary Nicholas Ridley, were unconvinced by the concept of 'strategic planning'.[11]

LPAC's work was to prove to be a key building block in the intellectual evolution which occurred in relation to London from the late 1980s up to 1997. By developing a consensus about the capital's development and self-image that all the boroughs and the City signed up to, LPAC demonstrated that there were benefits to research-led planning. The LPAC-commissioned *London: World City Moving into the 21st Century* report, published in 1991, provided a popular, outward-looking analysis of how planning could shape London and expand its economy.[12] The report was published just as it became apparent that London's population was beginning to rise again and that the 1986 'Big

Bang' reforms to financial services had created a dynamic and globally focused sector where London was a world-leader.

Separately, the two London borough representative organisations began to work together more cooperatively. As wounds healed after the struggle over the abolition of the GLC, the LBA and the ALA – led, respectively, by Sir Peter Bowness (leader of Croydon Council) and Margaret Hodge (leader of Islington Council), both of whom went on to important parliamentary careers – increasingly found common cause, for example in negotiations with central government over financial settlements. Business organisations were also becoming more active. The Confederation of British Industry's London region and the London Chamber of Commerce and Industry produced policy on a range of issues, but in the interregnum after 1986 both organisations became more concerned with issues such as London's international representation and marketing.[13]

Indeed, the business sector made a significant move in 1992 by creating London First and its marketing arm, London First Centre (LFC), which were to become key players in the emerging consensus about the need for a new and reconstituted London-wide government.[14] London First was formed by a number of London-based international business leaders, notably Allen Sheppard (chief executive of Grand Metropolitan) and Colin Marshall (chair of British Airways). The proposal was that London First would act as a research-based promotional institution which would work with the boroughs, central government and other agencies to ensure that London's business voice was heard both nationally and internationally.

By the early 1990s, and particularly in the wake of the publication of LPAC's *London: World City*, dozens of reports were published by organisations such as London First, London Regional Transport (LRT), the London Research Centre, the King's Fund, the City of London, the boroughs' associations, academics and voluntary organisations. The vacuum created by a city as large as London having no city-wide government or thought leadership encouraged other players to step in. Reports were published and conferences held as these bodies vied for prominence in the 'London industry' that flourished from 1990 onwards.

AFTER 1990: MODERATION RETURNS

Another key reason for the growth in this kind of activity was the change in national and local politics. Margaret Thatcher had been dethroned in November 1990, to be replaced as Prime Minister by the more emollient John Major. Major had, coincidentally, been a well-regarded housing chair in Lambeth during the period the Conservatives were in control from 1968–71.[15] Labour's under-par performance (after eleven years in opposition and with the poll tax causing the government major problems) in the borough elections in May 1990 had, separately, convinced a number of the party's London politicians that the time had come to move away from the left's more radical policies in councils such as Lambeth, Southwark and Brent and instead to concentrate on the delivery of decent local services.[16] Thus, from the end of 1990 onwards the stage was set for a more rational and considered approach to politics in the capital.

The government created the post of transport minister for London, in part to implement investment policies outlined in the Central London Rail Study, which had been published in 1989.[17] The publication of the study was another important stage in the recovery of London following the decline of the 1970s and 1980s. The report suggested the creation of new rail lines for the capital and focused a debate on the need to modernise the existing Tube and commuter rail services in the capital. Steven Norris was appointed as London's minister for transport by Major to oversee the building of the Jubilee Line extension and to drive forward other improvements such as the Heathrow Express. The City of London was active at this time lobbying for the proposed east–west Crossrail to be built. Separately and competitively, Olympia & York, the developers of Canary Wharf in Docklands, were also lobbying for both the Jubilee Line extension and Crossrail.[18]

In 1993, environment secretary John Gummer began to style himself as 'minister for London', and took particular interest in projects such as the pedestrianisation of Trafalgar Square and the strategic planning of the Thames. One of the less successful outcomes of the abolition of the GLC had been the difficulty of ensuring the central boroughs aligned their policies on matters such as development along the river and, more prosaically, parking charges in the West End.

With abolition-era politics now well in the past, the Major government concluded that Whitehall needed better government mechanisms to deal with London. Although both the Department of the Environment and the Department of Transport had their own, separate, regional offices for the capital it was decided to create a 'Government Office for London' and, indeed, for other regions of England. Crucially, the Government Office for London (GOL) would be headed by a civil service deputy secretary, a rank higher than in other regions. From 1994 onwards, GOL became an influential conduit of policy between central government and the capital's proliferating governance institutions such as the boroughs, business organisations, NGOs and London Regional Transport.[19]

The roles of Norris, Gummer and the GOL, backed up by demands for infrastructure investment coming from organisations such as the City of London and London First, collectively implied that the post-abolition governance arrangements needed better coordination and leadership. By the mid-1990s, London's population was rising each year and a new service-based economy was replacing more traditional industries lost between the 1950s and 1980s. In Docklands, the Isle of Dogs was emerging as a glitzy cluster of towers, a monument to Americana (or more accurately, given Olympia & York's origins, Canadiana).[20] A broad consensus about London was emerging: the city had begun to self-style itself as an open, international, finance-rich, tolerant, 'world' city. The publication of a *London Pride Prospectus* in

1995 – which was signed by a long list of government, borough, business and voluntary organisation leaders – can be seen as marking the apogee of the post-1986 transition from a grey city of politicised decline to one fit for the films of Richard Curtis.

NEW GOVERNMENT AND A MAYOR FOR LONDON?

In 1994, Tony Blair had become leader of the Labour Party following the death of John Smith. Smith had been a careful moderniser of a party which had by this time been out of office for fifteen years. From the start, Blair lifted Labour in the polls and appeared to be on course for a victory at the next general election. Much has been written about his apparent non-ideological approach and his government sought to ensure that there was no risk that a number of Labour councils would slip back into extremism or inefficiency.[21] As a consequence, it appears that he was an easy convert to the possibility that a new, elected, London-wide government might be led not by the leader of its majority party but by a directly elected mayor.

In April 1996, Labour published 'A Voice for London', a consultation document which outlined a new Greater London Authority, with the tentative proposal for an elected mayor for the city. At a mass public meeting entitled 'London in the 21st Century', held at Central Hall, Westminster, organised by the Architectural Foundation and the *Evening Standard* in May 1996, Blair endorsed the principle of an elected mayor.[22] By this time, it was widely assumed that Labour would win the 1997 general election and that the Conservatives would be out of office for the first time in almost two decades. Labour was also committed to devolution for Scotland and Wales, while the Liberal Democrats strongly supported the restoration of city-wide government, if not a mayor, in London. A sense that a Labour victory would change Britain's constitutional arrangements meant that any London government reform was seen at this time as being part of a wider modernisation of government rather than an attempt to 'recreate the GLC'. No one close to power within Blair's Labour leadership wanted to return to the style of government which had ended at County Hall only a decade previously.[23]

The fact that the Conservatives had been in power for so long was important in understanding the steps towards reconstituting London-wide government. Many commentators, including senior Conservative figures, had expected to lose the 1992 general election. They won it, although the period from 1992 to 1997 badly damaged the party's reputation for economic and political competence.[24] By the time they lost office in 1997 to a moderate and attractive Labour leader, the Conservatives were worn out. Their political power and influence had reached a nadir. This factor gave Blair's 'New Labour' government (which had a majority of 179) the capacity to drive through reform with little hindrance from the Tories, who had suffered their worst election result since 1906. Given the radical nature of the proposed London government reforms, which meant not just restoring a system that the Conservatives had abolished eleven years before, but also adding an American-style elected mayor, the enfeebled nature of the new opposition was an important factor.

WAS A MAYOR INEVITABLE?

The narrative summarised above suggests a logical and inevitable series of steps from the abolition of the GLC on 31 March 1986 to the election of the new GLA members on 4 May 2000. But, of course, it was not like that at all. History often looks neat when it is chronologically laid out from year to year but feels chaotic and random as it is happening. In the immediate period after the demise of the GLC there was little expectation that a replacement would be put in place for many years. Senior Conservatives, particularly in boroughs such as Bromley and Westminster (who had been instrumental in lobbying for abolition) were adamant that London had no need for a new metropolitan authority. The London Boroughs Association, representing all the capital's Conservative authorities, were willing to take part in the leadership of joint committees and other replacement bodies, but showed no interest in discussing further reform.[25]

Even national Labour politicians were circumspect. The reputational damage to the party that had resulted from extremism within a minority of Labour councils and the GLC, whether real or imagined, made party leader Neil Kinnock wary of accidentally re-empowering the left. The party was committed to the restoration of London's city-wide government in both its 1987 and 1992 manifestos, but Kinnock and the mainstream elements of the party were fearful of anything that looked like a return to Ken Livingstone's GLC.[26]

What moved the debate on was the coincidence of London's return to population growth, a decisive shift in the make-up of the city's economy, the emergence of a new 'global city' narrative, greater moderation of politics at the national and local government levels and, inevitably, time. By the mid-1990s London Labour councils were increasingly pragmatic and were embracing pro-growth policies via large developer-led schemes. The schism between Labour boroughs and those run by Conservatives or Liberal Democrats was finally removed by the creation of a single Association of London Government (ALG) in 1995 and also by the success of the London Pride Partnership, which also embraced the private sector. The ALG was subsequently re-named London Councils, today's moderate, efficient, representative body.

As the Conservatives' power corroded after 1992, Labour's grew in strength. A perception that Labour would almost certainly win the next general election meant that its policies were treated with great seriousness. Senior shadow Cabinet members went on a 'prawn cocktail circuit' to meet leading figures in the City of London.[27] Any threat to abolish the ancient City Corporation disappeared as the New Labour leadership sought to reassure the financial markets and businesses more generally. It is almost certain that a John Smith-led Labour

Party would have won the 1997 general election, though possibly not with the vast majority won by Tony Blair. If Smith had not died, it seems likely that any new London-wide government would have been a more traditional authority with a leader drawn from its majority party. Blair, as leader, facilitated the arrival of the concept of 'mayor' in Britain.

The Conservatives continued to oppose the restoration of metropolitan government in their 1997 manifesto. The main manifesto did not specifically refer to the issue but it did commit the party to privatise London Underground.[28] A separate London manifesto reiterated the view that a new city-wide authority was unnecessary. Once the election had been lost and the party went into opposition, it became necessary to respond to the new Labour government's paper offering a mayor and assembly for the capital. Given the new government's mandate, the Tories accepted the new authority (including the idea of a mayor) though they did unsuccessfully attempt to replace the proposed assembly with a committee of borough leaders.[29]

Thereafter, the Conservatives had to come to terms with the need to field candidates for mayor and for the assembly. Former transport minister Steven Norris was instrumental in convincing his colleagues that they would appear foolish if they did not now enter into the fray to win both the mayor and assembly positions. Gradually, the Tories came to accept that the abolition of the GLC was part of history and that they now needed to live in a new political world.

THE PARADOX OF GLC ABOLITION

The irony is that the Conservative decision to abolish the GLC created a political space within which it proved possible for Labour to build a government institution rather more powerful, more constitutionally resilient and arguably more appropriate for the political conditions of the 2000s. Instead of a 92-member council with a huge bureaucracy and a track record of being uncertain about its own role, the Blair government devised a small administration with clear responsibilities, led by a mayor.

The Mayor of London has become one of the most powerful and visible offices in British politics, given legitimacy by its vast electoral mandate. The GLA was to be given responsibility for transport, fire and emergencies, spatial planning and, for the first time ever for any London authority, aspects of policing. Latterly, strategic housing policy was also added to the mayor's duties.[30]

Creating the new mayor's office machinery at Romney House and City Hall is considered in the following chapter. But there can be little doubt that the recent history of the GLC played a powerful role in shaping what came next for the governance of London. A fear of political extremism, a concern not to recreate an over-large bureaucracy, the risk of a continuing cycle of reform and the need to avoid parochialism (an issue that has affected the capital for over two centuries) all influenced the thinking of the ministers and civil servants who created the GLA.

No London government system has proved permanent, and definitive. In one of the world's most centralised democracies the UK Parliament, often with misgivings, from time to time feels the need to try another institutional settlement for the ominously large city in which it is located. The Metropolitan Board of Works survived thirty-three years, the LCC seventy-six, the GLC twenty-one, an 'interregnum' fourteen and the GLA (to date) has managed twenty. During the lives of these city-wide institutions London grew to become the largest city in the world, then reduced sharply in population end economic power before resurgence took it to a population of 9 million in 2020. The future today looks more complex than at any point since 1945. This challenge will be considered in the final chapter of the book.

2

CREATING THE GLA

RICHARD BROWN

'A new dawn has broken, has it not?'

The New Labour government that was elected on 1 May 1997 was an administration in a hurry. It was determined to make its mark and to usher in the 'new era of politics' that Tony Blair promised when he spoke to the victory party outside the Royal Festival Hall, in the dawning light of the morning after the country went to the polls.

The government was quick to get to work, and a flurry of announcements and legislation followed over the first 100 days. The Bank of England was granted independence, welfare to work plans were announced, a new Department for International Development was created, and the Department for National Heritage relaunched as the Department for Culture, Media and Sport. The government banned landmine exports, signed up to the EU's 'Social Chapter' (a charter of employment rights), announced plans to incorporate the European Convention on Human Rights into UK law and introduced bills for Scottish and Welsh devolution.[1]

On 29 July, just ninety days after the general election, the government issued its green paper, 'New Leadership for London', which proposed an elected mayor and assembly for the capital.[2] The mayor and assembly, who would together form a 'Greater London Authority', would be a new type of strategic organisation, the paper argued. It would be streamlined but high profile, working through consensus, influence and voice as well as through direct powers.

This chapter looks at how those proposals became a reality but also at their origins, at their genesis as well as their journey from policy to reality. The account is not wholly objective; I worked in the transition team responsible for setting up the new arrangements from summer 1999, but I have sought to distinguish researched narrative from passages relying on my own memories or perceptions.

*   *   *

The 1986 abolition of the GLC had left a void in its place. However much Margaret Thatcher's government resented the municipal socialism of the GLC, and the impertinent challenge that was posed by County Hall thumbing its nose at Westminster from across the river, its abolition left London with a diminished voice, atomised accountability and deteriorating infrastructure. London, almost uniquely among global capital cities, had no unified civic government.

Authority was dispersed between the thirty-two London boroughs, the venerable City of London, and numerous joint committees, agencies, quangos and government departments. The capital's transport and police services – public services employing thousands of people – lacked any local accountability. Len Duvall, leader of the London Borough of Greenwich from 1992 to 2000 and a London Assembly member since then, recalls annual consultation meetings with the Met Police:

> Interactions with the Met Police were a yearly meeting between the boroughs and the Receiver of the Metropolitan Police, usually an old borough treasurer, who'd tell you how much money they would ask for [from council tax], and you'd have biscuits and it would be a nice chat. Until one of the meetings, when Toby [Harris, then leader of Haringey] and I started asking questions about the budget. This clearly wasn't the done thing; you were meant to be nodding it through. And with London Transport there was even

less engagement. So it was a messy situation and things did need to change.[3]

Alongside the democratic deficit, concern was rising about London's decaying infrastructure. Opening a 1991 debate in Parliament, Dagenham MP and shadow environment secretary Bryan Gould said: 'Our great capital, once the world's greatest city, which has so much going for it and so great a heritage upon which to draw, is gradually grinding to a halt,' adding that London's attempt to bid for the 1992 Olympics 'could not be taken seriously as long as there was no one to speak for London.'[4]

Sunday Times editor Andrew Neil sounded an apocalyptic note in an open letter to the government:

> No one governs London ... what's to be done? Roads are seizing up. For those living in the city, crime, vandalism and litter are at their worse ... In quiet residential streets, there seems to be virtually no control over what people can do to ruin their houses and the appearance of whole streets ... There is a strong feeling that nobody is in control, that London, once one of the world's best-planned and best-run cities, has run out of control.[5]

As these problems became more widely debated, ideas for renewed civic leadership began to circulate. Looking back to how things were under the GLC was treated as a taboo, avoided for fear of resurrecting old enmities, but there was a widespread acknowledgement that something or someone needed to take control, to give London a voice, a sense of direction and purpose.

The 1991 *London: World City* report argued that London needed a 'strategic planning and transportation body' to help it keep up with its global competitors. Sociologist Ralph Dahrendorf (who gave a television lecture entitled 'Does London need to be governed?' in 1990), and Labour MP and former GLC member Tony Banks, argued for a new mayoral model of government, but others were shy of institutional solutions. For example, in *The Crisis of London*, Michael Hebbert argued for a polycentric government by the boroughs, with a reformed Corporation of London taking on a coordinating function, while others in the same volume advocated for private sector-led growth coalitions and a greater role for community organisations.

The problem was clear, even if the solutions were not. By the time of the 1992 general election, both of the main parties were proposing reforms to London's government. Labour argued that London – 'the only European capital without the advantage of its own elected authority' – needed a new 'Greater London Authority'.[6] The previous year, Bryan Gould had set out more detail:

> A streamlined, professional, proactive, enabling authority that will take in hand the strategic planning of land use and economic development, the planning of our transport needs and the provision of our fire, police and emergency services. That authority will encourage our cultural life and will adopt an overall strategy to protect our environment.[7]

The Conservative Party manifesto rejected 'Labour's plan to recreate a bureaucratic and wasteful GLC'. Instead it set out detailed plans for investment in and reform of London's transport system – partly in response to the King's Cross Fire of 1987 – and committed to a private sector-led 'London 2000' initiative to promote the capital, alongside a new cabinet committee, and a dedicated minister for transport in London.[8] After the Conservatives' unexpected victory, this post was occupied by Epping Forest MP Steve Norris, who was immediately thrown into rescuing the Jubilee Line extension project following the collapse of Canary Wharf developers Olympia & York.

Five years later, the 1997 Conservative manifesto was silent on London's government, promising only to privatise London Underground. But Labour's manifesto laid out the essence of its plans for the capital:

London is the only Western capital without an elected city government. Following a referendum to confirm popular demand, there will be a new deal for London, with a strategic authority and a mayor, each directly elected. Both will speak up for the needs of the city and plan its future. They will not duplicate the work of the boroughs, but take responsibility for London-wide issues – economic regeneration, planning, policing, transport and environmental protection. London-wide responsibility for its own government is urgently required. We will make it happen.[9]

The adoption of the mayoral model had been hard fought. Following the death of John Smith in 1994, Tony Blair's leadership marked a change in direction with the abandonment of the Labour Party's totemic commitment to 'common ownership of the means of production, distribution and exchange' under Clause IV of the party's constitution. Blair's roots were not in the trade unions or local government, the traditional proving grounds of Labour politicians, and he came to power believing that Labour could be its own worst enemy. While a new generation of pragmatic council leaders had come to the fore in the 1990s, after the rise of Militant and the rows over rate-capping in the 1980s, Blair continued to regard local government leaders with suspicion.

Simon Jenkins, former editor of the *Evening Standard* and *The Times*, and persistent advocate for devolution, recalls going to talk to the new Labour leader in 1995:

I had chaired a commission on local democracy, and the one thing that came up repeatedly was mayoralty as a dominant force – in France, in the US, in Germany. I had worked for John Lindsay [New York Mayor from 1966–73], and he was very impressive, far ahead of anything we had in England. I wanted to know why London couldn't have one of these people.

But when I met with Blair he was quite hostile to the idea. He had brought about what I regard as his finest achievement

– revolutionising the Labour Party. But he was worried about local parties and local party leaders, and Labour-led councils, who didn't like him, and he didn't like them.

I remember saying that the whole point about local mayors is that in a sense they supplant party politics in local government. He said, 'What do you mean?' I said, 'Well anyone can stand for mayor. You normally stand with a party's support, but anyone can stand, including independents. And either way because it's a direct election, if you decide to stand as mayor, you're going to have to be reasonably plausible and charismatic in your own right.' And Blair almost leapt out of his chair; he bought it lock stock and barrel. 'But,' he said, 'I don't think Frank [Dobson, Holborn and St Pancras MP, and then shadow secretary of state for the environment] is going to approve of this.' And I said, 'Well you need to get it in the manifesto, otherwise it will just die a death.' And he undertook to put it in the manifesto there and then.[10]

Tony Blair began talking about the potential for mayors in London and other cities. His arm was strengthened in 1996, when Ian Hargreaves, former *Financial Times* deputy editor, published his proposals for a 'governor' for the capital.[11] Study visits to US cities and the rise of successful European mayors like Joan Clos in Barcelona and Francesco Rutelli in Rome helped to strengthen the case. Nick Raynsford, Greenwich MP and then shadow minister for housing and construction, describes walking across Trafalgar Square with the mayor of New Orleans: 'Suddenly he was mobbed by some people from the city who were in London on holiday. I remember saying at the time that I can't imagine any local government leader in the UK being recognised like that, let alone mobbed.'[12]

While Labour's policy document, 'A Voice for London', was more tentative in making the case for a mayor rather than a traditional 'leader of the council' model for London's new strategic authority, Tony Blair began to push the idea more assiduously throughout 1996.

At the 'London in the 21st Century' debate hosted by the Architecture Foundation and *Evening Standard*, he made the case for strong civic leadership to 'provide vision and direction for London's future, to drive the development of the city, to pull together the partnerships to make things happen ... for a vision, there does need to be a voice'.[13]

The contrast between tentative policy papers and bolder public pronouncements reflected the unease that some in the Labour Party felt over the idea of a directly elected mayor. As Blair surmised, Frank Dobson didn't like it, telling Simon Jenkins that it would happen 'over my dead body', and some borough politicians and officials shared this suspicion, worrying that a mayoralty would inevitably take influence if not power away from elected borough leaders. The tensions within the party can be seen in the care the manifesto took to emphasise that the new authority would not duplicate the work of the boroughs, and the commitment to a referendum to test public opinion on the matter.

This uneasy compromise limited the amount of preparatory work that could be done as the 1997 election approached. Nick Raynsford recalls briefing meetings with civil servants:

> I had meetings with [Department of the Environment permanent secretary] Andrew Turnbull in the run up to the election, official meetings where the opposition discuss their policies. We talked about housing and construction, and for both of those I produced a little paper. When we reached the third one, London government, he asked where the paper was, and I told him I couldn't produce it because of the Blair–Dobson differences. But, I said, in my view there was an absolute commitment to restore democratic government, and that if the party leader has his way it will be a mayoral system, but that he would have to put together a team of people who could develop the policy, because we don't have a rubric.[14]

* * *

Preparatory work was underway nonetheless. In Riverwalk House, an office block at the north-east corner of Vauxhall Bridge, senior officials at the Government Office for London were preparing policy options for an incoming government. GOL was one of the ten regional offices set up by John Major's government in 1994 to decentralise administration of government programmes on housing, regeneration, transport and education and skills. Since 1994, GOL had been headed by the ebullient and extensively networked Robin Young as director general, with Liz Meek as his head of policy. Meek had previously worked on London policy for John Gummer MP, the secretary of state for the environment. In the last years of the Major government, Gummer had become a 'proto-mayor' who had been energetic in promoting the capital in the absence of strategic government – through publishing glossy brochures entitled 'Making the Best Better', through the London Pride initiative that brought boroughs and business together to develop a prospectus for London, and through a cabinet committee for London.

As the 1997 election approached, Meek and Young stepped up preparations for the expected Labour government, and started putting together options for realising the manifesto commitment to an elected authority. As Meek recalls, different ideas were plotted on a 'mayor-ometer', with options on a sliding scale from a very powerful mayor with minimal checks and minimal powers, to much more balanced and collegiate models, with cities like New York sitting somewhere between the two. There was a degree of urgency, too:

> We all knew that if we didn't move with these proposals quickly, given that they affected the empires of every department in White-hall, they would stall. So we had to move while politicians were still interested in delivering a collective vision, rather than protect-ing their departments and their turf. So, on day one, when Nick Raynsford came along to meet us, we had a questionnaire for him with sixty-seven or so questions, offering options on what a 'strong mayor' would be, what he meant by 'small assembly' and so on.[15]

However, the green paper 'New Leadership for London' was also developed at a time of frantic and competitive legislative activity. Genie Turton, who took over from Robin Young as director of GOL after the election, describes the scene:

> When I started at GOL, it was like arriving at a railway station, with a whole lot of different trains ready to go and all with a different agenda, so you had development agencies over here, congestion charging here, PPP on the Underground here, all of which were government-run, and all of which were completely contrary to the idea of a mayor for London, but all of which were on the tracks and ready to go.[16]

Deputy Prime Minister John Prescott, who was in charge of the new 'super-ministry' Department of the Environment, Transport and the Regions (DETR), was not the greatest enthusiast for elected mayors, but was 'trooperish' in his promotion of the plans for London. Plans for elected regional assemblies – his real passion – were pushed to the next Parliament, with regional development agencies as their precursors. And congestion charging, which was intended to be a nationwide scheme, had to be introduced in London first.

While the green paper was formally published by DETR, its drafting and the legislation that followed it were in the hands of GOL, which was able to defend the 'purity' of the new arrangements from big departmental interests.[17] Other departments wobbled between ignoring and resisting the proposals, with disputes resolved in cabinet committees or through back-channel discussions with Downing Street, often brokered through Pat McFadden, later political secretary to the Prime Minister. The Home Office was particularly keen to defend its turf, and the nineteenth-century legislation about policing the capital, perhaps with one eye on the adversarial 'police committee' that Ken Livingstone had set up to monitor the activities of the Met Police while he was leader of the GLC. The idea that the mayor might have power to hire and fire the Metropolitan Police Commissioner, a power formally in the hands of the monarch, was fiercely resisted.

In another Whitehall office block, the Department for Transport (now part of Prescott's DETR) had never been comfortable with London Transport being overseen by GOL; now their focus was on the 'public–private partnership' (PPP) deal for London Underground. This would award thirty-year concessions to maintain and renew infrastructure to private sector consortiums. The consortiums would raise private capital to invest in everything from trains, to stations, to signalling equipment, then charge London Underground for using this infrastructure to run services. The plans for the PPP were announced in March 1998, with the intention that the deal would be completed before transport powers and assets were handed to the mayor.

Local government had to be carefully handled too. Some borough leaders were wary of the new proposals and worried that they would place an additional tier of government between them and the ministries that had become more directly engaged in London since the demise of the GLC. Housing was a particularly sensitive point: Conservative GLC leader Horace Cutler had angered Labour boroughs by promoting right-to-buy in the 1970s, and Labour leaders had responded by building new council estates in Conservative outer London boroughs in the 1980s. Ministers also had to reassure the City of London that the Mayor of London would not supplant or overshadow the Lord Mayor of London.

Policy reacts to its precursors. So just as the PPP was seen as a response to the cost overruns and delays of the Jubilee Line extension (which had been managed directly by London Underground), the powers and structure of the new mayoral authority were explicitly designed to be as far from the GLC as possible. The green paper proposed 'a strong executive mayor to provide firm leadership' with an assembly to act as a check on the mayor's power.[18] The mayor would be directly elected by around 5 million Londoners, and the assembly (a slight dilution of the 'strategic authority' proposed in the manifesto) would have twenty-four to thirty-two unpaid members, elected through a proportional method that would likely deprive any party of a working majority.

The paper acknowledged the successes of London's boroughs, but underlined the capital's continuing problems: of unemployment and poverty; of inadequate infrastructure; and of congested and polluted streets. Most powers would lie with the mayor in the new arrangements: they would set strategies, including an overarching land-use plan, and strategies for economic development, transport, environmental and cultural issues. The mayor would also set budgets for and make appointments to the boards of a new transport authority, a regional development agency, a police authority and a fire authority. Most employees would work for these new agencies ('functional bodies', as they were described in the paper), with a small core staff of around 450 to support the mayor and assembly.

In the white paper that was published in March 1998, most of the green paper proposals remained intact, but there was more detail on voting arrangements, on the make-up and powers of the assembly (which would comprise twenty-five paid members) and on the more limited powers that the mayor would have over the police and fire authorities, following opposition from the Home Office.[19]

As proposed in the green paper, the proposals for a mayor and assembly for London were also put to a referendum. Referendums were and are unusual features of British political life (there had not been one since 1979), and have on occasion been promised tactically for party political advantage, rather than through a strategic desire to ensure that reform is embedded in consent. While still in opposition, the Labour Party had agreed to hold referendums for devolution in Scotland and Wales; a referendum for London was consistent not only with these, but also with policy documents referring to a 'need for consent' for regional government changes.[20] As Simon Jenkins has observed, this insistence on referenda has stymied attempts to introduce mayoral models elsewhere.

Legislation for a referendum was introduced in November 1997. The Conservatives and Liberal Democrats proposed separate questions on the mayor and the assembly, and Ken Livingstone and others called for a separate question on tax-raising powers (as there had been in the Scottish Parliament referendum).[21] The government rejected these proposals, and their single-question referendum on a mayor and assembly for London was added to the ballot paper for the 7 May local elections.

The 'Yes' campaign was supported by politicians from all mainstream parties – many of them potential candidates – and featured a double-decker bus blasting out tunes by The Clash and Madness. When the results were tallied, the proposal was supported by a 72:28 majority, albeit on a paltry turnout of 34.6 per cent. Support was highest in boroughs such as Haringey, Lambeth and Hackney, and lowest in the outer suburbs, demonstrating that 'Victorian London was far more enthusiastic … than the inter-war boroughs.'[22]

In December 1998, the Greater London Authority Bill was introduced into Parliament. As well as working through legislative implications that stretched back to the 1829 Metropolitan Police Act, the bill also included clauses enabling the PPP that John Prescott had announced in March, although these mushroomed as the bill passed through Parliament and the complexity of the plans became more apparent. It also included clauses to enable the introduction of road-user charging, in recognition that the national scheme would not be in place in time. By the time that the bill had been enacted, it was being described as the longest Act of Parliament since the Government of India Act 1935, which reorganised colonial administration of a whole subcontinent.

Opening the second reading debate on 14 December, John Prescott made the case for the bill: 'London has struggled on without leadership or accountability. It is governed by cliques and cabals, shadowy committees, background deals and quangos. Its infrastructure is decaying, traffic problems are worsening, and poverty and social exclusion are deepening.'[23]

Gillian Shephard, speaking for the Conservatives, expressed support for the principles of the bill, but argued for an assembly made up of borough leaders rather than directly elected members. Simon Hughes, the Liberal Democrat spokesman, drew attention to the many powers that the bill reserved to the secretary of state, and argued for powers to recall a mayor through a petition signed by assembly members or citizens. Ken Livingstone also spoke, saying that he was looking 'forward to the voice for London having a distinctly nasal quality'.[24]

* * *

While the proposals for the mayor and assembly were being refined and narrowed down, the politics of the mayoralty were starting to expand, if not explode. Since the publication of the green paper, the names of potential candidates had been thrown about, as if in a civic government version of fantasy football. Some of the less outlandish suggestions included Westminster veterans such as Tony Banks, Glenda Jackson, David Mellor, Ken Livingstone, Margaret Hodge, Steve Norris, Chris Patten, Simon Hughes and Chris Smith; local government figures such as Toby Harris and Michael Cassidy; and a few figures from outside mainstream politics including airline bosses Bob Ayling and Richard Branson, and broadcaster and journalist Trevor Phillips.[25] In MORI poll of Londoners in March 1998, Branson attracted support from 39 per cent of interviewees despite expressing no interest in the job, Ken Livingstone and Glenda Jackson scored 28 and 18 per cent respectively for Labour, and Chris Patten and Jeffrey Archer led for the Conservatives with 17 and 14 per cent.[26]

Both Archer and Livingstone were larger-than-life characters, the type of high-profile outsiders for whom the mayoralty was purpose-built. But they both presented problems too – albeit of very different kinds – for their parties. So in 1999, while the legislation passed fairly smoothly through Parliament and the Liberal Democrats selected former banker Susan Kramer as their candidate, the headlines became dominated by lumbering machinations to secure the 'correct' outcome by the two parties, and to control selection of candidates for a position that was meant to transcend party politics.

Jeffrey Archer, a novelist and former Conservative MP, had resigned as deputy chairman of the Conservative Party in 1986 after allegations he had slept with a prostitute appeared in the *Daily Star*. He successfully sued the paper for libel the following year, and was made a peer in 1992. Despite continuing reservations from party grandees and stalwart opposition from *Evening Standard* editor Max Hastings, Archer made the shortlist of Conservative candidates alongside Steve Norris, and former council leaders Andrew Boff and Bob Blackman, and was selected as candidate by an 'electoral college' in October 1999. But the following month he stood down, following allegations that he had persuaded a friend to lie for him in his 1987 libel action, as a result of which he was jailed in 2001.[27]

Rather than handing the nomination to runner-up Steve Norris, the Conservative Party decided to re-run the contest. Then, following internal party debates about his private life, Norris was first excluded, only to be re-admitted when the party realised that they had lost their best-known and most popular candidate. Following another electoral college and members' vote, Norris was selected as Conservative candidate in January 2000, more than a year after the first selection process.[28]

Labour's processes were if anything more contorted. From 1997 onwards, Ken Livingstone looked like the obvious candidate. The abolition of the GLC had been opposed by Londoners, and he had come to public prominence in the campaign to save it, a prominence that had been cemented in the 1990s in his role as MP for Brent East, and through his presence on everything from panel shows, to TV commercials to a spoken-word part on Blur's 1995 song 'Ernold Same'. Livingstone maintained active engagement in left-wing politics, including as publisher of the *Socialist Economic Bulletin*, but his public image was a world away from when he was described as being the 'most odious man in Britain' in the tabloids in the 1980s.[29] Indeed on many issues – including gay rights and the need for negotiations with republicans in Northern Ireland – the mainstream had moved towards his 'extreme' positions by the late 1990s.

However, Livingstone opposed the very idea of a mayor for London. Speaking in Parliament a few weeks after the 1997 election, he warned about the risk of corruption in mayoral models, and argued that a new strategic authority for London would need revenue-raising powers if it was to have any true autonomy. Deploying his favoured hyperbole, he concluded: 'If the Treasury remains in control, the government that we create for London will have no more independence than the Vichy regime in France under the Nazis.'[30]

These were not comparisons that won Livingstone many friends in Downing Street, and Tony Blair notes in his memoir that Gordon Brown and John Prescott were particularly 'visceral' in their opposition to a Livingstone candidature. Blair cites Livingstone's opposition to the London Underground PPP as the principal issue at stake, though underlying this were deeper concerns about Livingstone's status as a totem of a pre-1994 Labour Party, and suspicions that 'Cuddly Ken' would actually be confrontational and corrosive if elected as mayor.[31]

The story of Labour's candidate selection process has been well rehearsed elsewhere, not least in Ken Livingstone's own memoir – which, incidentally, quotes Tony Blair on the back cover: 'I believe passionately that he would be a disaster, a financial disaster, a disaster in terms of crime and police and business.'[32] Initially, the party leadership hoped that Livingstone would burn himself out, or be overshadowed by a more acceptable candidate, but other potential 'names' – apparently including not only Richard Branson and Mo Mowlam, but also Delia Smith, Alex Ferguson, Martin Bell and Joanna Lumley – all remained the stuff of speculation and never put themselves forward to stand.

By mid-1999 it had become clear that there would need to be a contest, and that Livingstone would need to be challenged rather than ignored. Nick Raynsford was the first to launch a formal campaign in

September 1999, only to stand down when Frank Dobson stepped forward a few days later (to the apparent surprise of Downing Street as well as the other candidates). Rather than a simple vote among members as originally proposed, the party agreed a two-stage process. The first stage was a vetting panel to ensure that candidates would abide by the agreed manifesto (which included the PPP). As Tony Travers has observed, 'the extraordinary contradiction between Labour's commitment to devolution and the reality of centralised politics in Britain could barely have been more clearly demonstrated'.[33]

Livingstone survived the vetting panel, partly due to Dobson's threat to stand down if he did not do so, and, together with Dobson and Hampstead and Highgate MP Glenda Jackson, went through to the electoral college. This was designed to give equal weight to the London membership, to trade unions and affiliates, and to London MPs, MEPs and London Assembly candidates. Livingstone won the membership and the unions, but Dobson won the third college by such a large majority that he won overall (by 52 per cent to 48 per cent once Glenda Jackson's votes had been re-allocated), so he was announced as Labour candidate on 20 February 2000. Initially Livingstone and his team focused on lobbying Dobson to stand aside, but when they were told that the leadership would impose another candidate if he did so, Livingstone decided to stand as an independent, launching his campaign on 6 March – two months before the mayoral election.[34]

* * *

By this stage in early 2000, I was working as part of a small 'transition team' in Romney House, a 1930s civil service outpost in Marsham Street, Westminster. This had been set up in early 1999 to put in place the organisational infrastructure that the mayor and assembly would inherit, to build what one of the civil servants involved described as a 'minimally viable product' – a structure that would be operational from day one, but would not prejudice how its political leadership would wish to direct it. Given that the core task of the new Greater London Authority was inherently political – the translation of policies and priorities into strategies, budgets and appointments – this required a delicate balance.

Transition teams were typically run out of government departments, and there was some concern among GOL civil servants about the idea of an independent entity operating in advance of the election, but Nick Raynsford pushed for it. As the legislation had been run at arm's length from the big government departments, the transition team needed to be separate enough from civil service to be credible to an incoming mayor. Bob Chilton, director of local government studies at the Audit Commission, which oversaw audit and efficiency in English and Welsh local authorities, was approached to head the team:

> A year out from the election, I just had a desk, a PA and a phone. I call the team that we formed 'Dad's Army' – there were enthusiastic youngsters and more senior people who had become available for one reason or another. We had to blend them together to get a result against an immoveable deadline. I think it was quite amazing that we did it.[35]

Chilton's 'Dad's Army' included temporary appointments and secondments of civil servants, management consultants, lawyers and senior local government officers. The team also swelled in early 2000 when staff were taken on from the London Research Centre, the London Planning Advisory Committee and the London Ecology Unit, three of the residuary bodies that had been set up following the abolition of the GLC.

GOL civil servants had commissioned a new building at the south side of Tower Bridge as the long-term home for the mayor and assembly, but Romney House would be home to the new Greater London Authority for the first two years of its life. As the election approached, the transition team did everything from ordering office furniture and setting up finance and IT systems, to recruiting core administrative staff, to preparing briefing papers and draft diaries for the mayor.

We worked through scenarios of how the first 100 days might play out, discussing the statutory obligations – to make appointments, hold formal 'question times', publish specific reports – contained in the Greater London Authority Act, which received royal assent in November 1999. We also tried to plan how the staffing of this unusual new institution might work in practice. Would the GLA staff divide into two groups – those working for the mayor and those working for the assembly? Or would the mayor and assembly 'commission' work and tasks from a shared core of expert officials, with the head of paid service (the statutory chief officer role, held on an interim basis by Bob Chilton) managing workloads and allocating staff as required?

Without official sanction, Chilton organised meetings with Ken Livingstone, Frank Dobson, Steve Norris and Susan Kramer, so that they knew what preparations were and were not in place, and so that we could get an idea of their thoughts on a few critical issues, such as whether the mayor intended to chair Transport for London (TfL) in person, and what preparations could be undertaken for advertising critical roles.

The transition team effectively vanished on the day of the 2000 mayoral and assembly election, with members of the team being lent on a short-term basis to the new GLA. We had built a serviceable vehicle, with little idea about who would be driving it, or where they would want to go. On the night of 3 May 2000, on the eve of the election, we worked in a pizza-fuelled production line preparing briefing packs – instruction manuals explaining what had to be done, who needed to be met and what decisions might be taken by the incoming mayor and assembly. London was about to get the 'new deal' promised in the Labour manifesto three years earlier.

3

MAKING THE MAYORALTY:
2000-2001

RICHARD BROWN

'As I was saying, before I was so rudely interrupted fourteen years ago...'

Before Ken Livingstone had even finished the first sentence of his acceptance speech, some of the transition team members were already leaving the Queen Elizabeth II Conference Centre in Westminster to head back to Romney House, the GLA's transitional headquarters a few minutes' walk away.

We had been equipped with pagers – technology from another age – to let us know if the result came through overnight, but technical problems meant that there were delays in the result being confirmed – until midday on Friday 5 May 2000. Not only were the Mayor of London and the London Assembly entirely new institutions, they were being elected by new voting methods (the 'supplementary vote' and 'additional member' systems respectively), and using new electronic counting machines, some of which failed when fibres from old baize tablecloths became electrostatically charged and interfered with the scanners.[1]

By the time Livingstone arrived in Romney House, surrounded by journalists who were keen to celebrate a black eye for New Labour, staff were lining the corridors and staircases to applaud the new mayor. Livingstone's campaign as an independent had caught the public imagination, with almost as many Conservatives keen to cheer him on for his defiance of Tony Blair and the New Labour machine as there were Labour stalwarts backing him. He had won 39 per cent of first-preference votes against Steven Norris's 27 per cent for the Conservatives. Labour's official candidate Frank Dobson received 13 per cent of the vote and the Liberal Democrats' Susan Kramer received 12 per cent. Second-preference votes for those who had chosen Dobson, Kramer or other candidates were then counted, which gave Livingstone a majority of 58 per cent.

For the fledgling organisation's staff, this was the moment we had been waiting for. In the mayor's second-floor office, Bob Chilton – head of the GLA transition team – welcomed Livingstone, introduced his private office support and handed over the briefing materials that we had prepared.

Livingstone was in a unique position; he was the first elected Mayor of London, and the decisions he took would give shape and substance to the minimal organisation that the transition team had built. This chapter tells the story of the early months of the Livingstone mayoralty, and of the decisions, experiments and events that shaped both his administration and his successors.

THE FIRST BIG WEEKEND

Within a few minutes of Livingstone's arrival, members of his campaign team started turning up, with Simon Fletcher, Redmond O'Neill, Neale Coleman, John Ross and Mark Watts in the vanguard. If the new mayor looked tired, many of his team, still wearing their campaign T-shirts, looked exhausted as they scrambled for offices along the corridor that had been reserved for them. I asked the mayor who I should take a lead from, and he told me Simon and Mark, the core of his Westminster office, but also John Ross (who, he added, would probably upset people). The briefing files which we had prepared were handed over to Ross, and after a quick press conference, Livingstone headed home – evading the press by using Romney House's scruffy courtyard to hop into a taxi.

The following morning, Livingstone was back in the office to take a call from Tony Blair. The discussion was brief but cordial. The Prime Minister congratulated the mayor on his election; the mayor congratulated the Prime Minister on his progress in the Northern Irish peace process, and assured him that he would want to work with the government. After the call ended, I said that it had seemed surprisingly friendly. Livingstone replied that he and Blair had more in common than many would expect, both being uneasy in the mainstream of the Labour Party.

It was true that Livingstone had steered clear of direct personal attacks on Blair during the election campaign, focusing instead on his pledges to stop the London Underground PPP, to freeze transport fares in real terms, to boost police numbers and to reduce traffic congestion. Blair in turn played down any sense of personal animus, writing that he never felt as viscerally opposed to Livingstone as John Prescott and Gordon Brown did: 'I rather admired Ken's style, his quirkiness, which made him stand out as different, and his ability to communicate.'[2]

Whatever guarded respect there was between the new Mayor of London and the Prime Minister, Ken Livingstone was short of political allies within Romney House. The transition team had made arrangements for assembly members and the mayor to come in at the weekend, to set up their offices and sign formal declarations. But the nine Labour assembly members stayed out of the building and debated among themselves whether they should work with Livingstone; some had worked behind the scenes on the campaign, while others regarded him with deep suspicion as someone who had damaged the party.

Things eased once Livingstone had spoken to Blair and agreed that Labour politicians could take jobs in the administration. Labour assembly members also started arriving quickly enough when Bob Chilton let it be known that the Liberal Democrats were getting all the best offices. Len Duvall, who became the assembly member for Greenwich and Lewisham in 2000 and was deputy leader of the assembly Labour Group, recalls the discussions:

We decided to be very pragmatic towards Ken. If he got it wrong we would say so, but if he got it right, we'd support him. And Toby [Harris, leader of the Labour Group and assembly member for Brent and Harrow] and I agreed that we would take positions that would optimise influence and power for the Labour Group. I'd say we were pragmatic, flirtatious, but also independent.[3]

The Labour Group teamed up with the four-strong Liberal Democrat Group, giving them a working majority. Labour's Trevor Phillips became the chair of the assembly (alternating with the Lib Dems' Sally Hamwee), and Len Duvall chaired the GLA Appointments Committee – which would turn out to be one of the most influential positions in the weeks that followed.

The weekend ended with a final victory tour for the open-topped purple bus that had become an emblem of Livingstone's insurgent campaign (having previously served the 'Yes' campaign during the referendum), before work started in earnest on Monday 8 May.

MEETINGS AND MINISTERS

The Greater London Authority Act 1999 had given the first Mayor of London a luxury that none of his successors have had – a two-month running-in period between the election and the formal transfer of powers over the police, fire, transport and economic development agencies. Those first weeks were quickly filled with meetings, statutory duties and the events and decisions that bombard any new administration.

In preparing for the mayor's arrival, diary secretary David Hayward and I had fixed a number of meetings for the incoming mayor. On the Tuesday morning, I realised that I had arranged an all-staff meeting (by now there were more than 100 people in Romney House), but I hadn't briefed the mayor. I rushed through to tell him, apologising profusely. 'That's alright,' he said, picking up an envelope to scribble some notes on. 'What are people worried about?' I said that people were anxious that he saw them as being a bunch of 'dullards' (a favoured term) and civil service suits, that they were eager for policy direction, and that they wanted to know how to work with the mayor and his team.

Livingstone went downstairs, and spoke for ten minutes. He knew that people were worried, he said, but he had now realised that far from being civil service stooges, he was going to be working with some of the same people who had been at the GLC, and with people who shared his passion for London who wanted to work for a better city. He stated that he planned to have an open administration, where everybody's opinion would be valued. But, he warned, if people sought to undermine his decisions once they had been reached, there would be trouble – as some officers quickly discovered when they aired negative views about the mayor in public forums. His address was pitch-perfect and he judged his audience as precisely as he would when speaking to private faith group meetings, or at boozy gatherings of property developers, in the years to come.

Other meetings were fixed with relevant ministers, which we had done well to get in the diary before the election result came out; it would have been a lot harder after. I joined those with John Prescott (who sat with his arms folded, declaring 'I get council leaders in here all the time', and frowned even when Livingstone said he would push forward his beloved congestion charge), the Home Secretary, Jack Straw (who was courteous, carefully briefed but guarded), and the secretary of state for culture, media and sport, Chris Smith (who beamed and seemed genuinely glad to greet the mayor).

In all these meetings, and the many more I attended with him over the years, Livingstone's encyclopaedic knowledge of London, acquired through more than twenty-five years working in London politics, shone through. He knew the political history of every borough, sometimes every ward. If shown a site plan for a planning application in the furthest reaches of Zone 6, he would quickly orientate it to the nearest Tube station, public park or greasy-spoon café.

Alongside these meetings were the mayor's formal obligations: to take big decisions and delegate smaller ones; to prepare a report to the assembly every month; to answer assembly members' questions; to hold a 'People's Question Time'; to publish a 'State of London' report. One of the great things about working in a start-up is that there are no established ways of doing things (although it can be frustrating when you realise there is no way to do something as simple as ordering a bicycle courier). The systems that we worked with the mayor's advisors and assembly officials to put in place in those early weeks are still more or less intact twenty years later.

RECRUITING THE MAYOR'S TEAM

Within the Greater London Authority, almost all executive powers rested with the mayor, but he had limited powers of appointment. The legislation had made most staff appointments a matter for the assembly, a provision intended to restrain a spendthrift or corrupt mayor (this was amended in 2007). The mayor could appoint two political advisors (akin to ministerial special advisors), and ten more staff, who the legislators had seen as a French-style *cabinet* of senior figures, who would be appointed through an openly advertised process. All other employees were to be appointed by the assembly, in the light of the mayor's appointments and views.

These powers constrained the size and scope of the mayor's support team. So Livingstone sought an early meeting with the chair of the Appointments Committee, Len Duvall. The pair did a deal – probably one of the most important deals in shaping how the GLA would operate: if the assembly would work with the mayor to appoint the mayor's office staff that he wanted, the mayor would agree to the assembly having the funding for individual and party-group support.

Duvall secured consent from the party group leaders, and an advertisement was published in the *Evening Standard* at the end of the mayor's first week for a chief of staff, policy advisors and personal assistants. Interviewing was undertaken by Livingstone and Duvall for the most senior roles, then Simon Fletcher (when he had been formally appointed as chief of staff by Livingstone and Duvall) and the GLA HR officers handled the rest.

Many of the people that were appointed had worked with Livingstone on the campaign and before, although not everyone made it through the process. Fletcher, Mark Watts and Maureen Charleson had worked in Livingstone's Westminster office. John Ross (economy) and Redmond O'Neill (transport and stakeholder relations) had worked with him on the *Socialist Economic Bulletin* and campaigns on Northern Ireland (and along with Fletcher were associated with Socialist Action, a Trotskyist splinter group). Anni Marjoram and Jude Woodward, who took the lead on women's issues and culture respectively, came from the same political milieu.

Neale Coleman ('best value', housing and budgets), a former Westminster councillor and scourge of council leader Dame Shirley Porter, knew Livingstone from the Paddington Labour Party; Lee Jasper (policing and equalities) and Kumar Murshid (regeneration) had worked with him on anti-racism campaigns; Emma St Giles (press) was a former TV journalist, who had been press secretary on Livingstone's election campaign; Theresa Coates (Simon's PA) and Harry Barlow (communications) were former GLC colleagues; and Emma Beal (office manager) knew Livingstone from his work as restaurant critic for the *Evening Standard*. In a subsequent conversation with me, Livingstone contrasted his appointment of people who had worked with him for years in London politics with his successors' mixed record of appointing outsiders to act as advisors.

Others were less closely allied with the mayor, or even complete outsiders: John Duffy, a Brent councillor who had clashed with Livingstone when he had been the local MP, was brought in to advise on waste and Eleanor Young, who had worked at the Association of London Government, took a role as planning advisor. The recruitment exercise also included my job as mayor's office liaison manager, and David Hayward's as diary secretary.

For some of the civil servants involved in the GLA legislation and transition, the deal between Livingstone and Duvall, and the appointment of so many of Livingstone's long-term associates, made a mockery of the 1999 Act's carefully balanced powers and measures to limit mayoral patronage, and undermined their aspirations for a mayoralty that would go beyond tribal politics to appoint a cabinet of disinterested heavy-hitters.

But just as no battle plan ever survives first contact with the enemy, it was probably inevitable that political deals would be done the moment that elected politicians took control of the machinery that civil servants had built. The deal with Duvall allowed Livingstone to appoint a larger office and to keep his formal powers of appointment (the '10+2' as they were commonly called) in reserve for future appointments. That said, while most of the 'insider' applicants were judged to be readily appointable by Duvall and the HR team, some had a tough time proving their worth, and at least one was not appointed as planned.

In public, the mayor talked of wanting his advisors to be accountable to the assembly as well as himself, and of seeking to avoid a 'them' and 'us' situation for the GLA staff, but in reality these were clearly appointments of the 'mayor's team'.[4] They advised him, gatekept for him and represented his views – later on the mayor would describe them as being like junior ministers, capable of speaking for him on relevant issues.

To ensure clarity in 'lines to take', the advisors met every morning, and senior advisors also met with senior management once a week – meetings that initially had a frosty tone, but gradually became more collegiate. This mirrored the gradual thaw of relationships between the mayor's advisors and the GLA staff, as the former understood better how bureaucracies operate, and the latter became more politically attuned to the mayor's objectives.

APPOINTING BOARDS

The other appointments in the mayor's gift were more high profile – a deputy mayor, board members for the four 'functional bodies' overseeing transport, economic development, police and fire, and the Cultural Strategy Group that would sit alongside them. Despite the political and procedural complexities that surrounded advertisement, consultation and balance, the functional body boards were all in place by 3 July, when powers were transferred. The Cultural Strategy Group, chaired by Yasmin Anwar, Channel 4's commissioning editor for multicultural programmes, had its first meeting a few weeks later.

Livingstone's first job was to choose a 'statutory' deputy mayor, who was required to be an assembly member that would be capable of taking over if the mayor was incapacitated. Having cleared his lines with Tony Blair, Livingstone asked Nicky Gavron, who was the assembly member for Enfield and Haringey, to take the post, with specific responsibility for advising on strategic planning – a subject dear to Gavron's heart as chair of the London Planning Advisory Committee, which had been absorbed into the GLA.

The Home Office had been cautious about letting the mayor have any power over the Metropolitan Police. The Metropolitan Police Authority (MPA), which was established under the Greater London Authority Act 1999, gave London a similar model of oversight and scrutiny to that in place outside the capital. The mayor's powers were formally limited to setting the annual police budget and appointing twelve of the authority's twenty-three members from the London Assembly. Other members were magistrates, or 'independent members', with the secretary of state retaining one nomination.

Livingstone appointed twelve MPA members, nominated by the London Assembly in proportion to political make-up, and nominated Labour Group leader Toby Harris as chair.[5] This was not formally a matter for the mayor, but Harris was duly elected. However, Livingstone's attempt to secure a place for his policing advisor Lee Jasper was rebuffed. While powers to appoint and sack the police commissioner remained with the secretary of state (advising the monarch), the then commissioner, Sir John Stevens, lost no time in meeting with the mayor – not only as the elected representative of 7 million Londoners, but as the man who would be setting his budget in future years, thus establishing a pattern of 'soft direction' that would persist between different mayors and police commissioners.

The mayor's powers over London Fire Brigade were similarly constrained. The mayor had to appoint nine London Fire and Emergency Planning Authority (LFEPA) members from the London Assembly and eight nominated by the London boroughs. Livingstone appointed Labour assembly member Val Shawcross as chair (having offered the role to Trevor Phillips and Liberal Democrat Graham Tope), and appointed other assembly members in line with party nominations.[6] The appointment of borough members proved to be more difficult, as Livingstone refused to accept one of the Association of London Government's nominations. Following fraught discussions, the nomination was withdrawn, though the incident was an early indicator of potential tensions between London's tiers of elected government – and delayed the GLA signing up as a formal member of the ALG.

The mayor's powers to appoint and direct London's new economic development and transport agencies were broader, and in some ways gave the mayor more power than he had within the confines of City Hall. The London Development Agency (LDA) joined eight other English regional development agencies that had been established in 1998. These agencies – directly appointed by central government in other regions – were to promote economic development, skills, employment and regeneration, taking over European and 'regeneration' funds from government, land holdings from English Partnerships, and the promotion of inward investment from existing regional structures. The Mayor of London would agree the LDA's strategy, set its budget and have the power to give it directions, though the agency would also be hobbled by retaining fuzzy accountability to central government for national programmes.

The Greater London Authority Act 1999 had made specific provisions for the LDA board, stipulating that a majority of members were business people, and at least four were London Assembly members, City of London or borough councillors. Livingstone advertised for the posts, and John Ross helped to sift applications, and consult with London's business and trade union representatives. The board of fifteen included three assembly members, Hammersmith and Fulham councillor Sally Powell, chair of the City of London's Policy and Resources Committee Judith Mayhew, trade union leader Mick Connolly and business figures from manufacturing, advertising, public relations, hospitality, accountancy and property backgrounds.[7] Livingstone appointed George Barlow, chief executive of Peabody Trust, as chair, and Michael Ward, former chair of the GLC's industry and employment committee but more recently chief executive of the Centre for Local Economic Strategies, as chief executive. Much of the LDA's budget was already committed in 2000, but the agency would come to assume more importance in the years to come, particularly in preparing for London's Olympic Bid, as discussed further in Chapter 13.

Transport for London brought together the London Underground, street management, bus and taxi licensing services (though the handover of the Underground was delayed while the PPP negotiations continued). The mayor's hand was relatively free in relation to TfL: not only did he set its budget and strategy, but he could also chair it himself, and had freedom to appoint a board (but with a prohibition on appointing assembly members, MPs or councillors).

Livingstone chose to chair TfL, and appointed a board of thirteen, which balanced expertise, 'big tent' politics, and strong trade union and former GLC representation, including Livingstone's erstwhile mayoral opponents Steve Norris and Susan Kramer, trade unionists such as Jimmy Knapp, former GLC members Paul Moore and Dave Wetzel (who became deputy chair), disability rights advocate Kirsten Hearn and transport experts Stephen Glaister and Robert Lane, alongside British Tourist Authority chair David Quarmby and British Airports Authority chief executive Mike Hodgkinson.[8]

As chair of TfL, the mayor could also appoint a chief executive, or 'commissioner of transport' as he rebadged the post. Livingstone was determined to find someone who would be credible in the transport world, but would also be credible in trying to persuade Gordon Brown to drop the planned PPP. As one observer recalls, in contrast to the political board, the mayor was very clear that he wanted the commissioner's post advertised in the *Sunday Times* and *The Economist*, not *The Guardian*, so he had the right calibre of people applying rather than people who could be dismissed as the 'usual leftie suspects'.

The search was global in scope, and Livingstone's appointment of Bob Kiley, former CIA officer and New York transport chief, could hardly have been more credible or less predictable for those who expected a leftish placeman to be selected. Anthony Mayer, the former civil servant who had been TfL's interim chief executive, was meanwhile appointed by the assembly to replace Bob Chilton at the head of the GLA (a post that the assembly had advertised as 'chief executive' despite the fact that executive authority lay with the mayor).

The appointments made by Livingstone in his early weeks reflect the ironies and ambiguities of his position. A left-wing Labour politician elected as an independent mayor. A classic machine politician without a party group to support him. A veteran of 1980s municipal socialism elected as leader of a city of resurgent capitalism.

THE ADVISORY CABINET

The balance between inclusion and partisanship, between new and old civic government, can perhaps be seen most clearly in the 'Mayor's Advisory Cabinet' – which is one Livingstone innovation that has not lasted. The cabinet was to be a public forum for the discussion of policy issues, comprising functional body leaders and other advisors.

There would be no collective responsibility, and members would be free to disagree with the mayor. As well as Nicky Gavron and the functional body chairs, the cabinet included assembly members Liberal Democrat Graham Tope and Green Darren Johnson, Angela Mason from Stonewall, Sean Baine (who ran the multi-stakeholder London Civic Forum), Lee Jasper and Kumar Murshid from the mayor's office, architect Richard Rogers, the MPs Glenda Jackson and Diane Abbott (advising on homelessness, and women and equality), Judith Mayhew as City and business advisor, and John McDonnell to advise on consultation and local government.

The last two appointments show just how roomy the mayor's 'big tent' was. As chair of the City of London's Policy and Resources Committee, solicitor Judith Mayhew was the effective leader of the ancient local authority. As Livingstone recalls in his memoirs, the City had campaigned for the GLC's abolition, so her appointment surprised some, though Mayhew actively worked to establish herself as a supportive ambassador to London's business establishment that was still nervous about the new mayoralty.

John McDonnell, MP for Hayes and Harlington, was in turn a fervent advocate of the abolition of the City of London. He had been chair of finance and Livingstone's deputy at the GLC, where they had fallen out over rate-capping. After abolition, McDonnell had been chief executive of the Association of London Authorities, one of two politically defined groupings of London boroughs, before becoming an MP in 1997. At the GLA, McDonnell proposed undertaking a comprehensive policy review and consultation exercise with a view to preparing a 'prospectus'– and, as some of Livingstone's team suspected, establishing himself as chief policy advisor. The process quickly ran into the ground, and McDonnell retreated, complaining, as I recall, that the GLA organisation was not 'mature enough' to provide him with the support he needed.

Originally, the cabinet was intended to meet weekly, and early meetings discussed issues such as budgets, European Car-Free Day, and the mayor's management of Trafalgar Square and Parliament Square. But as is often the case with public meetings in political settings, discussions quickly became 'dignified' performances, when the 'efficient' debates had already taken place between the mayor and his advisors behind closed doors. Meetings became less frequent, and petered out in 2002.

However, the cabinet was not without value. It illustrated Livingstone's early aspiration to work across traditional party lines, in a sense counterbalancing the Greater London Authority Act's concept of unitary mayoral rule. It brought in external voices and the range of stakeholder interests that Livingstone, working through Redmond O'Neill, was careful to cultivate, balance and engage – from faith groups, to LGBT groups, to business interests. It also incubated other projects – including Glenda Jackson's commission on homelessness, and Richard Rogers's establishment of the Architecture and Urbanism Unit (which I left the mayor's office to set up and manage in 2001).

EVENTS, OPPORTUNITIES AND TRAPS

Delivery takes time in city government, particularly from a standing start. With less than four years before the next election, the mayor was keen to pursue his plans, particularly the big-ticket transport initiatives that had dominated the election campaign. But his first weeks in office also showed the inherent challenges in seeking to represent, let alone govern, a city of 7 million people. As crises and long-festering problems emerged across the city, all seemed to migrate to the mayor's office, to test out what the city's new leader could do.

On 10 May, Ford announced the end of car production at Dagenham Motor Works, threatening the loss of 2,000 jobs. Livingstone met with trade and industry secretary Steven Byers, and John Ross was immediately in touch with the firm's Detroit head office. The following day, Livingstone joined the Queen, and a roll-call of 'Cool Britannia' celebrities, at the opening of Tate Modern on Bankside. Hitching a lift in a police riot van from Bankside to the hotel where he was due to meet Nick Scheele, the head of Ford Europe, the new mayor travelled the breadth of London's economic terrain – from booming cultural industries revitalising the city centre, to manufacturing decline blighting the east.[9] The rapid response from Ford, who eventually agreed to open a new engine plant at Dagenham, showed how important a city mayor's intervention could be – at least from the perspective of US firms who were used to dealing with powerful city bosses.

If the Ford announcement came as a surprise, other problems had been waiting in the wings for their moment. In July, Livingstone was told that the replacement for Hungerford Pedestrian Bridge, running over the Thames by Charing Cross Station, was heavily over budget – with delays partly caused by the engineering complexity of pile-driving next to a London Underground tunnel, in a river bed where unexploded bombs from World War Two might still be lurking. Following discussions led by Neale Coleman with Westminster City Council, London Underground and others, a £20 million rescue package was assembled, but Livingstone declined to take on responsibility for the contract.[10]

The mayor also declined the opportunity to take over responsibility for completing Picketts Lock Stadium, which was intended to be the home for the 2005 World Athletics Championship, despite concerns that failure to do so would doom any hope of a London Olympic bid.[11]

Other escapes were more narrow. Livingstone committed to delivering a fireworks display on New Year's Eve 2000, but this quickly ran into trouble. Speaking at a London assembly the mayor set out the problem:

> About six months after the election, the government suggested that this was exactly the sort of thing that the newly elected mayor and assembly should take over. Like a fool I agreed: the GOL staff were transferred to us, along with the contract that had been negotiated

49

with 10 Alps [the event organiser]. Things puttered along in a fairly reasonable way, until, on 4 October, the train operating companies and London Underground dropped the bombshell that they broadly intended to shut down the public transport system.[12]

Negotiations with train operators and London Underground – which at this time had not yet been transferred to the control of TfL – didn't make headway, and the event was cancelled. Livingstone records that the assembly inquiry 'found government files showing that they only transferred the project to me when they realised it was going to fail'.[13] Evaluating risk and choosing the right battles was an important skill for a mayor with limited power and high visibility.

POLICY DELIVERY AND POLITICAL WRANGLING

During this time transport became the mayor's primary focus. The London Underground PPP and the proposed congestion charge had dominated the election campaign, and Livingstone underlined the importance of the latter, when answering an assembly member's question about his 'main goal' at the end of May 2000:

> I have not the slightest doubt that getting the congestion charge right is the single biggest issue facing the GLA. If we get it right it will become the pattern for changing transport usage throughout cities, throughout the country, most probably spreading to cities all over the Western world. No other city of this size has introduced something like congestion charge. If we get it wrong it will set the whole process back by a decade.[14]

The plan for a congestion charge had been controversial among Livingstone's team during the campaign, with several of his advisors expressing concern that charging drivers to enter central London would look like imposing a tax on working people. Livingstone overruled them, however, and his manifesto committed to 'consult widely about the best possible congestion charge scheme to discourage unnecessary car journeys in a small zone of central London, to commence during the middle of my term of office, with all monies devoted to improving transport.'[15] Its introduction – to an accelerated timetable – is discussed further in Chapter 9.

Livingstone also continued to press for an alternative approach to the London Underground PPP. This would involve private sector consortiums taking over London Underground infrastructure and raising private finance to pay for improvements, which Livingstone believed would be more expensive and less safe than direct delivery by reformed London Underground management.[16] He commissioned the Industrial Society think tank, led by former *Observer* editor Will Hutton, to review the scheme. This review concluded in September that the PPP was unsafe and poor value for money.[17] Following his appointment, Bob Kiley proposed alternative plans – for a bond issue through which TfL would borrow the money directly for infrastructure upgrades – but the plans were rejected. After a brief interlude during which Kiley was appointed chair of London Transport and allowed to negotiate with the preferred bidders directly, the government proceeded with its plans.[18]

Liz Meek, who had led the GLA policy team at GOL, and moved to Transport for London after the election, recalls secret dawn meetings at Bob Kiley's flat. There they were joined by Shriti Vadera (then a government advisor, later a life peer and Labour minister), acting as a go-between with the Treasury; Chancellor Gordon Brown steadfastly refused to meet Livingstone. But, with the clunking fist of the Treasury in the background, both John Prescott and Stephen Byers, his successor as transport secretary, stuck to the plan. 'It was the saddest thing,' said Meek. 'They absolutely knew we'd won the argument, but there was no going back. Perhaps I was naïve, but I thought if you talked it through enough, things would get sorted out.'[19]

Another early tussle with Westminster was over the comprehensive spending review, which set out public spending plans for 2001 to 2004, as Gordon Brown began to loosen the government's purse strings. Working with Neale Coleman, Livingstone quickly got to the detail of London's bid, and entered into intense and sometimes furious negotiations with Keith Hill, Streatham MP and minister for London. The outcome was what Livingstone described as a 'good deal for London' (£3.2 billion was granted over the period) – despite a last-minute row about liability for £100 million of the Jubilee Line extension overspend being passed to TfL.[20]

Alongside the high politics of the London Underground PPP, GLA, TfL and LDA staff began production of the mayor's eight statutory strategies, overseen by the mayoral advisors. The draft Transport Strategy, which provided further justification for congestion charging and against the London Underground PPP, came out in October 2000, and the draft Economic Development Strategy in December. However, it was 'Towards the London Plan', which was published in May 2001, that set out the clearest statement of the new mayor's vision for London.

The London Plan (officially the 'spatial development strategy') was intended to be the 'overarching' plan for the development of Greater London. At Romney House, an 'SDS steering group' was convened to hash out the details of the vision and the policy it would contain. The core of the group comprised John Ross, Nicky Gavron, Neale Coleman and Eleanor Young, with Young seeking to balance Ross's focus on world city growth and agglomeration economics, Gavron's long-held interest in sustainable development and 'smart growth', and Coleman's advocacy for affordable housing and social inclusion. The vision that emerged, also informed by the work of Richard Rogers's Urban Task Force, made explicit the choice that London would welcome growth in its population and economy, rather than seeking to divert or disperse this, and would use the momentum of this growth to make London an 'exemplary sustainable world city'.[21]

ONE YEAR THAT SHAPED TWENTY

A year on from Livingstone's election, media critics were already asking what exactly he had achieved. There were some visible successes, including a reduction in bus fares and a rise in passengers, and a rise in police numbers alongside continued preparations for the congestion charge.[22] But the mayor had achieved more than that in laying the foundations for his mayoralty: buying in world-class leadership for London's transport system, publishing strategies for the city's economy, planning and transport systems and getting a good deal out of a government that had every reason to punish him.

At the time of the GLA's formal inception on 3 July 2000, London Assembly chair Trevor Phillips warned Livingstone that 'this is a democracy, not a Kenocracy'. But the organisational structures of the mayoralty cannot help but embody the decisions made by their first occupant. As Livingstone himself reflected:

> We were starting from scratch. No modern British politician had ever had the opportunity I was now presented with to create a new body, recruiting staff and drawing up planning, transport and environmental strategies. Future mayors would inherit the machine I created.[23]

The three mayors to date have been very different in character, but all have operated within the framework Livingstone set: establishing a small team of trusted advisors; using influence and networks as well as powers to shape the city; alternately doing deals with and denouncing central government; and seeking to harness the momentum of growth to make London a better place.

PART TWO

EVOLUTION

4

'HAVING A MAYOR': TWENTY YEARS OF THE MAYORALTY

JACK BROWN

KEN LIVINGSTONE'S MAYORALTY: 2000–2008

EARLY DAYS

As Richard Brown has examined in Chapter 3, the early days of the mayoralty offered the post's first holder, Ken Livingstone, a unique opportunity to shape the office in his own image. This consumed a great deal of time and focus, occupying much of the first eighteen months of his tenure. Running and winning the mayoralty as an independent, the candidate formerly known as 'Red Ken' arrived at City Hall with a team of advisors drawn in part from the far-left Socialist Action campaign group. Yet, the radical new vision for the capital that they were preparing was far from that which their opponents had expected.

GROWING UP

The first draft London Plan emerged in June 2002, adopting a pro-growth stance that has since become an accepted orthodoxy, but at the time was far from inevitable. By the time the plan was finalised in February 2004, it predicted and accommodated for 800,000 more Londoners by 2016, alongside 636,000 new jobs. Over 450,000 new homes would be needed, focused primarily in central and east London, and around transport hubs. The plan aimed for 50 per cent of new housing to be 'affordable'.[1]

Ultimately, the entire plan was, through necessity, heavily reliant upon the private sector and central government to deliver. Seeking to create an 'exemplary sustainable world city' – but branded a 'corporate world city' vision by the Green Party – the plan proved extremely influential in shaping the direction of travel for the capital over the coming decades.[2]

The private sector – or rather parts of the property sector – was certainly interested in playing its part. A wave of striking tall buildings began to emerge under Livingstone, from 30 St Mary Axe (the 'Gherkin'), which remains one of Londoners' favourite skyscrapers, to London's tallest building (and second favourite), Renzo Piano's 'Shard of Glass', today commonly shortened to 'The Shard'.[3] Battles with English Heritage persisted throughout Livingstone's tenure, but the mayor was clear that tall buildings were an essential element in accommodating London's growth – a view that subsequent mayors have not substantially diverged from.

RELATIONS WITH THE CENTRE

Central government also proved willing to play its part in implementing Livingstone's plan. While the mayor reportedly found himself barred from meeting Chancellor Gordon Brown in person until the latter became Prime Minister in 2007, the Treasury parted with substantial sums for major investment in the capital throughout the Livingstone mayoralty.[4] This covered major transport infrastructure investments, such as the east London line extension (London Overground) and the development of the northern ticket hall at King's Cross, (spurred on by the upcoming Olympic Games, which was no small investment in its own right). It also covered everything from expanding and improving the bus network to building social housing (although Livingstone would not survive in office long enough to oversee the latter).

The mayor (together with secretary of state for culture, media and sport Tessa Jowell) also managed to persuade a sceptical government to back a bid for the 2012 Olympic and Paralympic Games. Following negotiation of a funding package involving a mixture of council tax, National Lottery and London Development Agency funding, the bid, which would prove so significant for the capital, was announced in the House of Commons by Jowell on 15 May 2003, and then with the mayor at City Hall the following day. Formally launched in January 2004, the bid would ultimately prove successful. A mayoral council tax precept to contribute to its cost was collected from 2006.[5]

Perhaps unsurprisingly, there were also points of near-constant conflict between the government and the mayoralty. July 2002 saw a bid by Livingstone to re-join the Labour Party rejected through the party's National Executive Committee.[6] The independent mayor continued to publicly fight the Blair government over the PPP deal for Tube upgrades for the majority of his first term. These attempts ultimately proved fruitless, and while the scheme has few defenders today, the deal survived in part until 2010, outliving Livingstone's mayoralty.[7]

CHARGING FORWARDS

While the debate over the PPP was fierce among politicians, it did not have a great deal of public 'cut through'. The experience of the vast majority of Londoners was of a gradual improvement in public transport as Livingstone's mayoralty progressed, as investment began to flow and innovations were introduced. The bus network was an area of particular interest. The introduction of the Oyster card in June 2003 was revolutionary, and provided for the subsequent expansion and better integration of London's transport network, but uncontroversial. The introduction of the congestion charge in February 2003, by way of contrast, was a much more contentious, attention-grabbing policy, which was also politically risky. The scheme introduced a new tax shortly before the next mayoral election and proved to be a make-or-break moment for the capital's first mayor. It is explored in further detail in Chapters 8 and 9.

In the event, despite the concerns of mayor, officials, and political advisors alike, the charge operated smoothly, reduced congestion significantly, and even proved popular.[8] The risk certainly paid off, with Livingstone later branding the charge 'the only thing in my career that turned out better than I had hoped'.[9] While Livingstone's subsequent westward extension of the charging zone, which came into operation on 19 February 2007, would later be rolled back by his successor at the end of 2010, and his pledge to introduce a higher charge for 'gas guzzling' 4x4s was derailed by electoral defeat, the success of the initial congestion charge has paved the way for a series of subsequent traffic reduction and air quality measures in the years to follow.[10]

LONDON AND LONDONERS

As well as implementing his own major initiatives, Livingstone also pushed forwards with projects that local authorities were unable or unwilling to deal with. An excellent example of the latter could be found in the pedestrianisation and upgrading of Trafalgar Square, completed in 2003. The square's regeneration, planned before Livingstone's arrival but helped along by the new mayor, cemented its role as an international, national and city-wide civic space, highlighting another aspect of the mayor's role – engaging London's diverse communities, promoting London-wide cultural events and marketing London internationally as an inclusive, dynamic city. The mayor introduced a number of celebratory national and religious events, and promoted the annual 'Rise' anti-racist music festival. Livingstone also used his mandate and his voice to lend support to other minority groups – which echoed a theme of his GLC administration – including introducing a same-sex register for civil partnerships, which had no legal foundation, but arguably helped to pave the way for the Blair government's formal introduction of civil partnerships in 2004.

SECOND TERM

After what had seemed to outside observers to be a slow start, Livingstone's first term had kicked into life with the success of the congestion charge. Livingstone won re-admittance into the Labour Party in May 2004, and was re-elected as Mayor of London again by beating Steven Norris (albeit by a smaller margin than in 2000) in June 2004. The GLA's staff continued to increase in number, reportedly surpassing the number of seats at desks in City Hall, and the mayor's office also expanded.[11] The mayor's council tax 'precept' increased annually by an average of 12.8 per cent throughout both of Livingstone's terms (although this average was roughly twice as high in the first term as the second), and complemented substantial central government subsidy, which allowed the mayor to increase police numbers and invest heavily in the capital's public transport network.[12]

The re-introduction of neighbourhood policing had been a significant first-term achievement, and Livingstone enjoyed positive relations with the Metropolitan Police Commissioner Sir John Stevens, and his successor Sir Ian Blair. Relations with the London Assembly were not always as positive, but were ultimately navigated successfully; while several of the mayor's budgets provoked disagreement – particularly the first, which raised the mayoral precept specifically to increase police funding – the assembly's electoral system meant that it proved difficult to produce the two-thirds majority required to block a mayoral budget and agree an alternative budget. Livingstone's first and last budgets were particularly contentious, but deals were done prior to avoid the 'nuclear option' of the assembly blocking the mayoral budget. At the time of writing, the assembly is still yet to use this power.

TRIUMPH AND TRAGEDY

Livingstone's second term – and indeed his mayoralty – was punctuated sharply by an intense two-day period in July 2005. On 6 July, the mayor was in Singapore, where London had been announced as the city that had been selected to host the 2012 Olympics. Despite a self-proclaimed complete disinterest in sport, Livingstone was particularly taken by the regenerative potential of an east London-centred games early on in his first term.[13] Winning the bid not only provided great opportunities for the regeneration of Stratford and the wider area, but also lubricated the flow of central government investment into the capital. However, like Crossrail, Livingstone's role was to negotiate for substantial future investment into a project that would ultimately be delivered after he had left City Hall. Such is the nature of electoral politics.

On the day after the announcement that London had won the bid, four Islamist terrorists exploded bombs on Tube trains at Aldgate, Edgware Road and Russell Square, and later on a number 30 bus at Tavistock Square, killing fifty-six and injuring nearly 800. The mayor's response, outlined in Chapter 19, was powerfully defiant yet sensitive, and remains a key moment in the short history of the mayoralty. The intangible benefits of having a city-wide spokesperson, providing a focal point for grief, pain and resolution, were clear; in times of trage-dy, the mayor could 'speak for London' in a way that no other elected political could.

'YOU CAN'T SAY THAT'

However, Livingstone's speech proved to be a relatively rare example of a public utterance from the mayor that did not cause widespread controversy. Despite claiming that he never sought celebrity status, Livingstone was regularly in the news for his controversial comments, and his second term saw this tendency increase. Comparing Jewish *Evening Standard* reporter Oliver Finegold to a Nazi concentration camp guard led to a four-week suspension from his job which, while overturned by a judge, left a sour taste in the mouths of many Londoners.[14]

The mayor constantly pushed the boundaries of acceptability, but managed to escape censure or serious punishment despite repeated serious incidents. Inviting the hard-line Muslim cleric Yusuf al-Qaradawi – whose previous statements on Jews, women and homosexuals were incompatible with the mayor's supposedly inclusive. outlook – to City Hall as an 'honoured guest' in July 2004 caused great offence, as did his invitation to return.[15] Livingstone's comments to the Reuben brothers, property developers born in India of Iraqi-Jewish descent, that 'they can go back to Iran and try their luck with the ayatollahs if they don't like the planning regime or my approach', achieved the mayor's goal of getting an alternative developer involved in Westfield Stratford, but was also fairly described as 'low-level racist abuse'.[16] Following comments on a trade trip to China in April 2006 that compared the history of Tiananmen Square to the poll tax riots in Trafalgar Square, *The Guardian*'s Simon Jenkins claimed that Livingstone had 'the diplomatic skills of Attila the Hun'.[17]

FOREIGN POLICY

Livingstone's second term saw his focus shift beyond London's boundaries. The GLA established small offices in China (in Beijing and Shanghai) and India (Delhi and Mumbai), to promote foreign direct investment into London and attract international students and tourism. A 'European office' in Brussels was also established.[18] London was also promoted worldwide by mayoral agencies Visit London, Study London and Think London. A major promotional effort to boost tourism following the 11 September 2001 terror attack in New York, and again following the 7 July 2005 attacks, also proved successful in keeping London's growing tourist economy afloat.

However, not all mayoral 'foreign policy' was as successful. Livingstone's inability – or unwillingness – to avoid commenting on whatever global issue caught his eye led to headline-grabbing comments on everyone from the Saudi royal family to US President George W. Bush. This did not necessarily help relations with central government or further the cause of Londoners. A February 2007 deal with Hugo Chávez's Venezuela, which pledged TfL transport advice to the Latin American nation in exchange for discount oil to fuel London's buses, benefitted Londoners, but seemingly at the expense of their Venezuelan counterparts. The deal barely outlasted Livingstone's mayoralty, with his successor Johnson branding it 'completely Caracas'.[19] A trip to Cuba was 'an almost totally unmitigated disaster', according to one City Hall official.[20]

Livingstone's global approach to running London had more success relating to environmental issues and climate change. In 2005, Livingstone convened representatives from eighteen global 'megacities' to discuss ways to combat climate change and reduce emissions together, laying the foundations for the 'C20' and later 'C40' group of cities, developed alongside the Clinton Climate Initiative.[21] The mayor published a 'Climate Change Action Plan' in 2007.[22] In addition, schemes such as the 'Green 500' and the 'Better Buildings Partnership' brought businesses and landlords together in London to retrofit buildings and reduce carbon emissions.[23] But the C40 offered the opportunity to orchestrate economies of scale that made retrofitting buildings and other emission reduction measures possible in a much more impactful way.[24]

CONCLUSIONS

There were some mayoral schemes that came to nothing under Livingstone. A bid to host Formula 1 racing in Hyde Park was much discussed but failed to materialise, and an aquarium at Silvertown Quays also never arrived.[25] Two new tram projects – the West London Tram and the Cross River Tram – and the long-anticipated Thames Gateway Bridge all also dragged on for several years before ultimately proving undeliverable.[26] But Livingstone's two terms are held in high esteem by many expert mayor-watchers to this day, for the sheer breadth of activity and the boldness of action taken. Alongside setting an ambitious, pro-growth 'world city' vision for London, there were several major achievements either secured or initiated between 2000 and 2008 that would have a lasting impact, and that are unlikely to have occurred without Livingstone's involvement: the congestion charge is a clear, radical achievement, but the pursuit of a transformative East End-focused bid for the 2012 Olympics and securing central government commitment to funding Crossrail were also lasting, significant legacies.

Livingstone was re-selected by Labour Party members as their candidate in 2007, and stood for a third term in 2008. However, accusations of impropriety on the part of his equalities advisor Lee Jasper, prompted by an ongoing campaign in December 2007 by the *Evening Standard*, damaged the mayor's reputation. The capital's regional development agency, the LDA, was tasked with economic development, regeneration and skills, and provided grants to bodies across London. It was alleged that Jasper had channelled grant money improperly to friends or associates. While Jasper was cleared by internal investigation, and a critical investigation ordered by Boris Johnson found 'ineptitude rather than corruption' at the LDA, some felt that Livingstone had failed to act swiftly or ruthlessly enough.[27] Others suggested that his foreign endeavours had distracted him from what was going on at home. Either way, the damage was done.

BORIS JOHNSON'S MAYORALTY: 2008–16

'BORIS'

Alexander Boris de Pfeffel Johnson, Conservative MP for Henley since 2001, entered the race to be the party's candidate for Mayor of London at the last possible moment, with a speech at County Hall on 16 July 2007.[28] Johnson won the Conservative nomination easily on 27 September, winning 75 per cent of all votes cast in a four-horse race.[29] Echoing the Blair government's initial hopes for their 2000 candidate, David Cameron had tried and failed to persuade a figure from outside politics to run, such as broadcaster Nick Ferrari, or former BBC director general Greg Dyke.[30] In the end, a candidate was found who was arguably both a politician *and* a celebrity.

Johnson's mayoral campaign began slowly, and was taken over and run by Australian elections guru Lynton Crosby at the behest of shadow Chancellor George Osborne at the end of 2007. The campaign pursued what became known as the 'doughnut strategy', targeting voters in the outer ring of boroughs supposedly neglected by Johnson's Zone 1-focused predecessor, and concentrating on the reduction of crime, and particularly youth violence. However, Johnson was also aware that he needed to offer something to the capital's liberal voters, and on the campaign trail praised London as a 'magnificent example of diversity and tolerance and cosmopolitanism', and pledged an inquiry into a potential amnesty for illegal immigrants in the capital.[31] On winning the mayoralty, Johnson adapted Tony Blair's famous 1997 pledge and declared that 'I was elected as New Boris and I will govern as New Boris'.[32]

Johnson won the 2008 election decisively, by 53.2 per cent to Livingstone's 46.8 per cent, once second-preference votes were allocated.[33] While Livingstone managed to garner more overall votes than he had achieved in 2004, Johnson motivated his voters to turn out.[34] The 2008 election had attracted widespread attention as two figures with truly national profiles competed for the mayoralty for the first time. Early on in the race, Livingstone described Johnson as 'the most formidable opponent I will face in my political career'.[35]

EARLY DAYS

Having announced his candidacy late on, Johnson's team was assembled at speed, and featured several former colleagues of 'acting chief of staff' Nick Boles – once the preferred mayoral candidate of the Conservative leadership until illness forced him to step down – from the Policy Exchange think tank and Westminster City Council.[36] This process is outlined in more detail in Chapter 7.

Perhaps unsurprisingly, then, the initial phase of the Johnson mayoralty was widely regarded as somewhat chaotic. One City Hall insider described the first few months of the new administration as an 'absolute A-grade shambles'.[37] A Conservative assembly member recalled that 'the first year was dreadful. We had some terrible problems.'[38] At the heart of the supposed shambles was what Johnson biographer Andrew Gimson called an 'embarrassingly high attrition rate'.[39]

Johnson was elected in May but by August he had already lost three advisors, with more to follow (a process also described in more detail in Chapter 7).

RIP IT UP AND START AGAIN?

Johnson's mayoralty also took a little while to find its feet in terms of policy. Many of the new mayor's early initiatives were focused on dismantling aspects of his predecessor's regime, with a focus on cost cutting and rooting out 'corruption': committing to improved transparency and cost reduction at City Hall; replacing the senior leadership of the London Development Agency and appointing a panel to investigate its work and finances; pledging to close the 'Kenbassies' in China and India (although these were instead 'put to review' and ultimately survived); abolishing the Livingstone-initiated *Londoner* newspaper and using part of the expected £2.9 million saving to plant 10,000 trees; ending Livingstone's Venezuela deal when it expired in August 2008; and repealing both Livingstone's planned £25 congestion charge for 'gas guzzling' 4x4s, and the western extension of the congestion charge.[40]

Johnson took an initially fiscally conservative approach to running City Hall. The mayoral share of council tax was frozen year-on-year, but TfL fare rises were tolerated when deemed necessary in order to raise additional funds.[41] The announcement of a ban on alcohol consumption on public transport from 1 June 2008 was an instinctively un-Johnsonite policy that tipped its hat towards the 'law and order' mayoralty pledged during Johnson's campaign, but was not the kind of bold and ambitious policy to set the mayoralty alight.

POLICING AND CRIME

It was reported that the mayor felt that he was still suffering from a 'vision problem' a year into his first term.[42] However, in the view of Johnson's communications director Guto Harri, 'The more he took charge, the more focused and determined we became, and the more we got done.'[43] Such an occasion came abruptly on 2 October 2008, when Metropolitan Police Commissioner Sir Ian Blair announced his resignation, seemingly at the mayor's behest, which is described in further detail in Chapter 11. It has been argued that this flexing of mayoral muscle 'established Boris as a serious player'.[44] With no formal power to do so, the mayor's use of 'soft' power to remove the Met commissioner demonstrated an authority and a seriousness that critics had suggested Johnson lacked.

Policing and crime were a major area of focus throughout the Johnson mayoralty. The mayor personally chaired the Metropolitan Police Authority until 2010. November 2008 saw the publication of the mayor's 'Time for Action' strategy to deal with youth violence, and the reduction of knife crime among young Londoners was a particular target. Kit Malthouse urged schools to install metal detectors as early as June 2008 and an increase in the controversial use of 'stop and search' powers followed.[45] The number of knife crime offences rose annually throughout Johnson's first term, but they reduced notably during his second.[46]

2011 RIOTS

Crime continued to be a major issue for Johnson throughout his mayoralty. On 4 August 2011, armed police officers shot 29-year-old Mark Duggan dead on Ferry Lane, Tottenham. A peaceful march on Tottenham police station on 6 August later erupted into violence, with looting and rioting spreading across London and to other English cities in the coming days. Johnson was holidaying with his family in Canada, and was either reluctant or unable to return to the capital immediately, eventually arriving back in the capital on 9 August, three nights into the riots. On his return, he was jeered and heckled at his first public appearance at Clapham Junction. His instinctive, perhaps opportune, response, brandishing a broom in a gesture of solidarity with the clean-up effort, won some of those present around.[47] But the mayor's initial response to the riots was not widely regarded as impressive.[48]

RELATIONS WITH THE CENTRE, PART TWO

The mayor dined with Prime Minister David Cameron at Downing Street on the evening that he returned to the capital. He declined to mention that he planned to criticise police cuts on BBC Radio Four's *Today* programme the following morning, leaving Cameron reportedly furious. Throughout Johnson's mayoralty, there were moments where there was clear political benefit in distancing himself from the (post-2010) coalition government, despite party allegiances. As Andrew Gimson has noted, the mayor 'retrieved his own position at the expense of his colleagues'.[49]

This was evidenced by Johnson's October 2010 comments on the government's proposed housing benefit cap, which saw the mayor tell BBC London that 'we will not accept any kind of Kosovo-style social cleansing of London'.[50] However, while some of this was about political positioning, there were also occasions when the mayor's comments were designed to leverage investment from central government, to the benefit of London and Londoners. Johnson established the London Finance Commission in July 2012 to investigate funding arrangements in the capital, and to see if there was a case for greater fiscal devolution to London, giving the capital more control of, and incentive to grow, its tax base.[51] Alongside this, Johnson lobbied central government for funding in the meantime. Johnson's mayoralty began in the midst of a global recession, and from 2010 onwards existed in a climate of national austerity, but the mayor was able to extract impressive amounts of cash for London from the Treasury.

A £90 million central government grant in January 2012 helped to keep police numbers up, following the riots and in advance of the Olympics, and police numbers increased slightly overall across the duration of Johnson's two terms as mayor, in a context of falling numbers across the rest of England and Wales.[52] Crossrail funding was preserved, with the mayor publicly stating in May 2009: 'When you are in a hole as big as Crossrail, it is absolutely vital to keep digging.'[53] A wider programme of necessary Tube upgrades and the extension of the Northern Line were also secured; a 'City Hall staffer' told *The Guardian* in August 2010 that 'we will die in a ditch for Crossrail and the Tube improvements', should central government not be forthcoming with the funding.[54] According to then TfL commissioner Peter Hendy, Johnson 'played an absolute blinder for us ... He held out when some people around him wanted to settle early and extracted an extra £700 million out of the government as a result'.[55]

TRANSPORT AND 'MEGAPROJECTS'

Under Johnson, as Livingstone, public transport remained the policy sphere in which the mayor could make the most visible, tangible difference. The mayor himself took particular interest in several large-scale, eye-catching projects, with varying degrees of success, but also made significant progress on less glamorous but important transport improvements.

The launch of a cycle-hire scheme for London, sponsored by Barclays and later Santander, which became known colloquially and inescapably as 'Boris Bikes', was a notable first-term success. While the political risk was undoubtedly lower, the scheme's profile, the rush to ensure that it was ready, and the uncertainty around its opening day success bear some comparison with Livingstone's implementation of the congestion charge.[56] While Livingstone had investigated the possibility of such a scheme, itself based on Paris's existing 'Vélib' scheme, towards the end of his mayoralty, the execution and risks of the project were very much Johnson's. Johnson's mayoralty also saw an increasing focus on cycling, which is explored in Chapter 21.

Johnson's experience with the capital's bus network was perhaps more complex, but also ultimately a broad success. Johnson was elected on a pledge to remove articulated 'bendy buses' from the capital's streets, citing safety concerns for cyclists, and introduced a newly designed Routemaster bus, notable for their 'hop on, hop off' rear platforms.[57] While the new buses attracted some early criticism, they have since been adapted and remain in operation.

The mayor's enthusiasm for a new airport in the Thames Estuary, inevitably dubbed 'Boris Island', was an ambitious idea that failed to materialise, despite the commissioning of a feasibility study that found no 'insoluble issues' with the project,[58] and the appointment of Daniel Moylan as mayoral 'aviation advisor'.[59] Plans for a 'Garden Bridge' in central London also failed and were cancelled by Sadiq Khan following a review, citing value for money, escalating costs and controversy around procurement and competition.[60]

The 2012 Olympic and Paralympic Games also brought about several projects that caught Johnson's eye. The mayor was a major enthusiast for the Emirates 'Air Line', a cable car which runs between North Greenwich and the Royal Docks, which was opened just in time for the games.[61] The games were more central to the genesis of the ArcelorMittal Orbit tower in the Olympic Park (initially dubbed 'The Piffle Tower'), which was later converted into a 'helter-skelter' slide. Johnson made much of the fact that both projects brought in private funding alongside public, although the ratio between the two was a topic of much debate.[62] While neither have proved great revenue generators, nor provide the most practical way of getting from A to B, both projects are now tourist attractions and recognisable parts of London's skyline.

BUILT ENVIRONMENT

London's skyline would become a contentious issue during Johnson's mayoralty. Johnson arrived at City Hall as a mild sceptic of tall buildings, pledging in 2008 that he would avoid London turning into 'Dubai-on-Thames'. By 2016, it was claimed that the capital had 400 towers higher than twenty-storeys in the pipeline.[63] *The Observer* and *Architects' Journal* founded the Skyline Campaign in March 2014 in opposition to the surging pipeline of tall buildings, and a great deal of ink was spilled attacking towers that had been planned and permitted.[64]

Of course, many of the towers that appeared on London's skyline during Johnson's mayoralty were approved or even under construction during Livingstone's mayoralty. A London View Management Framework was published in March 2012, in an attempt to ensure that key sightlines were preserved among the rush to build upwards.[65] However, Johnson did give permission to several particularly large or tall developments following the denial of planning permission at borough level; nearly twenty such developments were 'called in' and approved during his administration.[66] A notable increase in permissions, applications and completions was also observable towards the end of Johnson's second term.[67]

Perhaps of more direct consequence to the lives of Londoners was the mayor's response to London's housing crisis. Livingstone's percentage-based affordable housing targets were replaced by numerical targets; Johnson's first housing strategy, produced as part of new mayoral powers in the area, aimed for 55,000 units of affordable housing by 2011.[68] By the end of March 2016, over 100,000 'affordable' homes had been constructed during Johnson's mayoralty, with the GLA contributing funding directly to nearly all. While the definition of 'affordable' was altered, and these homes were at least partly the product of central government cash provided by the Brown government, this was a higher overall number than during the previous administration.[69]

Quality was also an issue: Johnson pledged to combat the construction of 'rabbit hutch-sized homes' in the capital in 2008.[70] He published a 'Housing Design Guide' in August 2010, promising an end to homes 'built to indecently poor standards – fit neither for Bilbo Baggins or his hobbit friends'.[71] However, a pledge to eradicate rough sleeping from the capital by 2012, via the establishment of the London Delivery Board in February 2009, failed to meet its target, with rough sleeping up 43 per cent on the previous year in 2011 to 2012.[72]

RE-ELECTION AND THE OLYMPICS

The 2012 mayoral election was in many ways a re-run of 2008. Livingstone and Johnson dominated, with opinion polls showing narrow leads flicking between each candidate in the months prior. Turnout was lower, at 38 per cent, and Johnson's margin of victory tighter, but he emerged victorious after second preferences were counted, winning by 51.5 to 48.5 per cent.[73] It was therefore Johnson who would get to enjoy holding the position of Mayor of London during the Olympic Games.

While it is still perhaps too early to judge fully the social impact of the 2012 Olympic Games on the regeneration of Stratford and the wider East End of London, it is clear that there has been tremendous physical change. The games were delivered on time and with relatively little controversy. The capital's transport system did not grind to a halt, and the games themselves passed without major incident. While the London Olympics were secured under his predecessor, Johnson oversaw preparations for the event, and put in place legacy delivery structures and plans (including the complex of cultural and educational facilities that he called 'Olympicopolis', and his successor rebranded as 'East Bank'), as well as basking in the warm glow of public enthusiasm for a widely successful games.

The image of the mayor 'stuck' on a zipwire, Union flags dangling in each hand, remains an iconic image of the 'Boris as buffoon' characterisation of Johnson. The zipwire incident, which occurred during a promotional visit to Victoria Park just after Team GB's first gold medal of the 2012 Olympics, placed the mayor front and centre of the news agenda in the midst of this rare moment of national positivity, enthusiasm and even pride. It did his reputation no harm whatsoever. Chancellor George Osborne being loudly booed when presenting a medal at the Paralympic Games contrasted notably with Johnson's 'Olympomania' speech at Hyde Park in the build-up to the games, where the mayor asserted that the capital was 'the greatest city on earth' and that 'the Geiger-counter of Olympomania is going to go zoink – off the scale'. Call-and-response chants with the excited crowd followed, interrupted only by chants of 'Boris! Boris!'[74]

The mayor would later upstage the Prime Minister when speaking at the ceremony to celebrate the 'tear-sodden, juddering climax of the summer of London 2012', where he addressed the Team GB athletes:

> This was your achievement. You brought this country together in a way we never expected. You routed the doubters, and you scattered the gloomsters, and for the first time in living memory you caused Tube train passengers to break into spontaneous conversation with their neighbours about subjects other than their trod-on toes ... and you produced such paroxysms of tears and joy on the sofas of Britain that you probably not only inspired a generation, but helped to create one as well. I can get away with that.[75]

Following the games, a ConservativeHome poll found the mayor emerging as clear favourite among Conservative Party members to succeed David Cameron as Prime Minister, with 32 per cent of votes to Osborne's 2 per cent.[76]

SPRINGBOARD?

Ultimately, the mayor's Olympic experience serves as a reminder that, unlike his predecessor, but potentially for all future holders of the office, few believed that Johnson's mayoralty was the peak of his ambition. Speculation around when, rather than if, the mayor would make his move on Downing Street occurred throughout Johnson's tenure.[77] As early as November 2011, former deputy mayor and advisor Ray Lewis proclaimed that Johnson was 'A man with a growing sense of destiny. London will be too small for Boris soon.'[78] In late 2012, the *New Statesman*'s Rafael Behr reported that Johnson 'told aides he intends to perform his mayoral duties on an unofficial part-time basis after the Olympics'.[79]

The accusation that Johnson was a 'part-time' Mayor of London was not limited to the post-Olympic years of his mayoralty. On becoming mayor in 2008, he declined to give up his lucrative *Telegraph* column, describing the associated £250,000 second salary as 'chickenfeed' in an interview on the BBC's *HARDTalk* programme.[80] A commitment to justify this continued second job by donating 20 per cent of his salary to charity (namely establishing a 'Boris bursary' for journalism students and supporting the teaching of classics at London state schools) was made public, but it is unclear whether this was delivered in full.[81]

The mayor also wrote and published two books – a history of London in 2011, and a biography of Winston Churchill in 2014 – while Mayor of London. For Johnson, his authoring of books was entirely compatible with his political career: 'If some lefty, snivelling opponent tells you that you can't combine writing and politics you can remind them that Churchill wrote journalism throughout his career.'[82] Ultimately, much of the latter part of the Johnson mayoralty was dominated by speculation on what would be next for Johnson personally. In 2015, having pledged not to run for a third term as mayor when his second expired in May 2016, Johnson stood for and won a seat in Parliament as the MP for Uxbridge and South Ruislip. Just over four years later, he became Prime Minister.

CONCLUSION

Johnson's two terms as Mayor of London had been a blend of excellent and extremely challenging timing. Johnson inherited major projects and a broad 'world city' vision from his predecessor, and had the great fortune of being in City Hall for the London Olympics. But he also took charge of the capital at the onset of a global financial crisis, and had to contend with riots as well as a national climate of austerity. Johnson succeeded in winning funding for the capital, and was good at selling London overseas, raising the profile of the mayoralty even further, and delivering some major projects. His personality was an asset; as self-proclaimed Johnson critic Julian Glover observed: 'When he talked of London as the greatest city on Earth he really seemed to feel it.'[83] Critics would argue that too much attention was sometimes paid to big, eye-catching 'vanity projects', which – of those that were actually delivered – did not always achieve value for public money.[84] Ultimately, Johnson's was neither a disastrous nor truly transformative mayoralty.

SADIQ KHAN'S MAYORALTY: 2016–

CAMPAIGN AND ELECTION

Johnson and Livingstone may have had hugely different upbringings, but the two are big personalities and they have more traits in common than either would like to admit. The 2016 election, by way of contrast, would focus on two very different characters. Sadiq Aman Khan, Labour MP for Tooting and a former human rights lawyer, was the council estate-born son of a bus driver, but also an astute political operator with an excellent feel for the Labour Party's internal machinations. Frank Zacharias Robin Goldsmith, Conservative MP for Richmond Park and a former journalist and environmentalist, was a man of great privilege, but a green rebel, a Eurosceptic, and an independent thinker within his party.

The 2016 mayoral election saw the highest turnout to date (46 per cent), and Khan won by 56.8 per cent to 43.2 per cent, the second highest margin to date (beaten only by Livingstone's first victory in 2000).[85] Achieving 1.3 million votes, Khan's mandate as mayor is the largest any single politician has ever received in UK history.[86] This decisive result emerged from a much more contentious electoral battle. Goldsmith's campaign repeatedly attempted to connect the former human rights lawyer Khan to Islamist extremists and extremism, as well as targeting specific ethnic and religious groups with tailored anti-Khan messaging.[87] Khan, for his part, had pledged to combat radicalism, committing to being 'the British Muslim who takes the fight to the extremists'.[88] Islamophobia, an undercurrent of the entire campaign, was visible in plain sight when the since-deregistered far-right Britain First Party's mayoral candidate turned his back on the new mayor during his inaugural speech.[89]

PLEDGES

Alongside shaping a strong narrative around Khan's own personal backstory, the mayor-to-be's campaign focused on the capital's housing crisis, pledging to provide thousands of 'genuinely affordable' new homes, with 'first dibs' for Londoners, establishing a 'Homes for Londoners' board to oversee this, and setting a target of 50 per cent 'affordable' properties on development on public land. Khan also committed to introduce a one-hour 'hopper' bus ticket to the capital, and made the eye-catching promise to freeze transport fares for the duration of his four-year term.[90] Aware of the potentially damaging impression created by his nomination of Jeremy Corbyn for the Labour leadership, he also eagerly pledged to be 'the most pro-business mayor ever'.[91] Other areas of focus included improving the capital's air quality, tackling gangs and knife crime, improving the skills offering available to Londoners and making the capital a 'living wage city'.[92]

EXTERNAL SHOCKS

Khan's mayoral term occurred in a time of great political turmoil both at home and abroad. Even before Khan's election, it became clear that a greater portion of his time at City Hall would be dominated by politics (with a capital 'P') than either of his predecessors. Some of this was to do with who the new mayor was, and some concerned what was going on in the wider world. Much required mayoral response and much risked completely derailing Khan's agenda.

On 23 June 2016, a month and a half into Khan's mayoralty, the United Kingdom voted to leave the European Union. London's 60:40 vote in favour of remaining in the EU placed the capital in stark contrast with the rest of England and Wales, and revealed that the majority of Londoners (but not all) agreed with Khan's vocal support for Remain in the build-up to the vote. Khan has maintained his anti-Brexit stance, stating that he is 'proud that London was the only region in England to vote to remain'.[93] He has repeatedly branded Brexit as 'the biggest act of economic self-harm' the UK had ever committed, and called for a second referendum in 2018.[94]

The result of the EU referendum has also had a tangible impact on London, with economic slowdown predicted and other European cities actively seeking to lure businesses and investment away from London. The mayor launched the 'London is Open' campaign in response to the referendum results, to promote the capital's inclusivity and diversity and attract visitors and investors from around the world, and to counteract the threat of other European cities luring investment away from London.[95]

A series of terror attacks across Europe also required Khan's response, beginning with the Paris terror attacks of 13 November 2015, which just preceded his mayoralty. Several terror attacks occurred in London in 2017, at Westminster Bridge, London Bridge, Finsbury Park and Parsons Green, as well as in Manchester at the Manchester Arena. The London incidents, which ranged from Islamist extremist-inspired attacks on civilians using vehicles and knives, to a man driving his van through a crowd of worshippers outside a mosque during Ramadan, were horrific in their own right, but also risked provoking further retaliation and division among Londoners.

In each case, the mayor's response was resolute, clear and calm, winning him plaudits across the capital and beyond. However, journalist Dave Hill was right to also acknowledge 'the disruption, the devouring of time and energy, the sheer, exhausting weight of responsibility'.[96] The horrific Grenfell Tower fire of 14 June 2017, whereby a small domestic fire in the kitchen of a fourth-floor flat spread through the tower's supposedly incombustible exterior to engulf the building, killing seventy-two people and injuring many more, also required a response from Khan. The mayor has been vocal about the fire, issuing a series of statements, writing to the Prime Minister advocating for residents and pushing for a public inquiry into the tragedy.[97]

Khan's mayoralty also came at a time of continued national austerity and at a time when the national government and the London government were no longer political allies. Khan's first term has been the first full term of any mayor where the national government has been entirely composed of an opposing political party (Livingstone's first term as an independent, having applied to re-join the Labour

Party and eventually succeeding in doing so, being an anomaly of sorts). Relations have been particularly poor: the mayor attacked Prime Minister Theresa May and her government as 'anti-London'; while Conservative MPs accused the mayor of being 'obsessed' with publicity and of 'never taking responsibility for his own actions'.[98] Relations with former Boris Johnson's subsequent government have been little better.[99]

Repeated and significant delays to the opening of Crossrail have been embarrassing, but also caused serious problems for TfL's finances, even before the Covid-19 pandemic struck. While blame for delay does not lie at the mayor's door, controversy over when Khan was first informed dominated newspaper headlines for some time in summer 2018.[100] That the foregone revenue and additional construction costs involved in the project's repeated delays came (and continue to come) at a time when central government no longer provides TfL with a direct grant towards operating costs of £700 million a year, and alongside an as yet unexplained decline in Tube ridership, make the situation particularly difficult for TfL and the mayor.[101] In a sense, the current Covid-19 pandemic is merely the latest in a chain of derailing events that have plagued Khan's mayoralty.

REPRESENTING LONDONERS

While events in national and international politics have presented Khan with repeated challenges, they have also helped to place him front and centre in national and international debates. On winning the mayoralty, Khan received a congratulatory tweet from Democratic presidential candidate Hilary Clinton.[102] An ongoing, highly public war of words with President Trump, who has called the mayor a 'national disgrace' and a 'stone cold loser', appears to only have boosted both the mayor's profile and his support among Londoners.[103]

Khan's popularity among Londoners has remained impressively high, although it is highest among women, non-white Londoners, higher social classes and those living in inner London.[104] But the capital's first Muslim mayor has also made a conscious and deliberate effort to reach out to a full range of London's diverse communities. From joining a vigil on Old Compton Street to support LGBT+ people following the Orlando nightclub attack, to making a point of breaking his fast at synagogues during Ramadan, Khan has been aware of the signals that his actions send, and arguably particularly so as a Muslim or a Labour Party politician. While all three London mayors have repeatedly praised the capital's diversity, Khan is perhaps the first occupant of the post who does not have a history of highly controversial statements that have been criticised as being contradictory to this sentiment.

POLICY

In terms of policy, Sadiq Khan's first term has lacked a radical, transformative centrepiece. The 'hopper' bus ticket has been a success. Delivering the 'Night Tube' on several lines has been an accomplishment that ultimately eluded his predecessor, and part of a wider stream of work on the night-time economy. Neither have grabbed much public attention. The mayor's fares freeze has proven popular, but will not be renewed in his second term. Khan has had much more success in raising the issue of air quality in the public consciousness. The toxicity charge ('T-charge') and the Ultra-Low Emissions Zone (ULEZ) built on the work of both predecessors. Plans to enhance the ULEZ in 2020, and expand it in October 2021, are more radical, but will fall outside of Khan's first term.

Housing was also a central plank of Khan's campaign. His mayoralty has seen another revision of the definition of 'affordable housing' and the targets for its provision. An inquiry into the effects of foreign ownership and investment on the capital's housing market reported in 2017, finding that such investment had broadly positive effects; 'Homes for Londoners' was established to drive delivery forwards; and Khan's London Plan saw a shift towards housing construction on small sites, particularly in outer London (although numbers were forced downwards following the inspector's report).[105] Members of the Johnson and Khan administrations have debated affordable housing delivery figures repeatedly, with starts, completions and the definition of 'affordability' used to boost either case.[106] In May 2020, Khan claimed a 'record-breaking' number of 'genuinely affordable' housing starts over the last year (17,256), alongside starts on over 3,300 council homes, 'the most in any years since 1984/85'.[107]

Levels of violent crime, and particularly the perennial challenge of knife crime among young Londoners, are another metric by which Khan's mayoralty will be measured. Responsibility for success and failure has again been hotly debated; in this case, between the mayor and central government. In April 2018, it was widely reported that London's 'murder rate' had overtaken New York's in February and March, and soon after Khan endorsed 'targeted, intelligence-led' use of stop-and-search by the Metropolitan Police to combat knife crime.[108] In September 2018, the mayor announced the establishment of a Violence Reduction Unit (VRU), based on the model of a similar unit in Glasgow, which seeks to take a more holistic 'public health approach' to addressing the issue. But while crime has remained an issue throughout Khan's mayoralty, he has repeatedly cited a lack of central government funding and consequent reduction in police numbers as leaving him fighting crime with 'one hand tied behind his back'.[109] Opinion polling from May 2018 showed that Londoners agreed with the mayor, by a sizeable margin, that central government was to blame for rising knife crime.[110]

RECORD

At the time of writing, Sadiq Khan has seen his first term at City Hall extended until 2021 due to the coronavirus pandemic, but he still remains firm favourite to win a second term.[111] His first term has been hit by a series of shocks and crises, but has also lacked a landmark policy achievement. The mayor has undertaken a review into London's terror readiness; another into the Garden Bridge project (subsequently cancelled); reconvened the London Finance Commission to investigate further fiscal devolution for the capital; and advocated for control over suburban rail lines. He has used his 'soft power' through the introduction of standards and accreditations in the vein of the London living wage, such as the Good Work Standard.

But if Boris Johnson's mayoralty was reportedly suffering from a 'vision problem' one year in, Khan's could be argued to still be suffering from a 'big policy' problem at the end of his first term. There is currently no infrastructure project, building or major initiative which has Khan's name as a prefix. A mayoral commitment to pedestrianise Oxford Street, a striking policy, has been frustrated.[112] Yet Khan has proved a popular mayor. He is committed to a major expansion of the ULEZ and has spoken of making the 2021 mayoral election 'a referendum' on introducing rent controls in London. Both could prove ambitious and potentially controversial second-term policies. In the longer term, Khan's mayoralty has also seen repeated speculation that he may be destined for a larger, national political role in the near future.[113]

5

INTERVIEW WITH KEN LIVINGSTONE

JACK BROWN

13 AND 14 APRIL 2020

JB: Can we start at the beginning? It's a lovely moment: 'As I was saying before I was so rudely interrupted fourteen years ago...' Where did the line come from, and how did those first few days as mayor feel?

KL: Well, I'd been sitting on the Tube and a guy leant over and said: 'When you get elected, you should say this...' So a stranger on the Tube came up with that line. It was brilliant. When Blair first said that he had had the idea of creating a mayoralty, I had no interest in running for it. But, there was just this huge wave of support, I couldn't walk down the street without people saying: 'You've got to run, you've got to stand.' It was amazing!

JB: What about the actual moment when you won, following this very contentious campaign?

KL: Oh, I loved it. I love running things. I also totally love being a Londoner. I think it's the most amazing city on the planet. Having grown up and spent my whole life in London, my life's been amazing. There's just so much you can do in this city, the theatres, the cinemas, the sports centres, the arts. We've got more of those sort of things than New York or Paris. People come to London from all around the world because it is an amazing place to be.

JB: Let's focus first on the early days. Being the first mayor, you had such an influential role in setting everything up, did you have any idea of how you wanted to run the GLA in advance of becoming mayor? And how did that compare to the reality?

KL: Well I'm not aware of any politician who has been elected to an office where they have turned up and there was nothing there. Normally you inherit a bureaucracy that's been there for centuries. But after the abolition of the GLC, there wasn't really anything there. The Blair government pulled together a handful of civil servants, but I remember going into the building and there were just a few dozen people, none of whom were there permanently. They were just there for the transition.

So I started bringing people in, like my key advisor John Ross and Bob Kiley to run the transport system. But if you look at some of the press coverage after the first year and a half, they were saying: 'Where's the mayor? What's he doing?' Because I wasn't out promoting myself, it was literally 24/7 work. I had to create the machine and establish twenty-year strategies.

I always knew I was going to run it with my key advisors and aides that had been working on political stuff with me since the mid-1980s. I had a really good team running my campaign, and they followed me into the building. Much to the horror of the government bureaucrats; seeing all these lefties stroll in and take over the offices on my floor!

JB: So did the expectation match the reality?

KL: Don't forget, I had spent so long being involved in local government, I knew what I was going to do. It was wonderful because my successors have inherited what I created. They can amend it and change it, but Boris largely left it pretty much as it was and Sadiq has as well. So getting to set that up was a legacy that went far beyond my two terms. The only thing that changed was my attempt to try and make it work like a council, which failed, and so I just got on running it like a chief executive.

JB: Yes, you started off with a really collaborative attitude: inviting the Greens, Lib Dems to work with you, and then that changed. Why?

KL: I had been opposed to having a mayoralty, just like Frank Dobson was. We both thought they should just bring back the council. And so, in that first year, I was trying to run it like a council, whereas Blair had brought in the American system, where the mayor is the chief executive and makes all the decisions. So in that first year I was trying to bring in the members on the assembly … and I actually only really worked well with the Greens. The Labour people had all been vetted by the Blair machine, so none of them were really great fans of mine! After about a year of this, I just accepted the system and ran it like a chief executive, so instead of running a load of meetings with assembly members, I just sat down with my staff and took a decision.

JB: You had a very close team and in your memoirs you said that 'nine times out of ten they knew what I wanted without even checking', was that true?

KL: Most of the time, yes. They were all from Socialist Action, which was the only left group – it seemed to me – that was actually interested in running things, rather than sitting around and day-dreaming about having a revolution. They were about delivering. John Ross, effectively the leader of that group, was just brilliant. He was totally on top of economics. And we assembled this great team, and then we just got on with running things.

There was never any disagreement. With one exception – all my key staff were worried that the congestion charge wouldn't work, and so they tried to persuade me to put it off until after the 2004 election. But I knew it was going to work. It had worked in Singapore! We monitored it constantly and the only thing that didn't work was that the number of people driving into central London went down by twice the amount that we had expected, so the company that we'd given the contract to were going to make a big loss, so we had to re-negotiate the contract, or they would have walked away!

JB: You said you had experience of how to run things, and you had the experience of running the GLC, but the mayoralty must have been so different. How did your previous experience help?

KL: Well, although it was a completely different structure, it still comes down to making something work – the transport system or whatever. And so all the experience I had of trying to get things done, working through council committees, had a real impact. The difference was that I didn't have to sit around at a committee meeting, I just took those decisions with my key advisors. We had a meeting once every week, like a cabinet meeting. For two to three hours, about a dozen of us would sit around the table, and discuss all of the issues that were coming up and how things were working. There was a real open, focused debate and I was taking decisions after a serious analysis of what had been going on.

JB: Like cabinet government but without collective responsibility as the responsibility and mandate is very much that of one person alone?

KL: Yep. But one thing I've always said is that if you put all this power into the hands of one person, you'll eventually get someone corrupt. When the developer came to me to build the Shard, I could easily have said: 'Okay, fine, I'll give it permission, just put £50 million in this Swiss bank account.' So, one day, you will get a corrupt mayor. And that's the weakness of the system.

JB: How effective were the assembly in holding you to account in that respect?

KL: Well, I would turn up, and they would question me for hours at Mayor's Question Time. I'd always answer their questions, and I wasn't doing anything that was dodgy, so there wasn't anything for them to find. The only real power the assembly has is that they can change your budget, but only if there's a two-thirds majority for an alternative. And that was not likely, frankly, because they all disagreed among themselves. But they always squeezed me to spend less, that was the basic issue.

I think there should be a proper council to scrutinise what the mayor's doing, which has the power to remove the mayor if they find evidence of corruption. I would give the assembly more powers, if I could.

They should have the power to come up with ideas, amend things the mayor is providing and so on, if they get the votes through. Given that the assembly was created on a proportional representation system, you can trust it. Because no one party was ever going to have a majority, they had to cooperate, debate and get stuff done.

JB: Does the assembly produce the sort of calibre of figures that it should?

KL: Part of the problem was that no one had any idea what the assembly was. About 260 Labour members asked to be on the list of candidates, but then Blair's people got rid of about 160 of them. So it was a very unbalanced Labour Group. There wasn't a lefty in it! Quite a lot of very talented people were just blocked from standing.

Toby Harris was brilliant, actually, he was a very good, competent council leader. And Len Duvall was, of course. I got on very well with my deputy mayor [Nicky Gavron] as well. I'd known her because we were involved in the demonstrations against the Archway motorway project, back in the 1970s, so I knew she'd be good.

JB: The boroughs also have some power in shaping what the mayor can do, right? They pushed you to raise council tax less. Did they have a role in sort of indirectly holding you to account in that respect?

KL: In the days of the GLC, the borough councils loathed the fact that they had to collect the rates, and pass them on to County Hall, because they always felt that they were being blamed by local people whenever it went up. But back in my GLC days, when I increased the rates, a third of the money came from big corporations in the Square Mile. It was a wonderful redistribution of wealth. So when I increased the rates to cut transport fares, it was a real shift of wealth from giant corporations to ordinary Londoners.

JB: Was that not the case when you were mayor?

KL: Oh no, it's still pretty much the case. The system has changed, and they don't call it the rates any more, but it's still basically the same. It's not as good in terms of the redistribution of wealth any more, but cutting fares by increasing council tax was still a redistribution of wealth.

JB: Let's go to some specific issues. PPP was a huge issue. It went on and on and on. Was it worth all the time, money and effort opposing it in the courts?

KL: Well yes, although in the end we lost, and it was imposed on us... The first time I met Gordon Brown after he became Prime Minister, I told him that the larger of the two corporations that were running the Underground was about to go into liquidation, in just four or five years, they faced bankruptcy. It was an appalling system. Every transport expert was opposed to PPP. But the trouble was that Brown in particular was obsessed by this private finance initiative approach to things. When Bob Kiley had a private meeting with Tony Blair, Blair was persuaded that it wasn't going to work. But he just didn't have the courage to face down Gordon Brown.

JB: Why was Gordon Brown so into the idea, do you think?

KL: That generation of Labour politicians had grown up with Thatcher dominating politics. I think they felt that they had to carry on with her economic strategy. I saw an interview a few years ago and Blair said he thought it was his job to build on what she achieved, not roll it back.

JB: To continue with transport – can we talk about relations with central government. Was it easier once you were back within Labour?

KL: Yes, it was brilliant, because once the congestion charge worked, my poll ratings went up notably. And within a couple of months, Blair had asked me to come back as the Labour candidate. So we then worked together – we never talked about the war in Iraq, or anything like that. We just focused on things that we could agree on. And I got billions out of them for investment in transport. It was great. We just concentrated on what we could deliver.

JB: To what extent did the Olympics boost your case for doing that?

KL: Well, when the Olympic committee came to see if I would

support a London bid, I said: 'As long as it's in the East End of London, and we use it to regenerate it.' That's what Barcelona had done. Most Olympics are just very expensive and don't have much of a legacy, but ours has seen the transformation of the old East End, and we're still seeing growth. So that was the reason for trying to get the Olympics. Blair was into the Olympics, so we worked together well on that.

JB: Would you agree that transport is the area in which the mayor is most able to get things done?

KL: By a mile. Almost everything else you have to do is persuading others to come along with what you want to do. And you had real, direct control, more than over anything else. Basically, when Blair created the mayoralty, it ended up with only about one tenth of the powers that the Mayor of New York has got. It was very limited. That was one of the reasons that almost all of the people that Blair asked to run for mayor wouldn't do it – they just thought, 'What can you even do with all this?'

But transport is key for a city like London to work. If the transport isn't working, the city will fail. When I announced I was going to run, the business community was telling me: 'Look, you've got to sort the mess out, London's not working, firms are going to start leaving.' So we did huge amounts on transport. We got rid of thousands of old buses, brought even more new ones in. There was a massive expansion of routes and frequency.

An absolute key thing was bringing Bob Kiley over, because the old Transport for London bureaucracy just wasn't dynamic. There were all these bureaucrats there just waiting to retire and get their pensions, they weren't vaguely innovative or anything. Once Thatcher took London's transport away from the GLC in 1984, it was just out of the political debate. There was no one pushing anything, no one drawing up a plan for twenty years' expansion or anything. So I knew, from the day that I was elected, that I would have to get rid of most of the senior bureaucrats in TfL, which is why we brought Bob Kiley and his team in. Bob Kiley had totally regenerated Boston's underground, and then New York's, so he was just outstanding. And then other good people like Peter Hendy came along.

So I think what everybody noticed was the transformation of the transport system. And of course you'd had the nightmare of congestion in central London. And although no one really believed that the congestion charge was going to work, it worked perfectly from day one!

Of course, the trouble now is that, when I became mayor you had 7 million Londoners, now you've got over 9 million, and we desperately need Crossrail 1 open, but you've got to have a Crossrail 2 and a Crossrail 3, because our transport system is absolutely packed. Trying to get on the Tube in rush hour is just a nightmare.

JB: But, Crossrail 1 isn't quite here yet itself…

KL: Well, I had a brilliant team around me that I'd been working with for years. We kept on top of all my projects. We didn't just give out a contract and leave it, like Boris would've done. And I think, broadly, all my projects in my eight years came in on time and on budget.

JB: Moving on to the police, did you ever feel in control of the Met?

KL: No. I had no power to order the police what to do. But I was very lucky because, just before I was elected, John Stevens had been appointed commissioner, and Ian Blair the deputy. We got on brilliantly. They were amazed that I was prepared to increase council tax in order to boost police numbers. When I became mayor, there were 25,000 police – we got it up to 35,000 police and PCSOs [Police Community Support Officers]. They both realised that the racism that was endemic in the old London police system had to be dealt with. So, from the moment we met, we got on well, and worked well together all the way through. And though I had no power to order them about, we just broadly agreed on everything we were doing. The only thing I had to persuade them to do was bringing back 630 neighbourhood patrol teams, which they thought was old-fashioned. But, of course, as soon as you brought them back, there was a real drop in crime, locally. I grew up in a world where the police were always coming around the corner, so you realised that if you broke the law you were going to be caught, but then they all moved into cars and you never bloody saw them. And I think a lot of kids were more likely to get caught up in crime and gangs because of the lack of policing.

JB: Was it just good fortune that you got on with these people?

KL: Oh yes, it could be very difficult. When I became the leader of the GLC, the head of the Metropolitan Police refused to meet me, ever. My Tory predecessor, Horace Cutler, had been having lunch with him two or three times a year. And he just said: 'I'm not having anything to do with Ken Livingstone.' There was nothing you could do about that.

JB: A huge thing that happens during your mayoralty is the emergence of tall buildings, particularly iconic ones like the Gherkin and the Shard. People get very exercised by tall buildings. Do you think that this is something that the Mayor of London should have so much say over?

KL: The mayor's got to have a twenty-year strategy for the growth of London and its economy. I would never have allowed us to turn into something like Manhattan, completely gridlocked with tall buildings. I mean, there was only a handful that went up. But each of the London boroughs had these ridiculous rules about density and height, and my view was that we should look at each scheme on a case-by-case basis – is it a good scheme? Is it going to work? I mean, the Shard would never have been built at that height if I hadn't intervened.

JB: There was the Hungerford Bridge early on, and Trafalgar Square too – you have described that you felt that you were 'picking up failing Westminster projects'. Did you mind picking up the tab, or was it a source of frustration that you had to step in?

KL: Well, when I was growing up, parents took their kids to Trafalgar Square once, and bought a packet of birdseed and fed the pigeons. That was the only reason for ever going there. The only other things that ever happened there were demonstrations, people showing up and holding rallies. If we closed off the north road and made it a larger space, you could transform it. Westminster wasn't interested in doing anything fast, so we pushed ahead and did it. And it just transformed it. The other thing we had to do was get rid of the pigeons – we brought some hawks in to do that. Because twice in my life, crossing Trafalgar Square, I got shat on by a pigeon. And now, there's so many events there, it's brilliant, it's become a real focal point. It's a much better place.

JB: I like the idea that you got shat on by pigeons and thought: 'That's it, I've had enough of this, I'm going to get rid of them for ever.' But in terms of the mayor doing something like that, arguably Westminster's business, how did you feel about that?

KL: One of the problems was, because the mayor had been given such limited powers, suddenly reaching out and doing something like that, or bidding for the Olympics, did help to make the job a lot more fun than it would have been if I'd just been confined by what Blair had devolved. I just like doing things, that's why I came into politics, to achieve change. The tragedy is that that isn't the norm any more.

JB: How did the 'soft' power of the mayoralty compare to its 'hard' powers?

KL: As long as I had some money to bring to something, even if the council members despised me, they were still going to work with me to get something done. Because the GLA covered such a big area, and its income was so good, we could do so much. There are one or two things I regret. We didn't get round to building a great big aquarium out in the East End, which I would have loved. There were two or three things like that which I would have liked to have gotten done, but we just didn't quite manage to get it passed and agreed.

JB: The celebrations for Saint Patrick's Day, the recognition of same-sex civil partnerships and the work with faith groups, how important is this kind of 'civic leadership' part of the role?

KL: What I found interesting was that we'd assumed that a lot of the Tory press would have berated me for starting the civil partnership thing. But it didn't. and I think that's why a couple of years later, Blair realised that he could get away with passing a law to make it legal. Then, of course, after Blair you had Cameron making gay marriage legal!

JB: How much time do you think that you spent on engaging with different community groups?

KL: Well, an awful lot. One of the things that I'm very proud of was that, in my eight years, antisemitic incidents recorded by the Metropolitan Police went down. It wasn't just that – in the days after the 7 July bombings, police didn't record a single attack on a Muslim. I was very proud of that. One of my jobs was to promote tolerance. So I worked with the Jewish community, Hindus, Muslims, Sikhs… It seemed to me that that is one of the key jobs of a politician. You've got the right-wing politicians who promote hatred and mobilise nasty voters around it, but the alternative is that you promote tolerance.

JB: And how do you do that?

KL: For example, very early on, I met with a delegation from the Board of Deputies [of British Jews], and we agreed to set up organisations that would promote events open to non-Jews, so that non-Jews could find out about Jewish culture. And these things were well attended. And a lot of that stuff was happening at Trafalgar Square. But I just think that it's part of the job of a politician, to actually change social attitudes. And you can do it from the right, horribly, or you can do it progressively from the left.

JB: You talked, quite early on in your mayoralty, about carving London into five large pizza-slice boroughs, called 'super boroughs'. Could you expand on that?

KL: My view was always that the problem that we had with our thirty-two boroughs was that there were too many, and that it would be better to have fewer. But I had forgotten that I had got it down to five! You look at America and Germany, half of all public spending is at regional and local level. Whereas here, the vast majority of tax all goes into Whitehall. We are such a centralised country. I remember explaining how our political system worked to the Mayor of Moscow when he came to see me, and he just put up his hands and went: 'That's worse than Russia under Stalin!' And it actually is! Britain is more centralised in Whitehall than it was in Moscow under Stalin.

Anyway, if you have bigger boroughs, they could take over running the NHS in their area, managing universities and more. At the moment, this is all allegedly run from Whitehall, but not terribly well. The idea of running an organisation as big as the entire NHS from Whitehall is just madness. So I was always in favour of devolution, so that local problems could be dealt with locally. But I had no power to do that. If I could reorganise the whole state, I'd devolve most things down to regional or local government.

JB: But you were able to gain some extra powers for the mayoralty, through negotiation, weren't you?

KL: Oh yes, we got the 2007 agreement [the Greater London Authority Act]. Just before Blair retired he realised that the mayor needed more powers and Brown carried on with that idea. But they only kicked in at the 2008 election, so I never got to claim them.

JB: Do you think it's been good for the capital, that Westminster and Whitehall are based here, and therefore the rest of the country thinks that London has more influence than it should have?

KL: Well, that's why so many people are angry in the rest of the country. London has had much higher levels of investment than any other part of Britain. And it's because not only the politicians are based here, but also the civil service as well. And so they're doing things for themselves, as much as anything else. And London has had this most dramatic growth … I remember at the end of my mayoralty, if London had been an independent state, we would have just qualified to be a member of the G20. It would have been the twentieth-largest economy in the world, and for nearly 8 million people, that would have been quite remarkable. But if we had real devolution, people in the north-east could get on with public sector investment, borrowing, they could open offices like I did in China and India, and attract private investment. There's just no one there making the case for the north-east, or the south-west right now, in the way that the mayor does for London.

6

INTERVIEW WITH SADIQ KHAN

TONY TRAVERS AND JACK BROWN

20 JULY 2020

JB: Can we start with an introduction to the job – can you explain what the Mayor of London does? What does a typical week look like?

SK: Well, firstly it's worth noting that when I became mayor, there was no handbook and no induction. When I was made a minister, each job I had, you were given a proper induction. You were given all these papers by the private secretary, and the diary is fixed for about two weeks where you can have briefings on a daily basis. There is a template. When I became mayor, there wasn't really anything. For the last year, Boris had basically checked out, and Eddie [Lister, chief of staff and deputy mayor for policy and planning] was running everything. The staff at City Hall were sort of in snooze mode – they are very professional, brilliant people, but there were no structures in place.

I had all these ideas from the campaign, the hustings, I'd spoken to mayors around the world, I'd read Ben Barber's book [*If Mayors Ruled the World: Dysfunctional Nations, Rising Cities*], I'd spoken to people involved in Ken's administration, I'd spoken to Guto [Harri, communications director] in Boris's, but when I became mayor, it felt like there was nothing there. Boris genuinely did do a three-day week, so I couldn't use his diary as a guide. So we had to start from scratch.

But in order to answer your question, I asked my diary secretary to review what I did last year. So in 2019, I had over 1,300 diary commitments. That included: over 300 events and visits; over 260 external meetings; thirty-five planning meetings; thirty appearances in the chamber; and twenty-five board meetings. That's how things have changed over the last three years. I've tried to move from a strategic, personality-driven body, towards a focus on delivery. Strategy is important, of course, but we're trying to deliver stuff: affordable homes, better air quality. I've tried to bring the boroughs in, through London Councils. I'll give you an example – there was a health board, before I became mayor, and they would meet informally in Boris's private office, three council leaders, one person from the NHS, no real minutes, no transparency. I've opened it up. They are now streamed live. We have five council leaders, from the various sustainability and transformation partnership areas, and I bring in someone from NHS London, Public Health England, mental health representatives and others. And so that's an example of how things have changed.

So a normal day would look like this: I get three emails in the morning that I absolutely have to read, from the Met commissioner, the transport commissioner, and my City Hall team. We've set up something called a London Situation Awareness Team, where we monitor what's going on across London. And I read those three emails religiously when I wake up, between 6.30 to 7 a.m., and that leads to a number of actions. Then I email my chief of staff, my four mayoral directors, and my head of office – six people who are basically in contact nearly every day of the week, most times of the day. We'd have a meeting every day – pre-Covid, face-to-face, which is now a Zoom meeting. It's got to be early, because it sets the tone of the day.

Weeks in advance, my diary is pretty much full. There is some flexibility if events necessitate, but I like to work in grids, work out the week ahead. And I will also do things at the weekend. Eid in the square, going to a black church, attending Pride – so I'm not just working the five-day week. I think that one of my roles is to be seen out and about at those cultural events.

TT: On the subject of the machinery, you obviously inherited a City Hall machine, run by officials who stay on. What lay behind the decisions that led you to the particular mayoral team you appointed, the deputy mayors you appointed and other appointments near the top of the administration?

SK: During any election I fight, I focus on the campaigning, and I am quite strict about this. I need maximum time to focus on the campaign. But David Bellamy, my chief of staff, who was my campaign manager, he was tasked to work on the transition. So he was working with Jeff Jacobs, the GLA head of paid service, and talking privately to a number of other people to help prepare for power. Now, I never take it for granted or tempt fate as to what we'll do if we win. But as the election day came nearer, I was spending more time on transition. This included things like deciding that I would not do a normal signing-in ceremony, which we did at Southwark Cathedral. That's just one small example.

We knew some of the deputy mayors before I became mayor, but not all of them. There were some areas where I knew I wanted a deputy mayor to be responsible for a certain area where we hadn't had one beforehand – for social integration and social mobility, or for the environment and energy. I wanted a beefed-up role for the deputy mayor for culture. But for some of those jobs we hadn't worked out who it was going to be. Some we had. There's a certain amount of appointments I can make – it's twelve, or 'ten plus two' – and we had to work out which of the inherited staff we would keep on, and which we would bring new people in for. There would be a natural churn, because without saying 'you're fired', some people would have loyalties to Boris Johnson and would not want to stay, and that's fine. I would have been astonished if Eddie Lister had said to me, I want to stay and be your chief of staff.

So we had an idea about who we wanted. Some we knew, some we advertised openly, some we headhunted, some we had a shortlist and I'd interview for the position.

TT: The Mayor of London is a bit of a hybrid between the British and American version of an office, but closer to the American system in terms of appointments. However, the instant changeover you have to deliver is more British. American Presidents and mayors get a two-month period, as did Ken actually, whereas the Mayor of London goes straight in, like the Prime Minister. Am I right to say that it's more difficult for a directly elected mayor, given the need to make these appointments so fast?

SK: Yes and no. Firstly, I mean, not in a cocky way, but I did know I was going to win. That helps. And if you're a member of my political tribe, you're not used to winning elections. And so there were a lot of members of my tribe that wanted to come and work with me. They used to compare us to Noah's ark, or a refugee camp, because all the Labour talent were desperate to work in City Hall and actually run things. We got the results on Friday night, and we were in on Saturday morning, early doors.

There were a few key appointments that we had to make very quickly. Transport has to run. I had to arrange to see the three commissioners of TfL, the Met and the fire service – Mike Brown, Bernard Hogan-Howe and Ron Dobson – right away, look them in the eyes and say: 'Listen, this is what I want to do. You've seen my manifesto. This is my mandate. Are you on side?' And we had those really frank, proper conversations right on day one, which is really important. So there is some pressure to make sure those appointments are sorted quickly.

There's a bit more time with the other appointments, which are less urgent. I think that there are some strengths in that. The thing that I've always said to my team is that no one should be appointed because they're my mate. You've got to be appointed on merit. One of the things that I also learned from Boris Johnson in 2008 was not to panic appoint. Because if you remember 2008, it was chaos at first. And that's a classic mistake that we wanted to avoid making. And I think all of our appointments have been good ones.

JB: Can you pick out something that's gone particularly well, a big achievement, and maybe something that you've found challenging, perhaps a frustration, in your first term?

SK: Well, we've had a whole list of achievements! From the ULEZ, to really good work on affordable and council housing starts, there's been a lot. But the things that have been challenging... I had a feeling a week before 23 June that the EU referendum wasn't going our way, for the simple reason that I spent a day outside of London campaigning. But for that, I would have been shocked. So we'd worked out a strategy for what to do, on the Friday after the Thursday, if we lost. I was on College Green at 7 a.m. the next morning, when the leader of my party and his shadow Chancellor were saying that we should leave straight away. I was saying something different, because of our planning. And that led to the London is Open campaign.

We didn't foresee, or we couldn't plan for, President Trump being elected, and some of the things that he has talked about are the opposite of our values. One of the important roles of the mayor is not simply the delivery role, not simply the convening powers, but to stand up for our values. That's one of our unique selling points, that's why people love our city. So we didn't foresee that. Grenfell Tower too. Not one but four terror attacks in 2017. And now we've seen what's happened with Covid-19. I remember someone joking with me recently, saying the only thing that's left is a plague of locusts, and I'll have had the full set.

Now, the terrorist attacks, we did plan and prepare for, so we're as ready as we can be. One simple thing we did was make sure that we had faith leaders of different faiths ready to go, God forbid, if there's a terror attack, to try and help avoid reprisals. So that's one of the fruits of good preparation. Some things you can't prepare for though – Covid-19 is a good example, I was asking to go to COBRA [Cabinet Office Briefing Room A] meetings back in March, and I was told there was no need to, but then I got a phone call on 16 March saying, 'Please come to the Cabinet Office for a COBRA meeting', and the rest is history. So those are the challenges, things outside of my control, that it's difficult to properly prepare and plan for.

JB: We tend to talk about the mayoralty as being a series of frustrations, and limited powers. But was there something that you wanted to happen that you found was actually quite easy to deliver?

SK: Well, air quality is a good story – the Ultra-Low Emissions Zone. People told me we couldn't do it. The government would be against us, they'd stop us. And then it worked so well that Michael Gove, when he was environment secretary, would make speeches name-checking me and what we'd done on air quality. We've seen the difference it's made in terms of nitrogen dioxide, carbon emissions, vehicle compliance – it's a great success story. And it's a good example, to be fair to the government, of us working well with them. They could have done stuff to stop it happening, but they didn't.

I'll give you another one. When I set up England's first Violence Reduction Unit, after a lot of time speaking to Glasgow, we were told that it couldn't happen, that there was no way that you'd get all those different agencies, from the Ministry of Justice to probation, councils, social workers, all around a table to talk about early interventions to prevent violence. But that's now happening. To the point where, to give him credit, when Sajid Javid was Home Secretary, Saj started supporting VRUs around the country, and would name-check London and VRUs. And so it's a good example of how sometimes government can work with us to make progress.

When Liam Fox was international trade secretary, our team worked closely with his team when I was doing international visits – promoting London overseas, saying that 'London is Open'. We had really good relations with the department, and with the City of London Corporation, and we'd speak with them before an international visit. So they're all good examples. Counter-terror too. Whether it's been Theresa May or Boris Johnson, when it comes to dealing with a terror incident, I've been really impressed with how we've worked together, in relation to those incidents.

TT: You've touched on this in the last answer, but of all the levers of power in City Hall, which ones work the best, and which ones seem to have nothing attached to them?

SK: Transport works the best, but – and this is an important caveat – I think the 2015 funding deal that I inherited, whereby TfL get no revenue funding, and they're reliant on business rates growth, doesn't work. But transport works in terms of having autonomy to do things – the hopper fare, for example. Freezing the fares. Reducing strikes by 73 per cent, and reducing the operating deficit at the same time, and increasing cash balances. I have the autonomy to do this.

Another example where it works pretty well is in planning, by and large. Again, until Robert Jenrick kicks off during a campaign. Jenrick thought that we had an election coming up in 2020, and threw his toys out of the pram in relation to the draft London Plan. Hopefully we can deal with that now. Policing works, to some extent, although the frustration is that, because we're a capital city, the Home Secretary gets more involved than she would in other parts of the country. The problem with policing is that I rely on the Home Office for funding for policing, which is why you've seen the police cuts.

Where it works well is in relation to the convening powers. I've worked really hard to get the London councils working with me, Labour and Tory councils, and the City of London. It's been a learning curve for all of us, but during Ken's time they felt really neglected, during Boris Johnson's time they felt he was quite tribal, and I've really tried to avoid that. And it's been challenging to make some Conservative councils feel that we're on the same side here. A good example is that [former Chancellor] Philip Hammond gave us a challenge over business rates, he expected us not to reach an agreement around the 100 per cent business rates retention pilot, and how to use the additional income this was expected to provide. But we did – which surprised the Treasury and Hammond. But it's a credit to the London family, to the local councils working with us, to try and persuade them that it was the right thing to do.

Another example of the 'suck it and see' approach to devolution was adult education. To give credit to Gavin Barwell, when he was minister for London, Theresa May was quite anti-devolution, but he became her chief of staff. Gavin said that while he couldn't give us more devolution, he would give us something, and if we could make it work, then it would help them be persuaded. They gave us a £300 million budget around adult education. Now, my frustration there is that it's a delegation, rather than a devolution, because of boring statutory reasons. Other mayors around the country, my colleagues in the Metro-9 [the group of nine English combined authorities, or 'metro' mayors], have proper devolution, when we still have a delegation, because of the deal that they got. But we're working around that, and we do have control over £300 million that we wouldn't otherwise have.

JB: You're the first mayor that has actually had the opposition party in power nationally for your entire term – Ken Livingstone doesn't count, because while he was an independent, he was Labour before and after – I wonder how you've found that? How has it constrained or enhanced your ability to deliver?

SK: My analysis is that if the government minister is confident in his or her abilities, it's far easier to do business. When you've got a government minister who is trying to make a name for themselves, or lacks confidence, or is frankly being childish, it's more difficult. Let me give you some examples of the fruits of grown-up relationships. The government initially said to us that they believed that the future lies in homes costing £450,000 or less – that's what they called an 'affordable' or 'intermediate' house. Now, James Murray did the work on my part, on my behalf, but Gavin Barwell was minister for housing, and the Ministry for Communities and Local Government secretary was Sajid Javid. And they agreed that I could include affordable housing at council rents, with a £4 billion deal. So that's a good example of a deal being made, and we met the targets that the government set us, we're making good progress, and we've had more genuinely affordable housing starts in the last three years than at any time before – and we've started more council homes last year than in any year since 1982 to 1983.

That's a good example of where it works, because it's a grown-up relationship, and we can do business. Saj, I had a lot of time for him as Home Secretary. He got the importance of bringing people together to deal on violent crime, and he started to make progress. But since Priti Patel has been Home Secretary, there's not been one meeting of this task force that Saj set up. Because what happens with politicians is that they want their own legacy. They don't like building on things from their predecessors. Similarly one of the churlish things that I could have done as mayor would have been to cut stuff for the sake of it. But I've kept the good stuff that Boris did – London & Partners, for example. Where I've stopped something it's because it was a stupid idea, like the Garden Bridge.

The problem with central government is that everyone wants a legacy. And so that can lead to relationships becoming challenging. And also, the nearer you get to an election, the more challenging relations can be. So, Robert Jenrick's childish behaviour with the Draft London Plan was simply because he wanted to do something politically six weeks before an election. But I get criticism from members of my party, because I am strongly of the view that you should work alongside the government, regardless of what political colour it is, to the benefit of Londoners, and put aside any silly differences. So, with Covid-19, I didn't play any party-political games, until the government started briefing against the TfL deal. So I had to respond to that, and explain what the deal was with [transport secretary] Grant Shapps. Sometimes, you even disagree with your own party, when they're not being sensible towards London – and that's one of the roles of the mayor, to be a champion and an advocate for the city, working with the government when it's in London's best interests to do so, but also not being scared to stand up to them when you have to.

TT: Just to move on in the other direction, given the boroughs are so important in quite a lot of delivery, how do you sort of corral and marshal them, and indeed the other elements of civil society such as faith groups?

SK: Actually, that's been the most fascinating part of the last four years. In my view, it's all about relationships. And making sure that we're all on the same side. Let me give you an example – when there is a homicide, in a particular borough, we will make sure we contact the leader of the council, and the local MP. When it comes to housing delivery, you need to work with the borough, in terms of what funding they need and what targets they can realistically deliver.

Because I spent twelve years as a councillor in Wandsworth, where there was a Tory council, I understand what it's like to be a councillor, but I also know what it's like to work with a party that's of a different colour to you. I respect the boroughs, because I see that they are crucial for London; 95 per cent of the roads in our city are controlled by councils. So if I want more walking and cycling, I'd better work with them. I've had well-documented, public fights with Westminster around the pedestrianisation of Oxford Street and cycle routes – I'm not sure whether that's because they're Tory, or because they're Westminster, I don't know. I've also had some disagreements with Labour councils, about a whole host of issues.

So the councils all matter. Civic society is important too – amenity groups, faith groups... I meet leaders of the black evangelical churches for breakfast on a regular basis. I go to churches, synagogues, temples, gurdwaras. The first event I did was with the Jewish community, Yom HaShoah. And these events can be small in terms of numbers, but they are crucial for a variety of reasons. You've got to make time for them. And I'm afraid the bad news for future mayors is that it ain't a nine-to-five job, Monday to Friday. If you want to be a good mayor, the convening power means that you've got to be working all the time to get the confidence of all of these groups.

Why do employers choose London over Frankfurt, Berlin, Paris, Madrid? It's because of our culture. And that comes from meeting with these groups. I don't want to just be a 'Zone 1 mayor', or a mayor just for Labour London. There was a route for us, in 2016, to win London by just focusing on the Labour boroughs. That's not the sort of campaign I wanted to have, and it's not the sort of mayor I wanted to be. I wanted to be a mayor for all Londoners. And that includes the Bexleys, and the Haverings, and the Suttons. And so that's about relationships, spending time with them.

JB: I'd like to ask you where you think that the mayoralty should go next? You mentioned 2024 earlier, but whoever wins the next one, and whoever wins the one after that, what additional powers, if any, does the mayoralty need?

SK: Well, there's good news and bad news. The good news is that we now have nine metro mayors, and other mayors that aren't metro mayors, Bristol and others. That's great. And actually – Michael Heseltine is right on this – it's a strength that you've got mayors from different parties.

But the bad news is that there has never been, in my lifetime, more of an anti-London feeling than there is now, in the civil service, in politics, in the country. And we've got to address that. But actually, you speak to the Mayor of Paris, or the Mayor of Madrid or New York – I know it's not the capital city, but still – there are similar animuses towards their cities. So it's not unique to our country, and we shouldn't be scared of it. But I hope the genie of devolution is out of the bottle. I hope that 'Take Back Control' means cities and regions getting more power. What I hope it doesn't mean is the hoarding of power in Westminster and Whitehall. And unfortunately the evidence of the last few weeks has not been good, in relation to the TfL deal with the Department for Transport, in relation to the government's response to Covid-19 – centralisation, command and control. We'll see how the local lock-downs work – we've had one so far in Leicester, and it's not a good example of trusting mayors and cities.

I'm a subscriber to what Wellington Webb, a former Mayor of Denver, said: 'If the nineteenth century was known as the century of empires, and the twentieth century as that of nation states, then the twenty-first century is all about cities and mayors.' We can move quickly, we're nimble, we're dextrous, we're closer to our population. But I'm well aware that people in Havering, for example, can feel as disconnected from City Hall as they do from Parliament. And we are always conscious to make sure we try and keep in tune with the entirety of our city, in relation to how they're feeling.

TT: When you're sitting in City Hall, looking out over a city of 9 million people, how do you get a feel for all of those neighbourhoods, all of those different interests and different civil society groups, private, public, business institutions all supposedly from one place?

SK: The size point is important. If you look at Anne Hidalgo in Paris, she is responsible for a central area of 2.1 million people. Ada Colau in Barcelona is responsible for 1.6 million, I think. Andy Burnham, Steve Rotherham, Andy Street, their populations are nowhere near that of Greater London [around 9 million]. So it's not comparable. Scotland and Wales put together still have a smaller population than Greater London. Bill de Blasio and Mike Bloomberg, they understand what it's like to be the mayor of a city of this size. Mike's first piece of advice was, 'Listen, if you have 90 per cent of your city loving you, that still leaves 900,000 people who don't.' And, by the way, 90 per cent of Londoners don't love me, as much as I'd like to think they do, 90 per cent of my family don't love me, to be honest! So we've tried to make sure we understand the different villages and town centres across our city.

I'm always conscious that 40 per cent of Londoners didn't vote to Remain in the EU, even though 60 per cent did. I've never been one of those people who said that those who voted for Brexit are all racist, or not patriotic, and I respect that. We've spent a lot of time engaging with and listening to some of the concerns they've got in the Barkings and the Haverings and other parts. But, I've still got a responsibility to represent the 60 per cent that did want to remain in the EU, and London's EU citizens, and often they're heartbroken, they're scared, they're anxious. What I've never had is an echo chamber; yes, I spend a lot of time with my mayoral directors, my close team, but I also spend a lot of time with people who have other points of view, to understand what people are thinking.

I think that one of the great things that the Greater London Authority Act requires of us is People's Question Time. There's nothing more sobering than going to a public meeting, in a part of London you may not have visited for three months, and have 500 to 600 people in an old-school town hall meeting. It's brilliant! I deliberately do regular phone-ins, radio shows, and other things, and we are really responsive. One of the other big advantages I have that nobody else really had before, or to the same extent anyway, is social media. I mean, people can literally tweet me, direct-message me, Facebook me, email me. I have more correspondence than any mayor in history, and we've had to take on more staff to deal with that. Internationally, domestically and in London. That also means a lot more hatred though. No other mayor has had a protection team with them 24/7, seven days a week. So there are pros and cons to the job I'm doing, but I would say that it's far easier for a Londoner to let the mayor know their views during my mayoralty than ever before.

JB: One final question. I've asked you what might come next for the mayoralty, but what next for the capital? You find yourself mayor in a particularly difficult time – what are you and your team thinking about at the moment, what are you planning for?

SK: So, my answer to your question would have been very different before Covid-19. So before Covid, the expectation was that we were going to carry on being the greatest city in the world, carry on growing, notwithstanding Brexit. We could withstand bumps and turbulence, because of the strength of who we are. But I think Covid provides additional challenges, because what is the role of central London post-Covid? Will we have a polarised recovery? That question becomes more profound going forward, for capital cities, but also for cities generally. How do we deal with this situation where, for the foreseeable future, we won't have the same level of fares income from passengers to pay for public transport, let alone address the infrastructure investment we need for the future?

What I've done is establish a London Recovery Board, which I co-chair with the chair of London Councils. The board has various task forces and we're trying to address inequalities, address questions like: what is the role for the City of London, if most employers there choose to start having their staff working from home?

How can we encourage a greater cultural offering in outer London, if fewer people will be travelling into central London? The London Borough of Culture was arguably ahead of its time in this. How do we make sure that we have a recovery that doesn't lead to a ghost town on Oxford Street, or in Westfields, or in the City of London? What is the future of Canary Wharf? How do we keep the sandwich bars, the dry-cleaners, the other shops that need footfall from struggling? What about the future of housing? Are people going to want to move out of London? It's only the past few decades that London's population has been growing. Prior to that, there were decades where it shrank. This is all so important.

The good news is, if you look at our environment strategy, our transport strategy, the London Plan, the Cultural Infrastructure Plan, look at some of the work that the chief digital officer has been doing – arguably, we were ahead of our game. The three big issues for London that I would have mentioned if you had asked this question six months ago, pre-Covid, would have been around leisure, and whether people go out for entertainment or just watch Netflix; shopping, because for some years there has been a shift towards online shopping; and working, with more people working from home. I think Covid has just accelerated these trends. And so there is grounds for optimism.

So I think we're in a fairly good place, subject to the government working with us. One of my jobs is to persuade them to calm down on the party-political rhetoric, and try and work better together. Because London contributes between a quarter and a third of all the nation's wealth. So it's in the government's interest not to try and punish London in order to punish me, because they will suffer too, not just London.

7

AN EVOLVING MAYORALTY

TONY TRAVERS

C reating a Mayor of London brought with it the need to create a 'City Hall machine'. On this occasion, there was no former authority to build upon. The winner of the May 2000 mayoral election would have to set up a mayor's office and appoint members to the boards of institutions such as Transport for London, which had been created under the Greater London Authority Act 1999. Preparatory work was undertaken by a transition team (see Chapter 2) but the first mayor had, by law, to make a significant number of appointments and begin the process of determining how power would be used within the Greater London Authority.

This process was very different from when the GLC had been created between 1963 and 1965. Although the creation of the original 'Greater London' authority had involved the setting up of an administrative entity to cover an area four times that of the former London County Council, there was a pre-existing County Hall machine which made it possible to utilise officials and processes already in place. The LCC bureaucracy and its headquarters simply moved across, adding more functions and staff, to a revised role of running the new GLC. Moreover, many of the first councillors at County Hall and in the new London boroughs had been members of predecessor authorities.[1] The LCC's education responsibilities were transferred wholesale to a special committee of the GLC.[2]

In 1999 and 2000, those creating the GLA needed to put in place sufficient administrative capacity to support a mayor's office, although there was no immediate need to do the same for transport, the police, and fire because each of these services had a separate, free-standing, head-quarters of their own. In the case of TfL, there was some need to absorb smaller functions, such as major roads and taxi regulation, into London Regional Transport, which had existed in various guises since 1933. The Metropolitan Police had had a separate operational and administrative existence since 1829 and the London Fire Brigade since 1865. The details of how each were made accountable to the GLA is considered below.

The need to create the GLA from scratch was very different from what had happened in Edinburgh and Cardiff the previous year when devolution to Scotland and Wales occurred. In both cases, the new devolved government took over from predecessor civil service depart-ments running, respectively, the Scottish Office and the Welsh Office. Thus, the new governments in each nation inherited a pre-existing civil service in offices that had been important centres of power for decades. In London, virtually every aspect of the former GLC's gov-ernment machine had been split up or sold off when it was disbanded in 1986. Only a few joint committees and their officials – for exam-ple, the London Fire and Civil Defence Authority and the London Research Centre – existed as they had under the GLC and thus were ready to hand back services to the new London-wide government.

Politicians and civil servants charged with creating the GLA were clear that they did not want to create a large bureaucracy of the kind that had existed at County Hall during its occupancy by the LCC and GLC. Nick Raynsford, the minister responsible for the proposed reform, wanted the GLA (unlike the GLC) to be 'streamlined and stra-tegic' with an explicit philosophy for metropolitan government.[3] This issue is considered in more detail in Chapter 2.

Inheriting the transition team created in 1999, the new mayor moved into the GLA's temporary headquarters in Romney Street, SW1, over the weekend from 5 to 7 May. Ken Livingstone had had a small team working with him at the centre of his independent mayor-al campaign and the most important of these became the core of the new mayor's office. The precise nature of the first mayor's office and its operation is considered in Chapter 3. Here, the evolution of both the style of successive mayors' offices and the evolution of the institutions controlled from them will be considered.

THE MAYOR'S OFFICE

Books about American mayors, particularly those of New York City, generally contain a section on the make-up and operation of the mayor's office, which outlines the style and appointment of key staff, the mayor's personal policy interests and policies adopted. Mayors' offices are key instruments in this particular form of government: directly elected executives have personal legitimacy to hire and fire individuals and, generally, demand loyalty.[4] Most of British government has (until the advent of directly elected mayors) consisted of collective leaderships with senior officials working in separate departments for individual leading members. The operation of 10 Downing Street and the Cabinet Office have perhaps been closest within the UK to the kind of dynamics found in American mayors' offices, acting as a coordinating fulcrum of national political power.

The three London mayors since 2000 have operated their offices in unique ways, with power held and operated differently under Ken Livingstone, Boris Johnson and Sadiq Khan.

LIVINGSTONE ADMINISTRATION

Livingstone, as first mayor (and as an independent), had an opportunity to create the core of the GLA from first principles. His term of office began with a two-month period, prior to 'vesting day' when he formally took power, during which he was able to put together the UK's first-ever mayoral administration.

He was thus the first mayor to use appointment powers under the Greater London Authority Act 1999. The transition team, under Bob Chilton, had been in place since April 1999 to create a shadow mayor's office. Chilton had put in place a basic administration, including personalised officials, such as a mayor's diary secretary, and had had papers prepared about the way that both the mayor's office and the assembly might operate. As if to reinforce the parallels with the concentration of power in the Prime Minister's office at Downing Street, the transition team staff gathered in the hallway of Romney House to welcome the new mayor.[5]

Livingstone's core team inherited this proto-machine and began the process of making it their own. In the best traditions of British government, Livingstone approached the legislative provisions flexibly. He struck a deal with Labour's Len Duvall, the former leader of Greenwich and the assembly member who emerged as an intermediary, to allow Livingstone a bigger mayor's office in exchange for the assembly being able to appoint additional research and support staff.[6]

Livingstone appointed a number of figures who had been loyal to him in the past in the GLC and London government and from the radical Socialist Action group. This element of the GLA's development is covered in more detail in Chapter 3.

Here they are considered, along with those inherited from the transition team, as the foundation of Livingstone's mayoral office. His period as leader of the GLC from 1981 to 1986 meant that he had extensive experience as a London-wide leader, though his policies were to differ substantially from 2000 onwards. As both leader and mayor, Livingstone took a keen interest in policy-making and its impact on the city. Against this backdrop, the mayor kept total control of appointments and the early days of GLA policy-making. The office was made in Livingstone's image and its members held their positions on the understanding that they accepted what the mayor was seeking to achieve and as his loyal agents. There was no room for interpretation of the mayor's views, nor for freelance action. When senior members of the mayor's office spoke, they did so in Ken Livingstone's voice. To stray from this true path would have resulted in an abrupt end of an appointee's role within the administration.

In appointing members of the boards that ran Transport for London, the London Development Agency and the London Fire and Emergency Planning Authority, Livingstone chose a mixture of former GLC colleagues, trusted outsiders and a small number of individuals (notably two of his opponents in the mayoral race) to signal he was creating a 'big tent' administration. Chapter 3 provides more detail about those involved.

Livingstone also created an advisory cabinet to work with his core team. According to Ben Pimlott and Nirmala Rao, this was 'to seek to counter political isolation by drawing in opponents and neutralising their opposition'.[7] In fact, this group had no executive authority (and met less and less frequently as time went by), and was a classic Livingstone grouping of different interests which signalled intent rather than granting power. The overall set of appointments 'were testimony to his hobby of collecting people he can trust and sticking to them'.[8]

JOHNSON ADMINISTRATION

This version of a mayor's office proved to be rather different to Boris Johnson's, which was appointed after he defeated Livingstone in 2008. Johnson had not been a minister or run a public authority before becoming mayor and he was known more as a political journalist than as a commentator on urban policy. Effortlessly popular and charismatic, he had beaten Livingstone partly because Labour was so unpopular nationally, but also partly because Johnson could reach voters who were not natural Conservative supporters. There was almost certainly some electoral resistance to a directly elected individual serving a third term in a relatively powerful position.

The forming of the second mayor's office was handled very differently to the first. Johnson brought in Nick Boles as chief of staff although the latter had not been part of Johnson's election machine. Boles had previously set up and run the moderate centre-right think tank Policy Exchange and later became an MP. Unlike Livingstone, Johnson had no close circle of potential appointees to (what was by this time) City Hall, which required Boles to seek outsiders to join the new administration. Boles had to cast about to seek potential nominees and ended up assembling a group of deputy mayors. 'Deputy mayor' was not a title given to Livingstone's senior team, apart from a single, 'statutory', deputy mayor, who by law had to be drawn from the assembly. Johnson's deputy mayoral appointments had never been his previous colleagues or confidants. Thus, Tim Parker was made chief of staff, Kit Malthouse was appointed deputy mayor for policing, Isabel Dedring for transport, Ray Lewis for young people and Ian Clement for government and external relations. Parker had been in business, Malthouse had been a senior Westminster councillor, Dedring had worked at TfL under Livingstone, Lewis was a community organiser and Clement was leader of Bexley Council. Board appointments to TfL and other agencies followed a similar pattern, with names assembled by the new Johnson team at City Hall.

There was a significant change in personnel with the change of mayor. Almost all of the senior Livingstone mayor's office left, although Neale Coleman was kept on by Johnson to assist with the preparation for the Olympics. Board members were in many, though not all, cases replaced. Non-political individuals such as Judith Hunt and Sir Mike Hodgkinson survived the change of administration, as did Peter Hendy the transport commissioner.

In an American city such as New York a change of mayor, even if of the same political party as their predecessor, generally heralds a changeover of virtually all senior office holders. The London experience at the point of the first change of mayor was a classic mixture of UK and US practice. One key member of the Livingstone core administration survived, as did a number of board appointees. The commissioners of services such as transport, police and fire continued in office, as did the chief executive of the Greater London Authority.

The original Johnson office suffered four resignations in just over a year. Parker, Lewis and Clement resigned for different reasons, while a fourth senior figure, James McGrath, had also stepped down.[9] The sense of chaos at City Hall was palpable at the time. It required the steady hand of Parker's replacement, Simon Milton, to create an effective and functioning administration. Milton, who had been leader of Westminster City Council, was succeeded (on his death) in 2011 by Edward Lister, leader of Wandsworth Council. These two figures between them created a mayor's office which allowed Johnson to settle into a more organised and effective period of government.

Johnson's office was significantly different to Livingstone's. Whereas Livingstone had operated with a tight group of close political allies and power that emanated directly from the mayor, Johnson's style was to allow his deputies more discretion within a broad understanding of his politics and interests. Johnson held a weekly 'cabinet' where he, the deputy mayors and senior officials discussed policy and delivery.

In fairness to Johnson, unlike Livingstone, he did not enjoy a two-month gap between election day and the point when he took control of GLA services. Whereas in 2000 there had been eight weeks to make appointments and determine policy, for Johnson there was an instant change-over of the kind experienced in all UK national and local elections. But there was a difference between the mayoral model and the traditional British Prime Ministerial or council leader changeover. When new administrations take office at Westminster or in town halls, they inherit a full, non-political, civil service (or council office) cadre to commence the business of government. In the US-imported mayoral model, many of the top people change, which creates the need to make rapid appointments and start policy delivery within hours. In American federal and local elections, there is generally a two-month period between the election and inauguration.

The key lessons from the senior appointments made by Livingstone and Johnson, and the operation of their respective mayor's offices, is that the mayor has considerable latitude to make appointments and to personalise their government. Appointments to City Hall and to boards were subject to some independent external oversight, but proposed individuals were rarely ruled out. The legitimacy of the mayor's mandate has been such that not only could appointments and style of government be personalised, but it has proved possible for mayors to override or ignore central government. Certainly, successive mayors have been able to make senior and independent appointments that suggest a greater degree of openness to creativity than central government generally achieves.

Boris Johnson effectively removed Ian Blair as police commissioner, a move that the Home Secretary was powerless to stop, as is covered further in Chapter 10.[10] Police commissioners can now only serve if the mayor has confidence in them. The appointments of Bob Kiley, Peter Hendy, Mike Brown and, most recently, Andy Byford (by Sadiq Khan) as transport commissioners have been made without central government intervention or approval. All four of these transport officials were seen as of the highest global standard (two were recruited from abroad), an achievement that stands in contrast to a number of UK government appointments within Whitehall. Similarly, fire commissioners have been appointed from among the most senior and impressive figures in UK firefighting. Sir Ken Knight, who was appointed by Ken Livingstone, went on to a series of senior positions in central government.

Intriguingly, the group which evolved around Boris Johnson at City Hall, despite its early difficulties, went on to form the basis of the team at No. 10 once he became Prime Minister in 2019. Ed Lister, who was chief of staff at City Hall, became chief strategic advisor in Downing Street. Munira Mirza, who became deputy mayor for culture, was made head of the No. 10 policy unit. Andrew Gilligan, who was responsible for the implementation of cycling policy at City Hall, became responsible for transport and infrastructure at No. 10. Kit Malthouse and Stephen Greenhalgh (the latter was deputy mayor for policing from 2012, then head of the Mayor's Office for Policing and Crime (MOPAC)) were appointed to ministerial positions. It is a tribute to Milton and Lister that their grip on Johnson mayoral office proved so effective that it paved the way for the machine that is at the core of UK government. City Hall took over No. 10 in many respects.

KHAN ADMINISTRATION

Sadiq Khan's City Hall administration included elements of both the Livingstone and Johnson approaches. As the third Mayor of London, the experience of a change of mayor in 2008 set an example from which to learn. Jeff Jacobs, the 'head of paid service' (effectively the chief executive), prepared for the changeover so as to reduce the pressure on the new mayor. In the event, Khan, like Livingstone, turned up at City Hall with a team which had worked with him in Parliament and in the Labour Party. David Bellamy (previously Khan's campaign manager) became chief of staff while Nick Bowes (previously Khan's policy chief and a former Wandsworth councillor) took responsibility for policy. Patrick Hennessey, a Fleet Street veteran who had worked for the Labour Party, became director of communications. Leah Kreitzman, who had a background in the Labour Party and in non-governmental organisations, took responsibility for external and international affairs.

It was very much a Sadiq Khan 'machine' which moved effortlessly into City Hall. Deputy mayors were appointed in larger numbers than under Boris Johnson, including the former mayor of Hackney, Jules Pipe (as deputy for planning, regeneration and skills), a former assembly member and Croydon councillor, Val Shawcross (transport), and a leading Islington councillor, James Murray (housing). Others included Justine Simons (culture and creative industries), Sophie Linden (policing and crime) and Rajesh Agrawal (business). Former MP Heidi Alexander took over from Shawcross in 2018, while Fiona Twycross became deputy mayor for fire and resilience in 2018. Joanne McCartney, who was appointed Sadiq Khan's 'statutory' deputy mayor, also took an education brief. Amy Lamé was subsequently appointed 'Night Czar', while Will Norman was made walking and cycling commissioner.

As when Ken Livingstone handed over to Boris Johnson, the appointment of board members to TfL involved many members being changed, though two continued between administrations. The two mayoral appointees to the fire authority changed. Commissioners, as had been the practice in 2008, remained unchanged.

Whereas Ken Livingstone had no deputy mayors (nor, really, analogous positions), Johnson appointed a number who assumed significant levels of personal power. Sadiq Khan's deputies, by contrast, are outside the key decision-making part of City Hall. The small team around Khan has in many ways been similar to the one Livingstone created, though his deputy mayors are in more representative rather than policy-making or delivery roles.

All three mayors have used the GLA officials for relatively traditional functions, including policy formulation involving TfL, the fire brigade and police. A key role for these civil service-type officers has been to prepare the detailed plans and strategies for which the mayor has responsibility, to undertake research and to operate the City Hall machine. Functions such as finance, planning and housing are handled by GLA officers working within a policy framework set by the mayor's office, subject to varying degrees of input from deputy mayors. The 'chief executive' role is broadly similar to that of a permanent secretary in Whitehall, effectively 'running the machine', as compared to a council chief executive where there is more scope for executive decision-making and delivery. At City Hall policy development is primarily a political matter. The mayor, by being a directly elected executive position, leaves officials with rather less political space for creativity than is the case within much of British government.

MAYORAL BOARDS, AGENCIES AND POWERS

The Greater London Authority Act 1999 created four 'functional bodies': Transport for London, the Metropolitan Police Authority, the London Fire and Emergency Planning Authority and the London Development Agency. As discussed above, the mayor made a number of appointments to these bodies, though the pattern varied from one to another. Thus, the mayor appointed all the board members of TfL and the London Development Agency and a majority of the boards for the other two bodies. The MPA board was modelled on the membership format for police authorities outside London, whereas LFEPA's board was appointed by the mayor from assembly members and borough nominees. Mayoral appointments to TfL and the LDA were at the mayor's discretion, while those for the MPA and the LFEPA had, by law, to be assembly members. The chairs of TfL, the LDA and the LFEPA were all mayoral appointments, as were the chief officers of TfL and the LDA. The police commissioner continued to be the Home Secretary's responsibility.[11]

This classic New Labour mixture of 'American' and 'British' systems, overlaid by a need to respect national practice, finding jobs for assembly members and the boroughs' former role within the fire service, had led to a tangle of accountability and control. Policy was set by the mayor for some services but not for others. In the years from 2000 to 2020, a number of steps have been taken to sort out accountability and, indeed, to give the mayor additional direct responsibilities.

The arrangements for TfL remain broadly as they were in 2000, although the emergency financial settlement agreed by ministers with TfL during the spring of 2020 as a result of the Covid-19 pandemic led to two government 'observers' being imposed on the TfL board, which included the aforementioned Andrew Gilligan.[12] The LDA was abolished in 2012, with its responsibilities for economic development, regeneration and promotion being taken into the City Hall administration, though two mayoral development corporations (for the Olympics 'legacy' and at Old Oak Common) were subsequently created. The MPA was abolished in 2012 as part of England and Wales police reforms. Its role was transferred to the mayor's office for policing and crime, where a deputy mayor leads the office.[13] Finally, the LFEPA was abolished in 2018, with the mayor (again through a deputy mayor) taking direct responsibility for fire brigade policy and governance.[14] Assembly committees were reorganised to reflect the need for new arrangements to scrutinise reformed mayoral powers.

Thus, by 2020, there is a far clearer line of responsibility about budgets, chief officer appointments and policy than there was in 2000. The mayor, through deputy mayors, is clearly more directly accountable for policing, fire and economic development. Accountability for transport policy and delivery was always relatively straightforward from the creation of the GLA.

City Hall has assumed greater powers over housing since 2000. Initially, the mayor was specifically excluded from any role in housing other than through the London Plan process.[15] The Greater London Authority Act 2007 and the Localism Act 2011 conferred new housing powers on the mayor, notably giving them land acquisition and social housing powers, including receiving grants from central government in relation to housing purposes.[16]

TWENTY YEARS OF EVOLUTION

The operation of the mayor's office and the reform of the functional bodies have, taken together, reinforced the powers of the mayor as compared to the objectives of the Greater London Authority Act 1999. Some of this accretion of power came about because Ken Livingstone set the stage for his two successors to operate the office in a way that gave the mayor tight control over the size of the office, the key positions within it and the control of the policy agenda. TfL and the Metropolitan Police, as large, well-resourced and long-established bodies, have undoubtedly been able to sustain a degree of autonomy throughout the twenty years of the GLA's existence, but they, too, have found that the mayor's office has been capable of overriding the long-evolved power of 'London Transport' and the 'Met'. Mayoral policies in relation to the appointment (or removal) of chief officers, over particular transport policies and over budgets have undoubtedly strengthened City Hall. The reformed governance of the police, fire and economic development all shifted power into the mayor's office.

Mayors, like Prime Ministers, have different levels of interest in policy and operate their offices in different ways. Livingstone, Johnson and Khan have pursued policies that are distinctively theirs. Congestion charging would almost certainly not have been introduced were it not for Livingstone, Johnson's pro-bicycle policies changed London's roads permanently and Khan has delivered anti-pollution policies which evaded earlier mayors and central government. The office of the directly elected Mayor of London was intended to personalise the leadership of London's city-wide authority and it has achieved this objective.

PART THREE

OPERATION

8

TRANSPORT

STEPHEN GLAISTER

Transport is arguably the policy area over which the Mayor of London has the most direct influence. However, central government has reserved much of the ultimate power over funding. For the majority of the first fifteen years of the mayoralty and after the creation of Transport for London, government grants were generous and borrowing was permitted. This allowed London's mayors to improve levels of service, to support a switch from private to public transport and to invest heavily without greatly increasing fares. But recently, less generous funding, coupled with a downturn in revenue from fares and delays in delivering Crossrail, has precipitated a funding crisis which has constrained the mayor.

LONDON TRANSPORT BEFORE 2000

London's transport services were all private sector ventures until 1933, when London buses and underground railways were brought into one public trust, the London Passenger Transport Board.[1] In 1948 this became part of the nationalised British Transport Commission, which also incorporated the mainline railways. A directly elected local administration, the GLC, took on the buses and the Underground (but not the mainline railways) in 1970. Legislation gave the GLC control over fares but major investment policy remained constrained by central government's powers over funding. The bus and Underground systems broadly paid for themselves from fares revenue up to this point.[2]

An important consequence of this mixed public–private heritage is that public transport in London remains an industry primarily paid for by charges to its users, albeit one that is heavily regulated and subsidised. The inescapable link between policy on the level of fares and the reliance on the national or local taxpayer for financial support is transparent and, in principle, a matter for explicit debate. This differs from continental Europe where the constitutions of many transport bodies define them as public services, a prime responsibility of the state. This point was well illustrated by the 'Fares Fair' episode in the GLC era in the early 1980s. Ken Livingstone, the radical left-wing leader of the GLC, announced an overnight reduction in bus and Underground fares. The London Borough of Bromley brought a judicial review against this move, which ultimately ruled that the policy was inconsistent with London Transport's duty to operate the bus and Underground networks with 'economy and efficiency'. Fares had to be restored immediately, and the debacle brought to a head a simmering dispute between Margaret Thatcher's national administration and the GLC. London Transport was re-nationalised in 1984 and the GLC abolished in 1986.[3]

The 1997 Blair government committed to recreating a directly elected London government with delivery of transport as one of its principal functions. Yet prior to the first mayoral election in May 2000, the government negotiated the PPP for the London Underground with the private sector.[4] The intention was that the thirty-year contracts for the PPP would be in place before the new Greater London Authority took its powers. It also researched what eventually became known as the congestion charge.[5] This reflected central government's reluctance to 'let go' and leave the new London administration to decide how it was going to do things and how it was going to pay for itself.

THE ADMINISTRATION OF TFL

The Greater London Authority Act 1999 established the GLA with a directly elected mayor and assembly, and TfL as the executive. The mayor was given the right to chair the board and so far all mayors have chosen to take up this position. The mayor appoints the members of the board and sets the policies that are to be executed by TfL, subject to scrutiny by the London Assembly. All three mayors have been assisted by unelected advisors and have used their power to appoint deputies: both Boris Johnson and Sadiq Khan appointed a specialist 'deputy mayor for transport'.

Under the legislation the mayor must produce a transport strategy and a spatial development strategy (the London Plan). The process of drafting and public consultation for these strategies has often been tortuous and they tend to be long and 'aspirational' documents. They are an opportunity for respective mayors to set out their general philosophies and lists of projects, and TfL's annual reports record progress. But they are not well known to the general public and appear to be quickly forgotten: there is little attempt to hold the mayors to delivery of these strategies.

A somewhat independent executive authority was common to all of TfL's predecessor organisations since 1933. London Buses Limited and London Underground Limited were set up as wholly owned subsidiaries of London Regional Transport in 1985 and they continue as such within TfL, which creates a degree of independence and financial transparency. The mayor is accountable for policy, with the TfL board responsible for running the various transport 'businesses' in accordance with such policy. The other main 'businesses' in 2001 were Street Management (which became London Streets), Docklands Light Railway, Dial-a-Ride, Croydon Tramlink, Victoria Coach Station and London River Services. By 2020 these had been joined by London Overground, TfL Rail, Emirates Air Line and Cycle Hire (initially branded as Barclays Cycle Hire and latterly as Santander Cycles).

The mayor and TfL have direct responsibility for the TfL Road Network, which accounts for 5 per cent of the London road network by length but carries about 30 per cent of traffic.[6] The thirty-two London boroughs and the City of London remain the highway authorities for the remainder.

On taking office as the first Mayor of London, Ken Livingstone set about creating a strong organisation at TfL. He appointed big names from North America, led by Bob Kiley as commissioner (chief executive). Some of the terms and conditions of Kiley's appointment were unheard of for UK local authority officials or civil servants.[7] Well-paid posts were also created further down the organisation and for a period TfL enjoyed much of the nation's transport planning talent.

In Boris Johnson's regime talk turned from self-confidence to 'efficiencies'. In a number of annual reports, the mayor and the commissioner (from 2006, Sir Peter Hendy) discussed efficiency programmes to save several billions of pounds and to reduce the cost base. There have been further rationalisations under Sadiq Khan and commissioner Mike Brown. A review in 2018 by the London Assembly's Budget and Performance Committee concluded that 'we have to recognise that TfL is quietly forging ahead with huge efficiency drives. It is doing remarkably well on this and, whilst this Committee would like more detail on where exactly savings are being made, the headline figures we see are encouraging.'[8]

LONDON BUSES

One of Livingstone's first actions as mayor was to increase the public funding for buses – made possible by an increased operating grant from central government – from almost zero in 2000 to around £600 million per annum by 2005. This figure has remained between £500 million and £700 million under Johnson and Khan (see Figure 1).[9]

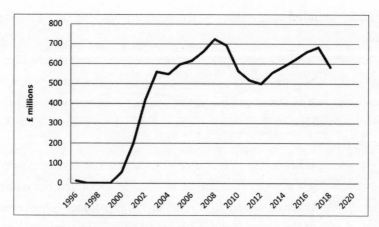

Figure 1. Financial support for London buses, £ millions at current prices

Source: Author's calculations from TfL annual reports 2000/01 to 2019/20
and other official documents

Fares were reduced and service levels increased. Figure 2 shows Livingstone's real fares reductions in his first term. Johnson increased real bus fares somewhat. Khan declared a 'fares freeze' (thus reducing them allowing for inflation) and introduced the 'Hopper' fare in September 2016, which allowed passengers to take a second bus or tram journey within an hour of their first one free of charge. This was good news for passengers, but reduced revenues to TfL.

Figure 2 shows how the real average bus fare paid generally fell up to 2008 and then stabilised. Similarly, the average fare paid on the Underground has remained remarkably stable even though business plans under all three mayors have typically worked on the basis that Underground fares would rise by at least 1 per cent faster than inflation.

Lower fares were good for passengers, less so for TfL finances and the balance between farebox and subsidy. Even where advertised fares have risen, as they did under Boris Johnson, concessions and customer behaviour have limited their effect on what each passenger pays on average.[10] The TfL annual business plan for 2020 to 2021 identifies ten concessions costing a total of £361 million in forgone revenue in 2018/19.[11] Figure 2 shows the discrepancy.

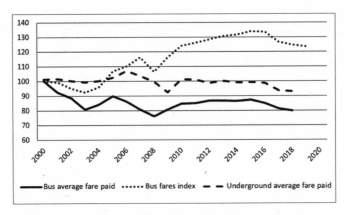

Figure 2. Bus and Underground fares (adjusted for inflation), index 2000 = 100

Source: Author's calculations from TfL annual reports 2000/01 to 2019/20,
Department for Transport (2020) and other official documents

Livingstone substantially increased bus service volumes and these have been broadly sustained since (see Figure 3). From 2003 bus service reliability in central London benefitted from the introduction of the congestion charge. Also, bus lanes have been expanded, from 162km across London in 2000 to 279km by 2008, improving service reliability. Most of this increase was on TfL's Road Network.[12]

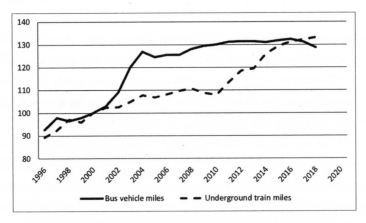

Figure 3. Bus and Underground service volumes, 1996–2018, index 2000 = 100

Source: Author's calculations from TfL annual reports 2000/01 to 2019/20
and other official documents

The reduced bus fares and – particularly – the much improved frequency and reliability of bus services greatly increased their popularity. Bus passenger volumes grew strongly until 2008 (see Figure 4). A contributory factor to the decline from 2015 was the decline in bus speeds and, as discussed later, that was partly due to the reduction in road space available to traffic.

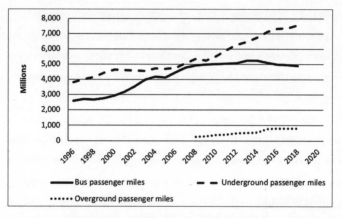

Figure 4. Bus, Underground and Overground passenger volumes, 1996–2018

Source: Author's calculations from TfL annual reports 2000/01 to 2019/20 and other official documents

Livingstone had expressed his intention to increase the proportion of bus services operated by a crew of two, partly to protect the numbers of employees in the London bus industry and partly because of the popularity of the iconic Routemaster vehicle, with its open-back platform providing the opportunity to hop-on and hop-off. This plan quickly came up against the factors that had driven the trend towards one-person operation for several decades prior: a poor safety record; difficulty finding two crew members available for every departure; inaccessibility to the less able; and the prohibitive expense of employing a second crew member. Livingstone increased the number of traditional Routemasters until 2005, thereafter operating only two 'heritage' routes, the 9 and 15. Johnson retained these routes, though their operation was cut back to one route operating on summer week-ends and bank holidays only by Sadiq Khan in 2019.

Another Livingstone innovation was to procure single-deck, artic-ulated vehicles (widely referred to as 'bendy buses', and still found in many cities around the world such as New York) 'which provided both a higher capacity and faster loading/unloading than standard double decker vehicles'.[13] They also had the benefit of being more easily acces-sible. Mayor Livingstone's spokeswoman noted in 2008 that: 'There's a perception that people don't like them but in customer satisfaction surveys people are pleased and say they meet their requirements'.[14] Al-legations that they caused a hazard to cyclists were not supported by the evidence, and allegations that their multiple-door entry allowed excessive fare-dodging were not accepted by TfL at the time.[15]

Nevertheless, Boris Johnson had pledged to get rid of the bendy buses and once elected he ran a design competition for a 'new Routemaster' (the 'Boris Bus'). The new bus would have three doors for rapid boarding, including an open rear door and a second crew member so passengers could once again hop on and hop off. It was to be a fuel-efficient, low-emissions, diesel-electric hybrid double-decker bus, with sufficient capacity to replace the articulated vehicles.

In the event, 1,000 of these vehicles were eventually commissioned and purchased (12 per cent of the TfL fleet), at a cost of over £350,000 each, which was considerably more than designs available 'off the peg'.[16] The bendy buses were retired. However, Johnson soon discov-ered that the operating cost of a two-person crew was prohibitive: the second crew member disappeared by 2016 and the hop-on and hop-off rear doors were replaced by a standard, closing door. Latterly, entry by the centre and rear doors was also stopped to control fraud. Technical failings in the construction of the buses compromised their emissions performance and the design received a mixed reception from users, poorly designed ventilation being a particular problem. No other op-erator has purchased the design.

Over the last twenty years investment in new vehicles has held the average age of the London bus fleet at around six years, compared to over eight years for the rest of England.[17]

LONDON UNDERGROUND

When Tony Blair's New Labour government replaced the Conservatives in 1997 there was a wide measure of agreement that London Underground needed substantial investment.[18]

Having tried and failed to secure a direct grant for this purpose, John Prescott, deputy Prime Minister and secretary of state for transport, devised the public–private partnership for the Underground, which was announced in March 1998. Three contracts, based on groups of lines, were to be awarded to the private sector after a competition, for the repair, maintenance and enhancement of the fixed infrastructure, signalling and trains. Each contract had a thirty-year term. Two-thirds of the existing employees on the network would remain in direct TfL employment to drive the trains and staff the stations. The government ultimately failed to complete the Underground PPP before the Greater London Authority Act came into being. Ken Livingstone and Transport for London's first commissioner Bob Kiley repeatedly attempted to persuade the government that the deal was poor value for public money. Kiley and others also proposed alternative means of raising the necessary finance.[19] An attempt by judicial review to prevent the government from imposing the PPP on the GLA was unsuccessful and the deals were executed in late 2002.[20]

The PPP contracts under Metronet – one of the two companies chosen to implement the PPP and responsible for the operation of two-thirds of the Underground network – went into administration in 2007. The company's responsibilities were taken over by TfL. While Metronet's shareholders lost their investment the banks (who had provided the greater part of the capital) were repaid most of their lending under the terms of the agreements. Tube Lines, which had assumed responsibility for the remaining third of the Underground network, was absorbed by TfL as a going concern in 2010.

So ended one of the greatest-ever procurement failures of British government.[21] A number of official reviews by parliamentary select committees and the National Audit Office both during and after the negotiation of the PPPs were critical, particularly in relation to the poor value for money that the contracts would have delivered, not to mention the delay and resources consumed in the abortive negotiations.

Traditionally maintenance on the Underground has been conducted in the early hours of the morning, and this was written into the PPP contracts, thus precluding passenger service at this time. However, with the night-time economy growing, successive mayors have wanted to run an all-night service. The demise of the PPP made this possible and in 2014 Boris Johnson announced all-night services on Fridays and Saturdays on several Underground lines. However, this precipitated an industrial relations dispute which delayed the introduction of the service and meant that it was Sadiq Khan who inaugurated the Night Tube in 2016.

CONTRACTING WITH THE PRIVATE SECTOR

The London Underground PPP was only one of nine examples of service provision under contract with private sector providers that TfL inherited: new trains for the Northern Line; Docklands Light Railway services; Croydon Tramlink; electrical power supply; an emergency radio communications system; the A13 road; British Transport Police accommodation; and ticketing. All were discontinued by TfL when the opportunity arose and the only contracts which survived were for the Northern Line trains and the Docklands Light Railway.

However, the private sector remains very much involved in London's public transport. For example, the congestion charge was administered by Capita from 2003, until it lost the contract to IBM in 2009. Throughout London's bus services have been procured from private sector providers on short-term, route-by-route contracts with TfL retaining control of the contract specification, passenger fares and revenues. This has proven highly successful and both Livingstone and Johnson continued the system after reviewing it. The new London Overground is operated in a similar way.

A significant proportion of the rail commuting into London and most of the rail movement in the suburbs is on the national railway, and outside the policy control of the mayor. Arguably, this is an anomaly. All three mayors have argued they should take over the suburban services, so as to be able to run them as an integrated part of the London system. Bob Kiley even worked up a proposal for a London Rail Authority.[22] Yet successive national governments have been unwilling to concede this, citing issues of competition for rail capacity between local services and longer-distance services centred on London. Exceptionally, some within-London suburban services were transferred in 2015–16, thereafter branded as the 'London Overground', with a distinctive livery and branding. The Overground has been highly successful and lines are operated under concession agreements with private train-operating companies. Sadiq Khan has continued the campaign for rail devolution initiated by his predecessors.[23]

CROSSRAIL AND THE NORTHERN LINE EXTENSION

Secretary of state for transport Cecil Parkinson gave the 'go-ahead' for Crossrail – now named the Elizabeth Line – as well as for the Chelsea–Hackney Line now known as Crossrail 2 – in October 1990.[24] However, no secure funding plan was put in place.

Crossrail was revived by Ken Livingstone, who secured a funding package for a £14.8 billion scheme in 2007 following negotiations with Ed Balls, deputy to then Chancellor Gordon Brown. This was a remarkable development in light of the previously poor relationship that existed between Livingstone and Brown.[25] The support of London businesses was a crucial factor.

For the first time the GLA was to be accountable for funding a significant portion of a major infrastructure investment: £4.1 billion was to be borrowed, serviced by a supplementary levy on property rates paid by London businesses. A further £1.9 billion of borrowing would be serviced out of TfL's revenues. The Department for Transport were to give a direct grant of £4.96 billion and a further grant of £2.3 billion through Network Rail. The remainder was to be funded by the sale of surplus land and property (£0.55 billion); contributions by the Corporation of London and London businesses (£0.35 billion); the Community Infrastructure Levy (£0.35 billion); and contributions from developers (£ 0.3 billion).[26]

The business rate levy was a recognition that, once built, the line would enhance the value of the land that would enjoy improved access: a mild form of recovery of the value created by the line.[27] Crossrail is the first major infrastructure project to be partially funded from the GLA's own resources. While each of the three mayors was a partner with the Department for Transport in the governance of the scheme, it was outside TfL control.

Construction began in May 2009. All appeared to be going well until a few months before the scheduled opening in December 2018, when TfL and mayor Sadiq Khan discovered that the scheme was far behind schedule and over budget. By June 2020, the total cost had risen to £18 billion: government made further loans of £1.4 billion and Crossrail was requesting a further £400 to £650 million.[28] Crossrail's opening has been delayed until late 2021 or beyond. There will be significant lessons for public infrastructure projects in the future – including High Speed 2 (HS2). The delay has had two important effects on TfL's finances: planned revenues from the new line are not available and TfL is bearing a significant portion of the additional cost of completion.

In 2012 Boris Johnson announced a novel funding arrangement for the extension of the Northern Line to serve new developments at Nine Elms and Battersea.[29] The government would permit borrowing to finance construction on the understanding that incremental business rates income from the new developments would be ringfenced and this, alongside developer contributions, would fully service the debt. In February 2019 there were press reports that the opening was to be delayed by a year until 2021 and that the net cost to the taxpayer is estimated to be about £1.1 billion.[30]

The Crossrail and Northern Line experiences illustrated that new infrastructure in London is expected to increase land values and that there are mechanisms whereby part of the increment can be 'captured' to pay towards the capital cost. But they also illustrate the difficulty, in practice, of fully funding these schemes in this way – even when the beneficiaries are readily identified – and the impossibility of transferring all the financial risks away from the public authority.

LONDON CONGESTION CHARGE

The introduction of the congestion charge was Ken Livingstone's best-known innovation on the international stage. He chose one of the schemes set out in a previous Government Office for London study,[31] which was similar to the GLC's proposed 1974 supplementary licensing scheme.[32] The project had been designed to ensure that it could easily be implemented within a mayor's first four-year term of office, the rules were readily understood and the charge would require no modification to any existing vehicles. The requirements for a proven technology explain the somewhat out-dated and expensive technical approach that was taken.

Throughout the debate surrounding the introduction of the charge, Livingstone was clear that the scheme was about managing traffic congestion: the raising of money was incidental. The net revenues were modest because the geographical coverage made up a small part of

London and did not cover the places where the traffic volumes were highest.

The congestion charge survived two judicial reviews. The introduction of the scheme had been clearly specified in Livingstone's mayoral manifesto, as well as the first mayoral transport strategy, which was itself subject to consultation. Nonetheless, it was widely considered to be a considerable political risk.[33] There was much nervousness, closely observed by the world's press when the scheme went 'live' in February 2003. It worked well and much as the models had predicted.[34]

Following the initial success, Livingstone subsequently extended the zone to the west in February 2007. This had the effect of including a much larger residential population, who then qualified for a 90 per cent discount for the whole Congestion Charge Zone. The western extension was less successful and Boris Johnson followed through with his manifesto promise when he removed it in January 2011. However, Johnson did not remove the original scheme, and the congestion charge ceased to be a controversial issue by the 2012 and 2016 elections.

ROADS

London's roads carry all of the capital's freight deliveries and many services. They are used by all bus services and by taxis. They provide for what remains the majority passenger transport mode share – the private car.[35] Yet road infrastructure has received little attention from successive mayors.

It was largely absent from Livingstone's policies, apart from the congestion charge which successfully improved traffic flow. On taking office, Johnson developed a policy of 'smoothing the traffic flow … delivering more reliable journey times, and more free-flowing travel conditions than at present'.[36] In 2012 he set up an independent Roads

Task Force to advise him.[37] This body produced a remarkably coherent view of the various functions and needs for roads in London and in March 2014 the mayor responded with a commitment of £4 billion to be spent on improving roads in London.[38] This was the only attempt at a coherent roads programme by any of the three mayors. It appears to have since been forgotten.

In January 2018, when the consequences of the loss of operating grants and declining revenues from fares were beginning to be noticed, Sadiq Khan told the London Assembly: 'As a consequence of this government's policies … less money will be spent on London's roads to maintain them. We can't run away from that. In the short to medium term, TfL will have to significantly reduce their programme of proactive capital renewals on the road network.'[39]

The TfL business plan for 2020 to 2021 shows the prospect of stagnant road and footway asset condition and remarks: 'In the long-term, we must identify adequate funding for London's roads, which does not force us to prioritise between serving public transport users and maintaining the strategic road network.'[40] This observation relates to the TfL Road Network. The 'Annual Local Authority Road Maintenance Survey' suggests that only 63 per cent of London's roads are in a good state of repair, which is similar to the national average.[41]

An important practical development affecting roads was TfL's Surface Transport and Traffic Operations Centre, which opened in 2009. This brought into one place the monitoring and coordination of responses to traffic congestion, incidents and major events and includes the London Buses Command and Control Centre, the London Streets Traffic Control Centre and the Metropolitan Police Traffic Operation Control Centre.

TfL data and a recent statement from the mayor suggest that average traffic speeds have been falling across London fairly consistently from 2000 to 2020, with the exception of a temporary post-congestion charge increase in speeds in central London, which had disappeared by 2005 to 2006. Traffic volumes also decreased until around 2014, and highway capacity has also been falling significantly.[42] There have been four main reasons for the reduction in capacity on London's roads: changes to give more space and priority to pedestrians; road works; the creation of bus lanes and the conversion of road space to cycleways.[43]

It is sometimes said that after its initial effect the congestion charge stopped working.[44] But it was the congestion charge that allowed these other changes without an even more damaging impact on traffic speeds.

It is well-understood that converting road space to cycling facilities would have a negative effect on road traffic speeds. For instance this was discussed in a TfL board paper of 4 February 2015.[45] The paper analysed the east–west cycle superhighway scheme and predicted that the disbenefits from increased journey times across much of London would greatly exceed the benefits to cyclists.[46] In the event the predicted reduction in bus speeds has turned out to be one of the factors in reducing bus patronage and revenues.[47]

TAXIS

Taxis (Hackney Carriages or black cabs) and private hire vehicles (minicabs) are important modes of transport for some people, at some times of the day and in some areas. They account for twice as many trips as motorcycles and one tenth of the number of bus trips.[48] Between 2000 and 2018 the number of trips by these modes grew by 24 per cent. Competition between the licensed taxi trade and the private hire trade has always been fierce.

Policy on taxis and private hire has been problematic for all three mayors. The mayor and TfL inherited the licensing of taxis from the Metropolitan Police, while private hire had been more or less unregulated. There was criticism of the behaviour and probity of minicab drivers – much of it from the competing licensed trade – and Ken Livingstone responded by introducing quality licensing of private hire.

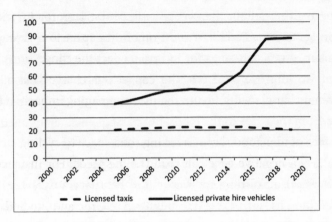

Figure 5. Numbers of licensed taxis and private hire vehicles (thousands), 2005–19

Source: Department for Transport

Two factors contributed to a rapid rise in the number of taxis and private hire vehicles on London's streets. First, under pressure, Livingstone granted taxis an exemption to the congestion charge. Second, one of the most fundamental technological changes for the transport industry occurred: the advent of the smartphone. Uber first exploited this in San Francisco in 2011 to offer a highly responsive, cheap, door-to-door taxi service provided by individuals who had a vehicle and time available. It came to London and many other world cities in 2012.

Uber proved to be attractive to the travelling public, but less so to the competing service providers and to the labour unions that represented some of their drivers. There soon followed allegations of unfair conditions of employment and poor behaviour by drivers. The number of private hire vehicles on the road in central London has also been blamed as a cause for worsening congestion. In 2019 TfL withdrew Uber's licence, citing concerns about passenger safety, although the company has been able to continue to operate in the city pending appeal of the decision.[49]

RIVER CROSSINGS

New crossings of the Thames to the east of the city have been a topic of controversy throughout the twenty years of the mayoralty. The Dartford Bridge and the Blackwall and Rotherhithe tunnels are congested. A number of new crossings for rail passengers have been created but attempts to improve road crossing capacity have all failed. Central government developed schemes that were approved by two public inquiries from the 1970s to the 1990s, but subsequently abandoned them in the face of opposition from local interests.

Ken Livingstone became convinced of the need for a new crossing and TfL made a planning application for the Thames Gateway Bridge from Beckton in Newham to Thamesmead in Greenwich in 2004. This again proved controversial and it was the only topic which came to a vote at the TfL board during Livingstone's tenure. Nevertheless, by 2008 there was a scheme in place with full funding from a mixture of charges and central government support. Although the planning inspector had recommended against the scheme the secretary of state for communities and local government had said she wanted a new inquiry to investigate further whether the bridge would lead to regeneration, and its potential impact on pollution.[50]

One of Johnson's first acts as mayor was to cancel the scheme. However, during his term Johnson was involved with several river crossing schemes of his own. The controversial Garden Bridge was proposed as more of a leisure facility than a transport link; however, it could not be funded and was cancelled by Sadiq Khan in 2017. The Emirates Air Line, a passenger cable car which opened in 2012 to coincide with the London Olympics, was underpinned by commercial sponsorship. However, the press reported that there were only a handful of regular commuters in November 2013.[51] Patronage has been falling and in 2018/19 it carried just 1.3 million passengers.[52] The net cost to the taxpayer is obscure.

Meanwhile, the need for more road passenger and freight crossing capacity remains – unless the overall demand for movement by road is reduced in some way. In 2012 Johnson announced a river crossing at Gallions Reach, in the same location that Livingstone had proposed a crossing. However, nothing came of this proposal. A Silvertown Tunnel has the support of Sadiq Khan and has secured a development consent order. This road tunnel will be tolled, as will the Blackwall Tunnel.[53]

PROMOTION OF PUBLIC TRANSPORT AND ACTIVE TRAVEL

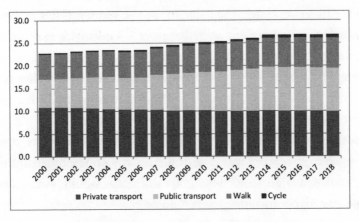

Figure 6. Trips per day (millions) by mode, 2000–2018

Source: 'Travel in London Report 12', Transport for London

An aspiration of all three mayors has been to 'get people out of their cars' and increase the shares of trips by public transport, walking and cycling: in other words, to reduce the proportion of trips that are made by private car. Figure 6 shows that this has been achieved to a degree, but there has only been a small absolute fall in the number of private transport trips and a bigger increase in public transport trips as London's population has grown. The share of public transport trips has grown from 27 per cent to 35 per cent. That is due to the growth in public transport use. While the share of private transport has fallen from 47 per cent to 36 per cent the absolute number of private transport trips has only fallen by 6 per cent and it remains the biggest single mode.

There has been much emphasis on promoting cycling and this mode has grown from 0.3 to 0.7 million trips per day. Boris Johnson made promoting cycling a headline policy and invested heavily in physical measures such as the cycle superhighways.

The cycle-hire scheme, modelled on the Vélib network in Paris, was announced by Livingstone close to the end of his term, and enthusiastically expanded by Johnson. In 2018–19 there were 10.9 million hires, representing about 5 per cent of all cycling trips but only 0.15 per cent of all trips in London.[54] The value for public money of this scheme is not known. A number of competing private sector cycle-hire schemes have since appeared, but all except a couple of the electric bike schemes have been withdrawn.[55] The non-electric schemes have found it harder to stay financially viable in London than in some other cities, partly because of higher rates of theft and vandalism.

But across Greater London, cycling makes up only 3 per cent of trips taken. It remains geographically heavily concentrated in inner and central London and demographically among the young, male, white and higher income groups.[56] So despite its salience, particularly under Boris Johnson, cycling is not an important element in the travel of the bulk of the London public.

Sadiq Khan announced a particularly ambitious aspiration to reduce car use, but TfL's business plan for 2019 to 2020 noted how difficult such a change would be to achieve:

> To support London's growth and achieve the 2041 target of 80 per cent of all journeys being made by sustainable methods, bus patronage will need to increase by 40 per cent. This is in the face of recent trends, whereby increased congestion, particularly in central London, has led to declining speeds and contributed to falling demand.[57]

The London 2012 Olympics demonstrated that the travelling public and commercial traffic could be persuaded to modify their travel behaviour, at least for the duration of the games, and that the array of authorities responsible for administration of transport in London could be made to work together. Properly managed, the railways can sustain high loadings and demand management is a viable way of adjusting the calls on the system. The need to serve the Olympics also expedited agreement with government for the east London line extension, the Northern Ticket Hall at King's Cross, Stratford Station and a number of other rail infrastructure improvements in east London.

The London Olympics are generally considered to have been a success in transport terms. Yet they were quickly forgotten and London returned to business as usual.

AIR QUALITY

Air quality and carbon dioxide emissions have become much more important issues during the first twenty years of the GLA.

When Ken Livingstone was introducing the congestion charge the benefits for air quality and carbon emissions were mentioned as additional benefits but the policy was primarily about easing congestion. Cars with low carbon emissions were exempted from the charge and have remained so.

In February 2008 Livingstone introduced the Low Emission Zone, which imposed an additional charge on non-compliant vehicles entering the congestion charge area. Boris Johnson progressively tightened this to a schedule he set out at the start of his period in office. Although Johnson did not introduce any major new initiatives, he set them in motion for his successor. In October 2017 Sadiq Khan introduced the toxicity charge on older, more polluting vehicles and the Ultra-Low Emissions Zone charge from April 2019. These are supplementary charges, additional to the congestion charge, for non-compliant vehicles.

All of these policies have only applied to the Congestion Charge Zone in central London so they had limited effect elsewhere, but Khan has said that he intends to extend the ULEZ to the North and South Circular roads in late 2021.[58]

All three mayors have continued the programme to improve the emissions performance of London's bus fleet, mainly by ensuring that they are all hybrid vehicles; 3.6 per cent of buses in the city are pure electric or hydrogen-powered vehicles.[59]

London's carbon emissions fell by 8 per cent between 2000 and 2007 and by 37 per cent between 2008 and 2015. Concentrations of oxides of nitrogen and particulates showed a mild declining trend throughout this period, and there are early indications that they have fallen by about one third in the ULEZ area.[60]

TFL FUNDING AND FINANCE

Since 2000, successive mayors have set the financial contribution to TfL from local tax at modest levels. Once it became established, the congestion charge has yielded an average net income of about £155 million per annum, which is only about 3 per cent of TfL's total income.[61] The main sources of funding for TfL are revenues from fares and central government grants, although in recent years grants have largely been replaced by retained non-domestic rate income. Prudential borrowing is used for financing, but debt must be serviced out of income in the longer-term.

Figure 7 shows revenue and capital grants to TfL, excluding Crossrail and excluding grant funding for the London Underground in the early years under the PPP.

Substantial government funding was agreed with Ken Livingstone in late 2007 in a 'ten-year settlement'.[62] This covered nine years rather than one year as had been previously the case – but there has since been a return to much shorter settlements.

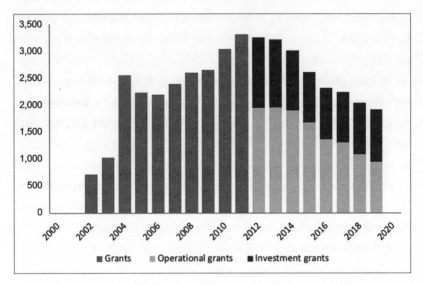

Figure 7. Revenue and capital grants, £ million, 2002–11 total grants, 2012–19 operating and investment grants. Excludes Crossrail and London Underground during PPP. After 2012 'Investment grants' includes items for Metronet and London Overground

Source: TfL annual reports and TfL private communication

It appears that the government commitments implicit in the ten-year business plan of November 2008 were honoured except, perhaps, in the final year. In light of the national and international financial crisis following 2007 this is a remarkable testament to the regard in which TfL had come to be held.

In November 2015, central government announced that from 2018 there would be no further general grants for the day-to-day running of services at TfL. While this was partly mitigated by retention of business rates, the government envisaged this being applied to capital spending.[63] This was a significant change in policy away from specific subsidy for operating buses, compared to the ten-year settlement of 2007.

Historically under-investment in London's transport assets has been a problem. But over the twenty years of the GLA there was considerable investment in the bus fleet. Investment in the Underground was £1 to £1.5 billion per year, mainly as a result of the programme of renewals and capacity enhancements promised under the London Underground PPP. Underground revenue is similar to operating cost, so this investment was broadly funded from grant. There was also substantial growth of investment in London rail up to about £1.9 billion in 2016 to 2017. Some of this is preparatory work for Crossrail, but a significant portion is the development of the London Overground. However, capital maintenance spend on TfL and borough road infrastructure has arguably been inadequate.

An important innovation from 2003 was that TfL was given the authority to borrow. After the first year that borrowing was permitted, debt grew steadily and is predicted to stand at around £12 billion by 2021, with further increases anticipated in future years.[64]

TfL could have borrowed from the Public Works Loan Board.[65] However, for its first major borrowing of £3.3 billion in 2004 the TfL board decided to borrow on the commercial markets at a higher rate of interest. This was partly to establish a degree of independence, but also to introduce for the first time the disciplines of transparency and accountability imposed by commercial markets. TfL therefore had to publish an information memorandum which set out its business transparently and in great detail.[66]

This combination of generous central government grants until 2018 and access to borrowing helped Livingstone and Johnson to avoid raising fares a great deal while expanding services and continuing to invest heavily in renewing and enhancing London's transport infrastructure. But since 2017 patronage on the Underground has not been growing as fast as had been forecast, while bus patronage has declined (see Figure 4) and average fares per trip have declined. Alongside delayed revenues and increased construction costs from Crossrail, reduced fares-yield growth has contributed to the severe financial situation that developed during 2019.

CONCLUSION

The TfL story began with a bitter struggle between national government and the first mayor, Ken Livingstone, over control of maintenance and investment for the London Underground. Once that had been settled – in favour of the government – relations improved quickly, and there followed fulsome financial support from national government and large-scale prudential borrowing. The average fare paid on buses was not greatly increased and service levels and reliability significantly improved. The congestion charge was successfully introduced. There was sustained investment in the Underground and the bus fleet. Funding for a ten-year plan was agreed with the government in 2007 and delivered despite a climate of austerity following the global financial crisis. The funding for Crossrail was agreed and was provided through central government grants, a special supplement on business rates, revenues from increased passenger numbers, revenues from the congestion charge and through new borrowing. With the exception of Crossrail, there has been no other significant call on London taxation since 2000 by TfL.

TfL has had some success in responding to the increasing concern surrounding air quality and carbon emissions. The proportion of trips made by public transport, cycling and walking has increased, but absolute numbers of trips by private car have reduced little and they remain the dominant mechanised mode. Cycling has become more popular and has been strongly promoted by all three mayors, but it remains a minority mode of transport as it is generally confined to particular geographical areas and particular types of users.

When central government operating grants were removed from 2018, TfL was faced with a more challenging environment: revenues from bus and Underground began to soften and there were delays to receiving revenues from Crossrail and cost overruns on the project. By the end of 2019 TfL had had to deliver significant efficiencies, but still ran into considerable resource difficulties. By this time, under three different mayors, the organisation had accumulated a total debt of £12 billion.

The situation was complicated in early 2020 when Covid-19 struck. Nothing could have prepared TfL's finances for the catastrophic loss of revenues as people stopped using public transport across the capital. TfL's financial position by the end of 2019 had already left the mayor in a weak position when negotiating with central government about the conditions under which London's transport finances would be rescued. In the circumstances it is unsurprising that central government would take the opportunity to insist on imposing changes to the mayor's policies in a way that it had refrained from doing throughout the existence of the regime since it was created in 2000.

9

INTRODUCING THE CONGESTION CHARGE

MICHÈLE DIX

The day that the congestion charge was introduced was a momentous one for London. On the morning of 17 February 2003, as co-director of congestion charging for TfL, I was waiting anxiously in the London Traffic Control Centre with my co-director Malcolm Murray-Clark, Derek Turner and the rest of the team to see what would happen.

Many other people were also looking on apprehensively. Capital Radio's 'Flying Eye' traffic-monitoring helicopter was buzzing around London's skies looking for queues and chaos at the boundary of the charging zone and watching to see if traffic levels remained unchanged within the zone itself. Others were looking out to see if public transport was being overloaded, or to see if Capita's congestion charge system would collapse under the stress of people making last-minute payments.

Would congestion charging work? Would people abandon their cars for public transport, to walk or cycle? Would businesses in central London rearrange their deliveries? Would they go out of business? Would residents not be able to access services? Would drivers who were accustomed to using central London as a cut-through divert around the area, causing chaos? Would inner London become a huge car park for central London? There were many concerns.

I had spent the previous eight years of my working life looking at the need for a congestion charging scheme for central London. In the years before the mayoralty existed, I had worked on a study for London First (a business campaigning group) examining the options and making the case for such a charge. Later, I worked on the Government Office for London's 'Road Charging Options for London' (ROCOL) study for the incoming mayor. Then, following Ken Livingstone's election, I joined Transport for London to work for the mayor, after he chose to use the new powers provided under the Greater London Authority Act to introduce congestion charging in central London. This moment had been a long time coming.

The scheme was a world first. The ROCOL work identified that it would take four years to complete the development, consent, procurement and delivery stages that were necessary to get the congestion charging scheme operational. However, the mayor also had to make sure that the scheme was part of his transport strategy, which itself had to be written and consulted on. A scheme order, consistent with the mayor's Transport Strategy, was then required in order to define the scheme in detail. The new Greater London Authority was established in July 2000 and the inaugural mayoral term would run until May 2004. The scheme order had to specify the time and date that the scheme would commence; this was problematic because the ROCOL delivery programme indicated that the scheme could not be up and running before the next mayoral election.

Nevertheless, a start date of 17 February 2003 was agreed as it allowed a year before the next mayoral election and also meant that the scheme would be introduced during a school holiday, when the traffic would be lighter. It was decided that charging hours would run from 7 a.m. until 7 p.m., although the end of the charging period was subsequently brought forward to 6 p.m., in response to theatre and evening businesses lobbying for an earlier end time.

And so the exact start time and date were set. The programme would have to work within these constraints. Changing the date or time would require a new scheme order consultation as it would have an impact on businesses and road users. As a result, rather than the steps of the programme running sequentially, it was decided that, where possible, such steps should run in parallel to enable the delivery of the scheme by the ambitious target date.

As well as defining the start date and times of operation, the scheme order also defined other key elements: the exact boundary for the charge; the specific level of the charge itself; exemptions and discounts; and what would be done with the money raised from the charge. The central aim of the scheme was to charge private vehicle drivers in order to deter them from using central London and to use the net revenues to support public transport. The scheme order therefore set out where monies raised could be spent.

Determining exemptions and discounts created the most debate. Many different groups of road users – by vehicle type, job type and location – made powerful cases arguing that they should receive a full exemption or discount.

The support for the scheme was strong at the beginning of the mayoralty. Most people agreed that there was too much traffic in central London and that something had to be done about it. The provision of more public transport was the favoured solution, but who would pay for it? Of the options – increased fares, increased local or income taxes or charging those who caused the congestion in the first place (i.e. private vehicle drivers) – the latter was preferred, and this is how the circular argument for congestion charging was made.

However, as the scheme was developed and started to become increasingly real, support began to waver. Concerns increased about the likely effectiveness of the project, both in terms of reducing traffic and achieving the environmental and economic benefits that were predicted. Advisors around the mayor started to become concerned. However, we had undertaken a huge amount of analysis to understand what journeys were being made, by whom, and for what purpose. We had run different modelling approaches and tested different assumptions in order to be as confident as possible that the scheme would work. We had considered every angle of the scheme when we had developed it – its effects, its operation, its enforcement and the robustness of the technology supporting it. We undertook extensive risk analysis and identified a range of mitigations. We sought to control everything that we could!

One thing that we could not control was what would be done when Tower Bridge (which was part of the congestion charging boundary route) would need to be raised for river traffic, as boats that are coming up-river can request passage through the bridge in a given period, which is then dependent on the tides.

Throughout all of this, the mayor remained confident that the scheme would work. And so, at 7 a.m. on 17 February 2003, the scheme went live. When the day passed without any serious incident, there were feelings of relief, joy and exhaustion all mixed together. The scheme had worked. The mayor had made the right call and his popularity rating increased. With some in the mayor's office having initially feared that the introduction of the charge was too close to the next mayoral election, Livingstone's only regret was that perhaps the charge should have been introduced in February 2004 after all!

10

POLICING, CRIME AND PUBLIC SAFETY

RICK MUIR

The establishment of the Mayor of London introduced for the first time city-wide accountability for the Metropolitan Police. Prior to 2000, Scotland Yard was largely accountable only to national government in Westminster and Londoners had few direct levers for holding their police service to account. Alongside the creation of the Greater London Authority, the Metropolitan Police Authority was established as part of a complex set of arrangements for London-wide police governance. But this was the first step in what has gradually evolved into a more powerful role for the London mayor.

In 2008 the mayor was given the power to appoint the chair of the MPA. In 2011, the London mayor took direct control of police accountability in London, with the creation of the Mayor's Office for Policing and Crime. Although the commissioner of the metropolis is formally appointed by the Home Secretary, in making that appointment the Home Secretary must 'have regard to' the views of the mayor. In reality, sustaining the confidence of the mayor has become a necessary part of the role of Britain's 'top cop'.

What impact has the mayoralty had on policing, crime and public safety? This is not an easy question to answer, given that most of the causes of crime and insecurity lie way beyond the control of City Hall. Indeed, even in the area where the mayor does have powerful levers, in the oversight of the police, the constitutional position is somewhat complex and not entirely clear-cut. The mayor does not in their own right appoint the commissioner, and the commissioner, as with all chief constables in England and Wales, is 'operationally independent' of politics.

This chapter will assess the mayor's impact in five areas: holding the Metropolitan police to account; tackling crime and disorder; sustaining police officer numbers and in particular promoting neighbourhood policing; improving public confidence in the police and dealing with the lower levels of confidence in policing among minority communities; and responding to major events that have tested London's resilience.

POLICE ACCOUNTABILITY

The Metropolitan Police has been London's police force since its formation by Robert Peel in 1829, although it was only with the introduction of the London mayoralty that the Met became directly accountable to the people of London. Prior to that Scotland Yard was ultimately accountable to Whitehall.

The Greater London Authority Act 1999 introduced the MPA, which was made up of members of the London Assembly, independent members and magistrates. The MPA was responsible for setting the Met's budget and its local policing plan, as well as scrutinising its performance.

This complex model of governance was somewhat similar to that which existed for police authorities outside London and was intended to prevent too much power being placed in the hands of politicians. Local corruption scandals in the middle of the twentieth century sensitised policy-makers to the dangers of giving elected politicians too much control over police forces. As a result, since the 1960s, English and Welsh policing has operated within a 'tripartite' model of governance in which locally elected figures, the Home Secretary and chief constables share power. The police authority had the power to approve budgets and appoint chief constables. The Home Secretary distributed most of the funding and possessed some legal powers to intervene. Chief constables, or in the case of London, the Commissioner of the Metropolitan Police, had, and still have, control over day-to-day operational decision-making. Or as one former Home Secretary once told me: 'The chief constables have all the power, the police authorities have all the money and the Home Secretary gets all the blame.'

Even within police authorities the role of local councillors was balanced by the appointment of 'independent members', often magistrates and other prominent local people. This deliberately opaque model was the one that was introduced in London through the MPA in 2000.

These blurred lines of accountability characterise the way in which the commissioner was (and still is) appointed. Following the introduction of the Greater London Authority Act in 1999 the Home Secretary retained the power to appoint the commissioner (or strictly speaking to recommend an appointment to the Queen), but in making that decision the Home Secretary was required for the first time to 'have regard to' the views of London's representatives: the MPA and the Mayor of London. The photo opportunities that all mayors from Ken Livingstone onwards have enjoyed, with the mayor doing a walkabout on the streets of London with the commissioner, created an image of US-style mayoral control over policing. The constitutional reality has always been somewhat different.

From the very beginning the mayor did hold considerable influence, however, through the GLA's powers to set the budget for the MPA, and through the MPA for the Met, including raising funds for policing via the council tax precept. The mayor's tax-raising powers play an important role in providing the resources for London's police.

In 2018/19, according to the National Audit Office, 30 per cent of the Met's revenues came from London council tax-payers. Of course it should be noted that that still leaves 70 per cent of the Met's funding coming from central government grants.[1] Battles with Whitehall over the Met's budget have hence been a perennial feature of the London mayoralty, regardless of which party has held City Hall and which party was in power nationally.

Despite the limits imposed on the mayor's control over policing at the very start, the story since then has been of a gradual accumulation of mayoral power. The powerful electoral mandate of the mayor, alongside the relative successes of the London mayoralty as an effective model of city government, created a gravitational pull towards giving the mayor greater control over policing. In 2008 the mayor was given the power to appoint the chair of the MPA, a position briefly occupied by Boris Johnson, who had criticised Ken Livingstone for not chairing the body himself.[2]

In 2011 the Conservative–Liberal Democrat coalition government introduced police and crime commissioners (PCCs) to replace the old police authorities across England and Wales, with the aim of strengthening the accountability of the police to the public. The Mayor of London effectively became the PCC for the Metropolitan Police District, with the powers that PCCs hold elsewhere residing with the newly created Mayor's Office for Policing and Crime.

This means that the mayor now directly sets the budget and the police and crime plan. MOPAC has been headed under both mayors Johnson and Khan by a powerful deputy mayor, a model of delegation that recognises that the mayor's job is too broad to allow for a detailed focus on policing matters. Policing remains operationally independent, with the commissioner commanding the force and making day-to-day decisions. MOPAC is held to account by the Police and Crime Committee of the London Assembly.

The power to appoint the Metropolitan Police Commissioner remains with the Queen, upon the recommendation of the Home

Secretary, although the Home Secretary must have regard to the views of the mayor in making that recommendation. The mayor can suspend the commissioner and call upon them to resign or retire, but only with the support of the Home Secretary.

Although the mayor's powers to hire and fire commissioners are *de jure* limited, *de facto* they have proven to be decisive. In 2008 the then commissioner Ian Blair resigned from his post once it became clear that he did not have the support of the new mayor Boris Johnson.[3] This process is recalled by Kit Malthouse in Chapter 11. It was also widely rumoured that Bernard Hogan-Howe's decision to retire in 2016 was in part due to a strained relationship with the recently elected Sadiq Khan.[4] Having the confidence of the mayor has become essential for the person occupying the top job in British policing.

Some have argued that the role of commissioner has been politicised by the introduction of the mayoralty.[5] It is certainly true that the mayoralty may have contributed to a higher level of turnover in the role, with a new mayor typically wanting their 'own man or woman' at Scotland Yard. However, while this may have contributed to the early departure of some commissioners, there is little evidence that the mayor has intervened excessively in operational policing decisions, or at least no more so than politicians have typically done in this country.

There is no detailed statutory definition of 'operational independence'. It is a constitutional concept that has been developed largely by the courts when required to adjudicate over the relative powers of chief constables and those charged with holding them to account. At the core of the notion is the idea that day-to-day control over the deployment and direction of police officers sits with the chief constable, or in London's case the commissioner. The Police Reform and Social Responsibility Act 2011 set out that PCCs, and in London's case the mayor, can approve the budget, set broad strategic priorities (via the police and crime plan) and appoint the chief constable. There are however many issues which sit across this artificially neat divide between 'strategy' and 'operational matters' and that in reality require ongoing negotiation between the commissioner and the mayor. For example, there is a case for seeing the use of police tactics such as stop and search or tasers as day-to-day operational matters. Nonetheless, the use of such tactics is highly controversial politically and therefore it seems unthinkable that decisions around their use should be made without some reference back to the mayor.

There is no question that the creation of the GLA and the gradual increase in the powers of the mayor have made the Met more accountable to Londoners. Those standing for the position of mayor have generally made policing and crime a core part of their campaign. In 2004 Ken Livingstone made the re-introduction of neighbourhood policing in his first term a key plank of his re-election bid.[6] In 2008 Boris Johnson published a dedicated 'crime manifesto' as part of a bid to tackle violent crime, which he said had increased under Livingstone.[7] The increase in knife crime in London since 2015, and the global anti-racism protests held following the murder of George Floyd, have once again made the issues of crime and policing central to the campaign in the run up to the 2021 mayoral elections.

Through the mayoralty Londoners have for the first time had a direct say on policing priorities in the capital, which represents a significant step forward from the days when the Met's priorities were set 'behind closed doors' in Whitehall and Scotland Yard.

CRIME AND DISORDER

One of the main ways in which the mayor's performance is judged is their success in reducing crime. If we take the overall level of recorded crime in London (see Figure 1), we can see that crime as reported to the police decreased over the first decade and a half, under Livingstone and Johnson, but started to rise again after 2014, mid-way through Johnson's second term and throughout Khan's first term.

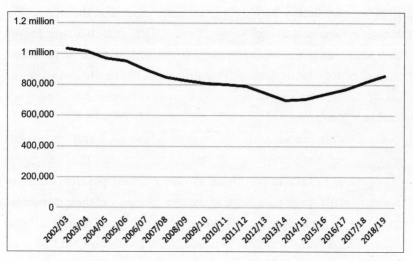

Figure 1. Total offences, excluding fraud, recorded by the Metropolitan Police

Source: 'Crime in England and Wales: Police Force Area data tables, 2015–19', Office for National Statistics and 'Historical crime data, 2002–14', Home Office

Breaking crime down into different offence types (see Table 1), we can see that most types of crime fell over the course of both Livingstone's and Johnson's periods of office. The main exceptions are a 33 per cent increase in violent crime under Johnson, alongside a 90 per cent increase in sexual offences, although the latter is likely to be as a result of increased reporting in the aftermath of a number of high-profile cases. Most types of recorded crime have increased over the course of Khan's term of office, including a big increase in possessions of weapons offences which reflects the recent increase in serious violence and police proactivity in responding to it.

What are we to make of all this in terms of an assessment of the three mayors? Taking this data at face value would lead to the conclusion that while Livingstone and Johnson were successful at getting crime down, Khan has been largely unsuccessful in doing so. However, there are a number of reasons for thinking that this assessment is unfair on the Khan administration.

Offence type	2002/03	2007/08	Percentage change from 2002/03 (Livingstone)	2015/16	Percentage change from 2007/08 (Johnson)	2018/19	Percentage change from 2015/16 (Khan)
Violence against the person	152,017	139,303	8 per cent down	185,675	33 per cent up	215,139	16 per cent up
Theft	604,834	437,389	28 per cent down	355,510	19 per cent down	427,460	20 per cent up
Domestic burglary	72,237	59,841	17 per cent down	43,901	27 per cent down	60,000	37 per cent up
Possession of weapons	9,393	7,833	17 per cent down	4,723	40 per cent down	7,564	60 per cent up
Sexual offences	11,002	8,423	23 per cent down	16,054	90 per cent up	20,433	27 per cent up
Robbery	42,493	37,045	13 per cent down	21,562	42 per cent down	34,341	59 per cent up
Vehicle offences	176,487	122,380	31 per cent down	82,848	32 per cent down	116,745	41 per cent up
Drugs offences	33,311	72,204	117 per cent up	39,535	45 per cent down	37,765	5 per cent down

Table 1. Offences recorded by the Metropolitan Police, 2002/03 to 2018/19

Source: Data for 2002/03 to 2008/09 taken from 'Historical crime data, 2002–14', Home Office, and data for 2015/16 to 2018/19 taken from 'Crime in England and Wales: Police Force Area data tables, 2015–19', Office for National Statistics

First, recorded crime statistics are a flawed measure of monitoring crime as it is actually experienced by the public. These figures measure crimes reported to and recorded by the police. Sometimes an increase can simply reflect proactive policing, or increased reporting. For example, the increase in drugs offences between 2002/03 and 2007/08 may reflect police proactivity, such as increased use of stop and search. Increases in crimes that were previously largely underreported, such as sexual offences, reflect factors such as an increased willingness to report. In this sense increased numbers of recorded sexual offences may be a good thing, indicating that more victims feel confident that the system will treat them seriously. It is also important to note that there has been a tightening up of crime recording standards in recent years, sending the figures upwards in a way that does not reflect crime as it is actually experienced by the public.[8] Second, the relationship between mayoral action and crime levels is complex. The mayor possesses important levers – most significantly oversight of the Met – and in that sense is clearly a contributor to the conditions in which crime can rise and fall.

Nonetheless, general crime trends across London can be the product of all sorts of factors way beyond the control of City Hall. For example, the recent increase in serious violence is almost certainly linked to changes in drug markets and the operating models of organised crime groups and networks involved in trafficking drugs.[9] Cuts to public services, such as local authority youth services, have also been argued as being contributing factors to young people getting involved in 'gang-related activity', which is linked to the increase in knife crime. Neither the evolution of global and English drug markets nor cuts to local authority services are within the control of the Mayor of London.

Equally, much of the national drop in acquisitive crime since 1995, picked up in the London data on theft, burglary and vehicle offences in Table 1, was due to improvements in home and vehicle security, rather than down to public policy success in London or even at a UK level. These crime types also decreased over the same period in Germany, the US and France.[10]

In fact, much of what we see in the London figures reflects wider trends. Figure 2 shows that the London pattern of a decline in recorded crime from 2002/03 and then a rise in recorded crime after 2013/14 was replicated in the rest of England and Wales. It is important to note that according to the Crime Survey for England and Wales, crime overall did not rise after 2013/14 but continued to decline somewhat. On that basis it is reasonable to hypothesise that a good chunk of the post-2014 increase in police-recorded crime is down to changing recording standards and increased reporting rather than a substantial increase in the overall crime rate.[11]

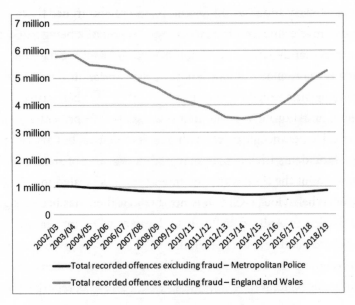

Figure 2. Total recorded offences excluding fraud
– England and Wales compared with the Metropolitan Police

Source: 'Crime in England and Wales: Police Force Area data tables, 2015–19',
Office for National Statistics, and 'Historical crime data, 2002–14', Home Office

Third, there was a shift in crime reduction priorities between the mayoralties of Boris Johnson and Sadiq Khan that is worth reflecting on. The Conservative mayor was very focused on tackling traditional volume crime. The so-called 'MOPAC 7' set of crime reduction targets sought to reduce crime by at least 20 per cent in seven categories between 2013 and 2016: burglary, vandalism and criminal damage, theft from motor vehicles, theft of motor vehicles, violence with injury, robbery and theft from the person. This unquestionably focused police activity on these priority areas and the Met was largely successful in meeting these targets.[12]

The targets were, however, scrapped by Sadiq Khan who argued that they distorted police efforts away from areas of crime that are hidden and do not show up in the recorded crime figures. The MOPAC 7 approach was also criticised by Her Majesty's Inspectorate of Constabulary and Fire and Rescue Services, who argued that a focus on acquisitive crime led to other areas of police work being neglected, most importantly child sexual abuse investigations.[13] Khan has subsequently reoriented MOPAC's strategic priorities towards tackling violence against women and girls, youth crime and hate crime, while allowing local boroughs to set their own local crime priorities.[14]

The police do not just deal with crime of course, but also a wider array of incidents where harm may occur. One area of significant national focus at the time when the mayoralty was created in 2000 was anti-social behaviour (ASB). It is notable that there has been a significant decline in ASB-related calls to the Met in recent years.[15] These are likely to capture only a portion of ASB incidents given that many complaints are made to local authorities, registered social landlords and other agencies. It is also unclear whether a fall in reporting is due to fewer incidents or as a result of people lacking confidence in the system and feeling that there is little point in reporting such issues.

Most of the levers for dealing with ASB lie at a borough level, where most preventative and enforcement activity is delivered. The mayor's role is largely in funding some of that preventative work and also in providing the police resource to support local efforts. It is notable that in 2018 the London Assembly's Police and Crime Committee criticised a lack of focus on the problem at City Hall and voiced concern at a reduction in funding for preventative work. The committee concluded: 'We are unclear as to how the mayor is leading the response to antisocial behaviour in London.'[16] The one area where the mayor has had an impact, however, is in relation to neighbourhood policing, to which we now turn.

POLICE NUMBERS AND NEIGHBOURHOOD POLICING

Each of London's mayors have promised to increase, or at least protect, the number of police officers serving the capital. In this, they have been largely successful, as shown in Figure 3. There was a substantial increase in the number of police officers under Ken Livingstone of around 7,000. Although he benefited from significant funding from national government at the time, it is worth pointing out that Livingstone also increased the council tax precept specifically to fund more police officers.[17]

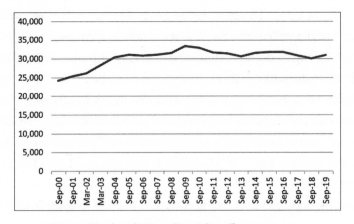

Figure 3. Number of Metropolitan Police officers, 2000–2019

Sources: 'Police workforce England and Wales Statistics', 2010–19, Home Office and 'Home Office Statistical bulletins archive', 2000–2010', National Archives

In 2008 Boris Johnson was elected on a promise to tackle crime, particularly knife crime and crime on London transport, and there was a bump in police officer numbers in his first years in office.[18] During the decade of austerity, in which the Met saw its central government grant fall by 29 per cent between 2010/11 and 2018/19, one might have expected the number of officers to fall as they did in the rest of the country.[19] But both Johnson and Khan have been successful in sustaining the number of officers in London at between 30,000 and 32,000 over the last ten years.

However, this success at sustaining officer numbers has not come without its problems. It has forced the respective mayors to find cuts in other parts of the police budget. For example, the number of Police

Community Support Officers (PCSOs) was cut from 4,247 in March 2008 to just 1,553 in September 2016, and then again to 1,273 by September 2019.[20] PSCOs were introduced in 2002 by the Labour government. They are not warranted constables but have some limited powers and tend to be focused on providing reassurance, through community engagement and visible patrols. There have also been reductions in the number of police staff, which fell by 42 per cent from 14,666 in 2007 to just 8,472 in 2019.[21] This may not be the most efficient way of reducing the size of the police workforce, as it is likely to have resulted in police officers having to do more desk-based tasks that police staff are better qualified to do, pulling officers away from front-line operational work.

Nor is it the case that 'more police officers equals less crime', although police officers deployed in effective ways can make a difference to local crime levels. Police effectiveness is affected by capacity issues of course, but it is much more closely related to what police officers do.[22]

Each of the mayors has supported a focus on neighbourhood policing, which is intended to meet the public's desire to see 'bobbies on the beat' in their local communities. There is good evidence that community policing can improve public confidence in the police and enable the police to be more proactive in tackling crime.[23]

London's safer neighbourhood teams were introduced by Ken Livingstone in 2004 and have been broadly sustained to the present day. Police Foundation research shows that between 2008 and 2016 the percentage of the Metropolitan Police workforce categorised as working in neighbourhood policing remained relatively steady at between 10 per cent and 15 per cent.[24]

However, the loss of PCSOs is likely to have impacted on the quality of neighbourhood policing in London. This is because such officers typically provide functions such as visible patrol, problem solving and community engagement activity which are hard to resource through warranted officers who have to deal with more serious matters requiring the use of police powers. Indeed, a reduction in the quality of neighbourhood policing is reflected in MOPAC's public perceptions data. Between 2014 and 2020 the percentage of residents who felt well informed about local police activities fell from 49 per cent to 38 per cent, and the percentage who knew how to contact their ward officer dropped sharply from 41 per cent to just 16 per cent.[25]

PUBLIC CONFIDENCE IN THE POLICE

The British model of 'policing by consent' rests on the idea that the police can only be effective if they enjoy the trust and cooperation of the public. Have London's three mayors made an impact on how Londoners feel about their police service? Most Londoners are satisfied with the service they receive from the Metropolitan Police, although the figures have deteriorated somewhat in recent years. In 2014, 67 per cent of Londoners agreed that 'the police do a good job in the local area', but this had fallen to 58 per cent by 2020. One positive indicator for the Met's legitimacy is that the overwhelming majority of Londoners perceive the police to perform their role fairly. The percentage of people agreeing that the police 'treat people with fairness and respect regardless of who they are' has increased slightly from 74 per cent in 2014 to 76 per cent in 2020.[26]

These views are not held equally among all social groups, however. Black and mixed ethnicity respondents are less likely than white respondents to agree that the police treat people with fairness and respect, with just 63 per cent of black and 61 per cent of mixed ethnicity respondents agreeing with this, compared to 75 per cent of white respondents.[27]

The London mayoralty was formed just a year after the publication of the Macpherson report into the murder of Stephen Lawrence, which concluded that 'institutional racism affects the MPS'.[28] Tackling racism and bias in policing was a major priority for Ken Livingstone as mayor. Twenty years on, the rise of the Black Lives Matter movement and the anti-racism protests in the aftermath of the murder of George Floyd in 2020 show that the Met still has a long way to go in building confidence among black communities.

At the centre of such concerns is the repeated finding that police enforcement activity disproportionately affects black people. In 2018/19 a black person was 4.6 times more likely to be stopped and searched by the Met than a white person.[29] Black people are more likely to be arrested and subject to use of force than white people.

Following the 2011 riots there was criticism of the use of stop and search by the Met, which it was argued had led to a breakdown of trust between young people and the police. These criticisms inspired a change in government guidance on the use of the power, which led to a significant fall in its use, not just in London but across the country. However, at the peak of the knife crime surge in London after 2015, the Met announced a renewed use of the power in order to recover weapons and deter young people from carrying knives. The number of stop and searches rose sharply from 13,085 in April 2018 to 30,608 in April 2020.[30]

Although the Met, and indeed the mayor, have emphasised that the power will now be used in an 'intelligence-led' manner, stop and search continues to be disproportionately used against black people and this remains a cause of considerable community concern.

Finally, it has long been a mayoral aspiration that those policing London should look more like the city they police. A recent Police Foundation analysis found that the proportion of BAME people within the Metropolitan Police workforce has increased, from 8 per cent in 2007 to 14 per cent in 2018.[31] However, this remains way below the proportion of London residents who are BAME, which stands at 40 per cent.[32] Moreover, while there has been progress with recruiting Asian officers, progress has been much slower with recruiting black officers.[33] The case of Shabnam Chaudhri, reported in the media recently, highlighted once again the obstacles that many BAME officers face when progressing through to more senior ranks in the Met.[34]

So, despite some progress in tackling racism and promoting diversity within the Met much more will need to be done both by the mayor and Scotland Yard if London's police are to enjoy the confidence of all communities in the capital.

LEADERSHIP IN TESTING TIMES

One of the most significant contributions of the mayor has been to provide visible public leadership at times of crisis, when the city's resilience has been tested and its cohesion has been shaken.

London is sadly a major target for terrorist attacks and there have been a number of these since 2000, including the 7 July bombings in 2005, and more recent attacks at Westminster Bridge and London Bridge in which many people died and many more were injured. The mayor has played a major role in ensuring that the capital is prepared for such major incidents, in particular by leading and coordinating the London Resilience Forum, which brings together all the main agencies in the capital who play a role in responding to such emergencies. The mayor is also typically involved in coordinating the response to such incidents with national government, through participation in the COBRA committee.

Leadership is not only about ensuring London's emergency services are prepared for such incidents, but it is also about providing an emotional rallying point for the capital at a time of crisis. Ken Livingstone's address at the time of the 7 July attacks may well be remembered as his finest hour as mayor. One also thinks of Boris Johnson holding a brush as he returned from holiday to help clear up after the 2011 riots. Sadiq Khan similarly used his public voice to rally Londoners in response to the Westminster Bridge and London Bridge terrorist attacks.

Recalling each of these events, clearly the actions and bravery of the emergency services represented the core of the state's response to these crises. Nevertheless, if London had lacked its elected mayor at those moments then a vital rallying point for the city would have been missing.

CONCLUSION

The 2000 reforms which brought in the GLA have had a significant and beneficial impact on crime, policing and public safety in the capital.

The model has provided Londoners with a direct line of accountability over these issues, which never existed before. If Londoners are concerned about the quality of service they receive from the police, the balance of police priorities, or about the way in which police officers go about their work, it is now very clear who they should go to for a remedy. The visibility of the mayor, as a single office holder with a big public profile, has created a very clear mechanism through which Londoners can exercise greater control over policing.

The mayoralty has also provided a mechanism for protecting the numbers of police officers in London, and provided a model of neighbourhood policing that has withstood the relentless pressures of austerity since 2010. It is hard to imagine the Met sustaining these officer numbers and this commitment to neighbourhood policing in the absence of an elected mayor.

There has been less success at tackling the lack of confidence in the police among some minority communities in London. The persistent racial disproportionalities in the use of police powers and the slow progress on police workforce diversity remain huge challenges for the Metropolitan Police as we enter the 2020s.

One of the mayoralty's greatest contributions to how safe and secure Londoners feel is perhaps at a more symbolic and affective level. At times of crisis, and there have been many, the Mayor of London has provided a city that twenty years ago had no city-wide government with visible and decisive public leadership.

11

GETTING CONTROL
OF THE MET

KIT MALTHOUSE MP

The departure of Metropolitan Police Commissioner Sir Ian Blair, announced on 2 October 2008, was a big moment for the mayoralty. It was an unfortunate thing to happen, in a sense, but it was a major step forward for the office. It really stamped the authority of the mayor on policing in London in a way that hadn't been seen before.

Boris Johnson's administration was elected in May 2008, against a backdrop of growing and significant alarm in London about knife crime. Young people were being killed on an almost daily basis. In the July following our election, there was one week when six people were stabbed to death.[1] And the numbers kept mounting.

We'd fought the 2008 election campaign very much on a law and order platform – we were going to sort this out, and we were going to take responsibility for it. During the campaign, Ken Livingstone had used this awful phrase to explain why knife crime was sensationalised by the media: 'If it bleeds, it leads.' But this just gave us a strong sense that there was an institutional indifference towards these young people being killed.

Then we got to City Hall. Boris Johnson made me deputy mayor for policing, and we met Ian Blair. Frankly, it was a pretty awkward relationship, because both Boris Johnson and I had written some pretty critical things about him in the papers. But, nevertheless, we wanted to give him a chance, and we went into the relationship with a cooperative approach. However, two things became clear early on. First, Ian was very distracted by internal problems at the Met. There was scandal after scandal, an assistant commissioner was pursuing legal action against him, and as he became more and more mired in controversy, and more distracted, it became clear that the senior management board at the Met was essentially dysfunctional. It was just not working, they weren't a coherent team. And so it was time to change the captain.

Second, and more worryingly, there was a sense of indifference towards this phenomenon of knife crime among young Londoners, on the basis of pure statistics. I was told more than once, and indeed, by Ian Blair himself, that we shouldn't worry too much about these knife killings because they ultimately involved a very small number of people: we were talking, at that stage, of roughly seventeen or eighteen people that had been killed, and that was statistically insignificant in a city of nearly 8 million people, I was told. I was horrified. Each one of these victims was somebody's child. Dead. Stabbed.

We did get a fair amount of movement early on, because Tim Godwin, who was the assistant commissioner territorial policing and Sir Paul Stephenson, Ian's deputy, did really get the issue. And so with our support, they launched 'Blunt 2', the stop-and-search operation, early into the mayoralty to drive stabbing numbers down. But as we got towards the autumn, it became clear that the confidence and the drive of the organisation really wasn't coming from the commissioner's office. And so we started to get a sense that the relationship between the commissioner and our administration wasn't going to work.

There were good things about Ian. Nobody is all good or all bad, and he was trying his best, but really we just didn't think that he was the person to drive the Met forward. The decision was taken that we were going to try and change the Met leadership. And so, on the fateful day, Ian showed up at City Hall for what was supposedly a routine meeting and Boris, Catherine Crawford, the chief executive of the Metropolitan Police Authority, and I accompanied Ian to Boris's office on the eighth floor of City Hall, and I guess the phrase that you would use is, 'persuaded him to go'.

The reason that we were able to do so was that there had been a small, but widely unnoticed change in the regulations that made such a change much more possible. Previously, the mayor could not be the chair of the MPA, they could only appoint the chair. The law changed that night, and so the following morning, Boris took control of the authority fully. Prior to that, we had been stuck with Len Duvall, the Labour chair, and I was vice-chair. We had asked Len to step aside, but he wanted to hold on to the job for some reason, possibly to frustrate us politically. But when Boris took over, we were able to use this change within the MPA to underline to Ian that a wider change in leadership was desirable as well, and so he agreed to move on.

Boris and I had discussed this over a number of weeks, and we had picked a particular moment to do it. But there was another aspect to our decision. Frankly, it was all part of a wider attempt by us to gently muscle the Home Office out of the picture. The governance of the Metropolitan Police had become very confused. The operational side of policing was rightly independent of political influence, but there was an odd, tripartite arrangement where the Home Office and City Hall had dual control of the priorities of the Met. The commissioner was spending as much of his time with the Home Secretary as he was with the mayor. And that was just going to be confusing – not least because we had a Labour Home Secretary, a Conservative mayor, and the poor old police in between. And so we tried quite hard to get the Met's attention, so that we could very much focus them on London's priorities, rather than their national role alone. Obviously the Home Secretary is very interested in counter-terrorism and national security, which is important, but there was a specific crime problem in London, and we needed full focus on it.

The following summer, when Sir Paul Stephenson was commissioner, I did an interview with *The Guardian*, and they ran a front-page headline saying that we had 'seized control of Scotland Yard' stating that we had our 'hands on the tiller' of the Metropolitan Police.[2] This blew up while I was on holiday in Italy, and it did not go down very well at the Met. It was of course a sensationalised headline, and there was a series of frantic calls back and forth to try and sort it all out, but in reality it was part of this wider positive mission on our part to lean into policing and effectively be the primary voice that the Metropolitan Police listened to.

When Ken Livingstone was mayor, Len Duvall was chair of the Metropolitan Police Authority, and my sense was that Ken and Len didn't really get on. Len wasn't part of Ken's inner team. My understanding was that the only other interaction that the mayor had with the police was through Lee Jasper, who was very focused on diversity, rather than dealing with crime. So there was no real drive on crime, no one directly setting the mission. And so we changed that, in my view, decisively and very successfully.

Replacing Ian Blair was a big moment for Boris's mayoralty, a sort of graduation to maturity. It was six months in, and it was the first really big, bold projection of the mandate, which then set a platform for increasing the power of the mayoralty. It showed that if you exercise the mandate with confidence, you could accrete power to the office, without necessarily even having the legislation to do so. I think it gave Boris personally a sense of the possibilities presented by his mandate. After that, we accelerated on all fronts.

12

ECONOMY AND LIVING STANDARDS

BRIDGET ROSEWELL[1]

HOW LONDON'S ECONOMY HAS CHANGED OVER THE LAST TWO DECADES

The year 2000 marked the end of a millennium and the opening of the Jubilee Line extension.[2] But it did not mark a shift in the performance of the London economy. Rather, it saw a confirmation of changes that were already underway. In the early 1990s, recession had hit London hard, with 'negative equity' first coming into common parlance, unemployment rising sharply and all services being affected. But by the mid-1990s this was over. Employment in central London was once more on the rise, and the transport system was filling up again too.

The big economic story of these years is one of a massive rise in services activity and a decline in manufacturing in London which changed the city's economic geography. This started in the 1970s and 1980s, so the fall in manufacturing flattened off in the early 1990s, largely because there was very little left to lose.[3] This was balanced by an increase in service sector employment. All through the 1990s, all parts of the service sector boomed, whether in administration activities, professional and scientific roles, information, communication and retail. Indeed, unemployment in the capital almost halved from 13.8 per cent in 1993 to 7.2 per cent in 2000.[4] It was no surprise that these years also saw pressure to recreate some kind of London government to deal with the implications, especially in transport but also in planning and support for growth.

It is important to remember that this switch to growth was not particularly about financial services, or the 'Big Bang' of the mid-1980s. This did make a difference and probably changed some attitudes, but the most significant increases were in the professional fields such as law, accountancy and management consultancy. In these fields 200,000 jobs were added between 1984 and 2000 at a steady rate. In the same period, a similar number of administrative roles and 120,000 information and communication jobs were also added. On the other hand, 230,000 manufacturing jobs disappeared, and financial services added only around 65,000.[5] Although considering comparable gross value added, output in financial and business services in the UK grew between 1970 and 2008 by some 350 per cent in real terms, doubling in the 1982–90 boom, and again in the 'long boom' of 1992–2008; a similar pattern to that reported in London.[6]

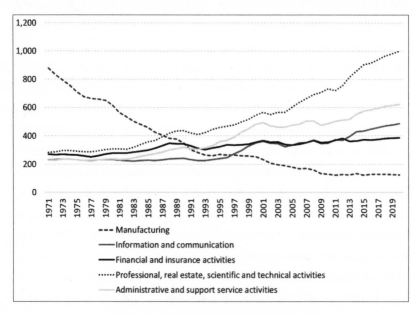

Figure 1. Sectoral employment (1,000), 1971–2019

'Total London and sector employment, 1971–2050', GLA 2020

This pattern was thus well established when the GLA came into existence. After 2000, it persisted, although the rise in administrative roles flattened alongside some information roles, while professional activity growth continued unabated, and has done so pretty much ever since.

Understanding this pattern has been very important to developing any attitude to shaping it. The idea that London was growing, and would continue to grow, was hard for some to grasp. Looking back, the role that technological change has played is crucial. Robert Solow, an eminent American economist, famously said that 'you can see computers everywhere but in the productivity statistics'.[7] But the inability to separate out the impact of computerisation on productivity does not mean it had no effect. The ubiquity of such machines made a massive difference across every field of activity. They made new kinds of business possible and allowed data to be accessed, checked and compared with ease. All of this became possible in the pre-2000 period. New firms sprang up and old ones morphed into something different. Audit firms became consultants, and consultants became advisors.

The GLA had to understand what was going on. When the Greater London Authority was established, and the first mayor elected, there was no agreed economic strategy for London, although the city was already growing fast. That vision had to be created as part of preparing the first London Plan. The mayor might have chosen to seek to slow growth or to divert it from London. However, Ken Livingstone's advisors, who had all worked with him for many years, were clear that this had to be a vision for 'world city' success. They were all clear that constraints had to be removed and difficulties swept aside. I remember sitting in one early meeting at which the growth potential was being discussed and the mayor's economic advisor was laying down the law. It took a while for me to chase down why this felt familiar, until I remembered the left-wing political meetings I had attended as a student and the rules of democratic centralism under which the decisions of the leadership are law.

This is not to suggest that there was explicit resistance to the vision developed in the mayor's office. Indeed, many felt liberated by the possibilities of a more integrated vision for London. It was just that it did require a shift away from habits of thought in, for example, the London Planning Advisory Committee, which had survived the end of the GLC, and the powers of which were limited and ambitions slim – although they had commissioned the *London World City* report in 1991.[8]

Elsewhere, of course, the campaign for the existence of the GLA had crossed party boundaries and the need for coordination and ambition recognised. Reports on London's future as a world city had been prepared throughout the 1990s, from the *London World City* report to Llewelyn Davies's *Four World Cities* report in 1996, and the establishment of London First in 1992.[9] All this is chronicled by Greg Clark in his book *The Making of a World City*.[10] So there was a strong following wind for the establishment of the GLA and for the vision for an 'exemplary sustainable world city' set out in the first London Plan, which was published in draft in 2002 and finalised in February 2004.

It remained to flesh out that vision and to support it with evidence. That evidence became the domain of GLA Economics, which provided the rationale for supporting the continuing shift to services in the city, the growth of the Central Activities Zone (London's core business district, comprising the West End, the City, the South Bank and peripheral areas), and crucially, the need for transport investment to sustain the continued productivity of that area. GLA Economics was set up in 2002 to provide a firm statistical, factual and forecasting basis for policy decision-making by the GLA and its functional bodies.

One of the first reports that the unit produced was on the creative industries, broadly defined. This looked at the self-employed and creatives in firms in general as well as creative firms themselves. It showed how important creative activities are to London and its economy, which was itself an insight that helped shape views about how London was about so much more than banking and the seriously rich. The report noted that:

> The growth of the Creative Industries is at the cutting edge of a fundamental transformation in London's economy that has been happening for the last three decades. Planning for London's Growth showed how Business Services have become the dominant sector within the city over this period, but alongside this a second process has been going on, which is now poised to take centre stage. The growth of the Creative Industries is the outcome of this second process, creating a major new source of economic expansion for the capital.[11]

Since the mid-1990s London's economy has grown by 5 per cent per year on average, with barely a dip, even post-2008. The city now represents 23 per cent of the UK economy (2017), up from 18 per cent in 1997.[12] That growth rate became established before the existence of the GLA, but it needed the GLA to establish policies both to support it and to help shape it.

GLA ECONOMIC IMPACT

The single most important thing that successive mayors have done to support and encourage the London economy is to support and finance the development of the transport system to enable more people to access the opportunities in the centre of the city as the service sector has grown. This has included more buses, the establishment of the congestion charge and the campaign to invest in the Underground, both in its existing configuration and with Crossrail. Twenty years ago, the Jubilee Line extension had just been opened, the Northern Line was known as the 'Misery Line', and the Victoria Line had an ancient signalling system.

The scale of investment in transport, and the battles over the PPP for London Underground, are set out in Chapter 8, but an account of London's economy cannot ignore the transport system, and the economic importance of investment. New buses, new information systems and bus priority lanes were implemented alongside new signalling systems and new rolling stock for the Underground.

Framing the case for new transport in economic terms was possibly the most important achievement in the new vision for the capital. The case for Crossrail could not have been won without a figurehead such as the mayor, backed by a strong lobby from London's business leaders, and it rested on the productivity benefit of being able to deliver more people into that central area.

This was important for London's shifting economic structure. Manufacturing activity, which largely took place along the radial routes such as the A13 and the North and South Circular roads, has been replaced over a generation by service sector activities which are much more centrally focused. Indeed, the Central Activities Zone and the northern Isle of Dogs are responsible for 40 per cent of London's employment and 45 per cent of London's gross value added while, at a sector level, these areas are responsible for 86 per cent of London's finance and insurance employment and 61 per cent of professional, scientific and technical sector employment.[13] Without a transport system which facilitates the movement of millions of workers into the city centre every day, that growth could not have happened.

Investment in transport has also been integrated into economic development and into managing the complexities of major development opportunities in London. Moreover, these drawn-out processes have involved long-term commitment from all three mayors over the last twenty years, even though their political approaches have differed. This long-term approach to identifying 'opportunity areas', listing them in the London Plan, and using transport investment, influence and planning powers to shape their development has been a fundamental shift and its impact should not be underestimated.

OPPORTUNITY AREAS

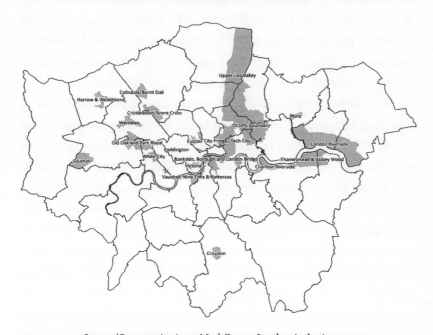

Source: 'Opportunity Areas Map', Greater London Authority, 2019

Three examples of specific opportunity areas are perhaps the most significant: Park Royal and Old Oak Common, the Olympic Park and Battersea Power Station. Park Royal, in west London between the A40 and the North Circular, had seen its manufacturing base shrink, with employment falling to around 30,000 people in 2016 compared to 45,000 in the 1960s.[14] Next door is Old Oak Common, where there are neither oaks nor a common but lots of railway sidings and infrastructure just to the north of Wormwood Scrubs. Old Oak Common was initially on the Crossrail route. After HS2's route was planned in 2009, Old Oak Common became the location where HS2 meets Crossrail.

To bring these strands together, without the GLA and its convening powers, would have been hard, if not impossible. Boris Johnson decided to establish a mayoral development corporation at Old Oak and Park Royal, using the provisions of the Localism Act of 2011. The Old Oak and Park Royal Development Corporation was set up in 2015 to make the most of the investment in rail infrastructure in the area, and to plan for 65,000 new jobs and 25,000 new homes within the 65-hectare site – essentially a new town around a transport hub. The ability to have ambition, to integrate policies and to take a long-term view is the result of the GLA coming into existence and gaining these powers.

The other mayoral development corporation is the London Legacy Development Corporation (LLDC), set up in 2012 to deliver a 'legacy' from the London Olympic and Paralympic Games of 2012. As well as maximising economic benefits and ensuring the utilisation of the Olympic Park land and facilities, the LLDC also aligns to the 'convergence' objectives of the neighbouring boroughs.[15] The goal is to reduce the gap in economic outcomes (e.g. skills and unemployment) between the population of the LLDC boroughs and the London average. The most recent data (from 2015 to 2016) notes that convergence has only been achieved so far with regard to the number of children achieving a good level of development at age five, though convergence appears on track for a further six indicators, four of which are education attainment indicators. However, the gap with the rest of London is identical to that in 2009 or has widened with regard to indicators such as median earnings, job density, physical activity and obesity.[16]

Overall, while a gap remains, it is noteworthy that the initiative has partly succeeded in narrowing the divide. Such changes, after all, typically take generations, rather than years, to achieve. This too was an initiative which was sustained by successive mayors and brought together transport and development initiatives, with a focus on legacy from the outset. I was (and remain) sceptical about the long-term benefits of major sporting events, but the existence of the London Overground owes quite a lot to the Olympics investment and has helped locations such as Dalston and Shoreditch increase their development capacity.

A final example of the effective integration of transport and planning powers can be seen in bringing the Northern Line to Battersea Power

Station and facilitating the redevelopment of this major site. The power station site had been the focus of repeated attempts at revival since its closure in 1980 and several major proposals, including significant leisure uses and the relocation of Chelsea FC's stadium. But development remained difficult until a new London Underground Northern Line spur from Kennington was proposed to service the development, with funding borrowed against future levies on development and business rates. At the same time, opportunity area planning was extended to cover Vauxhall and Nine Elms as well as Battersea. Now the iconic chimneys of the former power station have been rebuilt, with some housing already in occupation, and the American Embassy has been relocated between Battersea and Vauxhall. Erstwhile industrial sites are being developed to high densities both for residential and business use, which has made this area a real extension of London's Central Activities Zone just the other side of the river.

Shoreditch, which has become a hub for the tech industry, is a somewhat different example of the limitations as well as the powers of local and regional government. Start-up firms came to Old Street and to Shoreditch because they were cheap locations on the edge of the City, offering office accommodation within easy reach of the rest of London. Tech firms, marketing companies and creatives quickly moved in. Studies of the creative sector noticed this and started to talk about creative clusters, co-location space and cheap rents. None of this appears to have had much effect, despite the strongly expressed government support for 'Silicon Roundabout'.

Government policy interventions at places like Shoreditch have been based on a partially understood concept of 'clusters'. The term 'cluster' was first brought into prominence by Michael Porter, who looked at the conglomeration of textile firms in northern Italy, and how their supply chains worked.[17] This became narrowed to looking at the co-location of firms doing similar things rather than supplying each other, and a fashionable focus of policy. Even now, there can be too much emphasis on the desirable rather than the possible, as if policy creates businesses rather than removing barriers to others who can do so.

THE LONDON PLAN

The London Plan has been the vehicle for driving these opportunities and developing a vision of the economy. From the outset, the first London Plan was ambitious for employment and in arguing that projections for demand for different types of workspace and infrastructure needed to adapt to the changing nature of the economy, although this has remained a continuing challenge. GLA Economics was tasked with providing the analysis and the conceptual backing to understanding and arguing for these shifts. National officials had to be convinced that the plans were viable and realistic. As chief economist, I spent a lot of time with transport officials, and arguing the case for Crossrail and how transport is an economic driver and facilitator for economic growth.

As the GLA has developed, and different mayors have evolved different priorities, the London Plan has moved on. However, it has had a consistent thread supporting this economic pattern of high productivity service sector growth. From the beginning this also meant broadening opportunity, considering the links between central and outer London and thinking about the environment. The last of these has become much more prominent: Chapter 5 of the 2015 plan and Chapter 9 of the 2019 plan solely consider London's response to climate change and sustainable infrastructure, with key policies focusing on reducing emissions.[18]

The fundamentals of the London Plan have remained constant. There was an attempt to create better dialogue in the preparation of the London Plan on the employment prospects for individual boroughs. A triangulation process looked at how to compare historic trends, transport capacity and development capacity. The idea was to generate a debate within each borough about which of these trends might predominate. Perhaps inevitably, but disappointingly, this instead became a set of rules for which the mechanism could be adapted, and it never provided such a forum. Equally, in the wake of the financial crisis of 2008 to 2009, there were concerns that the future would look very different and that more cautious economic scenarios should be developed for the forthcoming revision of the plan. In the event, no agreement was reached on what form such alternatives might take, and further, no alternatives turned out to be necessary as growth rapidly resumed. The GLA's continued focus on growth and on maintaining infrastructure investment turned out to be the right call and prevented a damaging stop-start approach.

LIVING IN LONDON

The need to provide housing has also become far more important in recent years, with the latest London Plan outlining the need for 66,000 new homes each year.[19] Twenty years ago, we were not talking about a housing 'crisis' in London, although we were certainly talking about housing need and affordability. This is also an economic issue as quality of life (including quality and affordability of housing) is crucial to the success of the city, and affects the willingness that people have to live and work in it. Indeed, although ranked in the top three of the Kearny Global Cities Index for the past decade, London has been ranked at around forty out of 223 cities on the Mercer Quality of Living Index, putting it within the top 20 per cent; and around fifty out of 140 cities on the Economist Intelligence Unit Liveability Index, putting it within the top 40 per cent.[20]

Housing costs are one of the main distinctions between the living costs for Londoners and those living elsewhere in the UK. The median house price to income ratio is 12.8 in London compared to 7.8 in England.[21] In London, private renters can expect to spend 45 per cent of their gross income on rent, whereas the England average is 30 per cent, which is considered to be 'affordable'.[22] Commuting and housing cannot be separated, with much discussion during the preparation and public examination of each London Plan about the extent to which housing should match employment growth and the extent of cooperation with surrounding authorities – which has often been politically difficult.

Wages in London are higher than elsewhere but this doesn't always mean that living standards are higher. Median resident wages are 20 per cent higher than for the country as a whole, but there is a challenge both in the distribution of wages and in housing costs.[23] In 2016/17, the median household income before housing costs was £28,600 in London compared to £25,700 in the UK. However, after housing costs, income in London was £21,400; a decrease of 25 per cent compared to only 13 per cent in the UK.[24]

London's ongoing housing crisis has made it increasingly difficult for families to have adequate space and for younger people to get on the housing ladder; 7.6 per cent of London households are overcrowded compared to 3.4 per cent nationally and home-ownership rates in London's 25–34 year-olds have decreased from 42 per cent in 1997 to 25 per cent in 2017 (compared to 55 per cent to 35 per cent in the UK).[25] While this was a recognised issue when the GLA was formed, and respective mayors have fought to be able to do more in this area, they have had mixed success. The viability of housing schemes with desired proportions of affordable housing has been hard to guarantee, and in the wake of the financial crisis many housebuilders and developers have not been able to finance new developments.

Densification has been one response, but this has led in many cases to smaller rooms and reduced access to outside space.[26] In 2017/18, 35 per cent of approved schemes in London were within the density range recommended by the London Plan's 'sustainable residential quality' density matrix, and 59 per cent were delivered at higher densities than recommended by the matrix.[27] What kind of housing and where it should be built remains a significant challenge. Of course, this is not just true in London and the GLA's ability to do much about it remains limited. However, it cannot be counted a success as the continuing affordability crisis indicates.

On wages, the GLA has had more of an impact with the introduction of the living wage concept. The campaign for a living wage was started by Citizens UK (formerly London Citizens) in 2001, with the movement gaining mayoral support in 2004 and going national in 2011 with the launch of the first national living wage and the inception of the Living Wage Foundation.[28] Although there were sceptics, the idea that the national living wage was insufficient in London had merit. There is now an annual calculation and moral persuasion has been effective in getting firms to sign up to pay – and get their contractors to pay – a living wage. Now, some 4,700 employers across all sectors have joined the movement.[29]

Other forms of inequality are more intractable. In the early years of the GLA, under Ken Livingstone, there was a strong focus on gender wage gaps. This turned out to hinge on the highly paid – who were largely male. Further down the wage distribution there was less of a discrepancy, especially for full-time workers. While policies designed to ensure that women had full access to senior roles could be pursued and indeed have been by various initiatives, such as that for female representation on company boards, other alternative actions, such as targets for minority groups to tackle wage inequality, have had less support.

One factor affecting the wage gap is that more women work part-time: 32 per cent of working-age employees, compared to 11 per cent of their male counterparts.[30] At one point there was an argument about whether women 'should' work full-time or whether their choice to do part-time work was their own. There is no doubt that working part-time damages long-term earnings capability, but can be a desired choice. Moreover, there are relatively fewer part-time work opportunities in London, often because travel to work takes too long to make part-time work in higher-paid roles feasible. Childcare is also more expensive and more difficult to find. Policies to subsidise childcare more generously than elsewhere could not be funded under the mayor's powers.

London also has persistent patterns of inequality affecting people from black and minority ethnic groups. London has a much larger BAME population: the current estimate is that 40 per cent of the population belong to these groups (compared to 13 per cent across the UK). However, the employment experiences of different groups vary, and policies that have attempted to address this have struggled to make a difference. Some Asian groups, for example, have good earnings and good educational achievement too. Other Asian groups fare less well, and especially Pakistani women have low workplace engagement, while black and black British men face unemployment rates three times those of white men.

A WORLD CITY

London has been a world city since at least the seventeenth century. It has also been the subject of derision and distaste and was once described as the 'Great Wen', sucking prosperity and youth into destruction.[31] There is no doubt that the immediate post-war period saw London at its lowest ebb. Wartime destruction across Britain and a desire for better housing led to the establishment of more new towns – following on from the garden city movement of the 1930s – and de-densification. Like many large cities, during this period London seemed to be hollowing out. The age of the car was not kind to British cities, and road building privileged growth in smaller cities, suburbs and market towns.

But world cities do not die that easily. This chapter has already explained that by the 1990s, cities were becoming once more the place to be. In fact, cities are the place to be whenever change is happening. In the early 1970s when computers were just beginning to be used by businesses, they were located in the centre of cities, even though they required lots of space and massive cooling fans. By the 1980s large computer mainframes had moved out of our cities, but the micro-computer was making all kinds of new applications possible and the businesses that used them were starting up in cities where they could share ideas and find clients.

By the 1990s, reports were beginning to emerge on 'world cities'. Numerous bodies were calling for a London authority of some sort in order to better coordinate policy, promote the city overseas and maximise London's growing potential.

London has ridden the crest of the wave of the rise of the modern city, ranking often first, sometimes second to New York, in 'world city' indices. In the early years of the GLA, the media focus on financial institutions and conspicuous consumption perhaps overshadowed much of what was really going on in creative industries, in tech, in marketing and consultancy – all industries in which the UK and London have global positions. In riding that wave the existence of a Mayor of London, with the largest personal franchise of any UK elected official, has given the capital global clout and status akin to other world cities, many of which have mayors with far more financial power. Without the GLA, much would still have been achieved, but the changes would have been more difficult.

WHAT NEXT?

This chapter has focused on the period up to the beginning of 2020. It has not touched at all on the Covid-19 pandemic and its possible consequences as they are still unknown. Cities are obviously infectious places and London has been hit hard by coronavirus. Indeed, in the medieval period London was so unhealthy that constant immigration was required to keep the population level constant. But people came. They came because in times of change and opportunity, communication and ideas generation are the essence of innovation. Whatever comes next, London will remain important.

13

THE LONDON DEVELOPMENT AGENCY AND LONDON 2012

RICHARD BROWN

The venue was Holden Point, a sheltered housing block just north of Stratford town centre. On a grey day in February 2005, thirteen International Olympic Committee (IOC) grandees, their London hosts and sundry officials rode the building's elevator to the top floor, where London's future Queen Elizabeth Olympic Park was laid out before them.

The huge site, much of it still occupied by factories, car breaker yards and storage depots, was decorated with balloons to show where the various venues would be. On the future site of the aquatics centre, a bulldozer was already at work, preparing for a construction programme that would go ahead regardless of whether London won its bid for the 2012 Olympic Games. This earth-moving performance was not particularly urgent, but the display was all-important as a signal indicating London's seriousness about delivering its ambitious programme for the Lower Lea Valley.

Much has been written about how difficult it would have been for London to submit an Olympic bid without an elected mayor to represent the whole city. But if the bid was Livingstone's, and the event was to be Johnson's, the foundations were put in place by the LDA – an anomalous element of the 2000 governance reforms, but the right organisation in the right place for London 2012.

The LDA was grafted onto the mayoral machinery from another

root stock – deputy Prime Minister John Prescott's beloved regional development plans. But while regional development agencies elsewhere were government agencies headed by local business figures, London's had to be appointed by the mayor. In 2000, Ken Livingstone appointed George Barlow, chief executive of Peabody Trust housing association, as chair of the LDA, and his former Greater London Council comrade Michael Ward as chief executive.

The LDA took on urban thinker Greg Clark to prepare its strategy, and English Partnerships' Tony Winterbottom to oversee development of the substantial land holdings in east London that it had inherited from London Docklands Development Corporation. Most of the agency's budgets, programmes and targets, however, were still defined by central government, which led to misalignment between strategy and action. By 2002, the agency had objectives that included 'supporting London's economic growth, both as a world business centre and as a balanced regional economy' and 'developing London as a city of knowledge and learning', alongside the promotion of diversity, inclusive growth and environmental sustainability. However, £255 million out of a total budget of £300 million was tied up in land and regeneration programmes, which left just £2 million for tourism, £1 million for inward investment and £29 million for skills, business support and innovation.[1]

When the British Olympic Association approached Ken Livingstone about an Olympic bid in 2001, he insisted that the focus must be east London. The LDA commissioned Arup to look into the potential capacity for, and costs and benefits of, an east London Olympics, and this formed the basis of Livingstone's negotiations to get the government on board.[2] The LDA had no role in major sporting events, but they did have a remit for 'regeneration' – a conveniently stretchy and undefined term. Winterbottom sprang into action: commissioning masterplans for the Lower Lea Valley's 'regeneration' with or without an Olympic and Paralympic Games in 2012; beginning to look at options for relocating businesses and residents from the site;

launching an international design competition for an aquatics centre (which was won by Zaha Hadid); and part-funding the London 2012 'bidco' – the team, which was led first by Barbara Cassani and then by Seb Coe and was responsible for drafting and selling London's bid to the IOC's Lausanne luminaries.

By 2004, when the IOC evaluation commission arrived, Manny Lewis had replaced Michael Ward at the LDA, and the agency was getting ready to submit a simultaneous planning application to the four local authorities responsible for the Olympic Park area, so that the IOC would be able to see that London's complex democratic system of planning control would not stand in the way of the project. Outline permission was granted, in a highly choreographed evening at City Hall, within days of London's bid being submitted.

London's bid included plans for the Olympic Delivery Authority, which would build the venues and infrastructure for 2012. As the legislation to set up the delivery authority went through Parliament, the LDA acted as its shadow in signing some of the time-critical early contracts (e.g. to bury the high-voltage power lines that criss-crossed the site). It also hurried to assemble the site, launching a compulsory purchase process to buy up land interests, compensating and relocating occupiers, and cleaning up the contamination that had been left by a century of industrial use, before handing the site over for construction in 2007.

Boris Johnson's election in 2008 signalled a change for the LDA and for Olympic legacy planning, though the agency continued to fund training schemes and business support schemes to help Londoners to benefit from Olympic jobs and contracts. Manny Lewis was replaced by former Westminster City Council chief executive Peter Rogers, and plans were developed for a new 'legacy' body to take over after 2012. The government announced its intention to shut down regional development agencies in 2010, and Johnson agreed that the LDA's remaining land holdings, and some other functions, would be taken over by the Greater London Authority.

The LDA's achievements were not limited to the Olympics. The agency also partly or fully funded the Rich Mix centre in Shoreditch, the Thames Barrier Park, new public spaces in Brixton, Acton, Dalston and Woolwich, Wembley Stadium, the Laban Centre in Deptford; a host of public infrastructure projects of varying scale.[3] It developed grand plans for the east London 'Thames Gateway' area, for Crystal Palace and for King's Cross, and hosted Design for London, the mayor's architecture and urban design team. That said, the LDA struggled with its layered and incoherent remit and accountability. It was on occasion seen as being too lavish, and – as 'the mayor's piggy bank' – too easily influenced by the whims and preferences of mayors and their advisors.[4]

Without the LDA, there would probably have been no London Olympics. But by the time of the opening ceremony in July 2012, the LDA no longer existed as it had been closed down four months earlier.[5]

14

PLANNING AND DEVELOPMENT

DAVE HILL

The proof and the pressures of three decades of London growth are displayed in its development landscapes. As the capital's economy has burgeoned and its population has boomed, so its governance bodies have striven to respond to new kinds and quantities of demand while argument has raged on every side. Transformations in some parts of London – though not all – have been dramatic. For the past twenty of those thirty years, London's mayors have been significant players on these urban planning stages. They have operated within constraints imposed by others amid conditions that have been not of their making. Their formal powers, though they have grown, have remained limited. Even so, each mayor has been in the thick of how the city has been shaped.

New places and spaces have been created – combinations of flats, offices, shops and 'public realm' – while older ones have been adapted and transformed. Tall buildings have sprouted. Housing estates have been felled. Much of what has developed has been propelled by external forces – financial crises, footloose capital, demographic shifts – emanating from far beyond London's boundaries, presenting opportunities and challenges on the ground. Each scenario has been distinctive, but organised opposition, political priorities and pragmatic trade-offs (usually financial) have been recurring features. Tension between continuity and change is long-standing in London, but has intensified as the twenty-first century has aged.

The influence of London's mayors can be most plainly seen in big new features of the built environment. The Shard is the tallest. The largest and most triumphant is surely the Queen Elizabeth Olympic Park, which bears the hallmarks of each City Hall administration. The completion of its first iteration to host the sporting spectacle of London 2012 was largely down to mayoral leadership. The park still vexes sceptics, yet continues to morph and mature.

Other large projects have taken shape, attracting smorgasbords of fury and acclaim. The King's Cross regeneration is widely seen as a sensitive and beneficial melding of old and new.[1] There has been less enthusiasm for how the waterfront stretch taking in Vauxhall, Nine Elms and Battersea is being built out, with its contribution to the 'canyonisation' of the Thames.[2]

At the less successful end of the regeneration scale, a giant 'reimagining' of the Earl's Court area became hopelessly stalled, although not before the area's iconic exhibition centre was levelled. Part of the plan was to demolish two council-owned housing estates, sparking strong and effective opposition. A new developer has since taken over what remains of the original project. Housing estate regenerations have ranged from the stuttering (West Hendon in Barnet) to the more consensual (Woodberry Down in Hackney) to the wholly expunged (the Heygate in Southwark) and have often been focal points for 'social cleansing' accusations amid wider claims that London has become a soulless 'playground for the rich', with arts and entertainment enclaves closed and crushed. In the West End, the 'uplift' created by the promise of Crossrail has been criticised as threatening the character of Denmark Street, for decades London's rackety Tin Pan Ally.[3]

Debate about development has defined political positions and confirmed alliances. Protesting voices have infused words that might otherwise be positive with hostile meanings: 'regeneration' is used as a synonym for community destruction and private greed and 'gentrification', originally a critical but social scientific concept, is now a full-on dirty word, not only in London but internationally.[4] 'Luxury' is the adjective pejoratively attached to just about any new flat proposed for the open market, no matter how basic it would be. The neighbourhood identities of suburban areas have been fiercely defended against perceived threats to their dilution across the capital, in Islington and Lambeth as well as Bromley and Richmond. The proliferation of skyscrapers has sparked campaigns to protect the London skyline. There are often persuasive arguments on all sides.

Such are the minefields that London's mayors have had to pick through, encouraging, influencing, reconciling, declaiming, adjudicating and sometimes firmly intervening. Within contested and clamorous arenas, each mayor has sought to advance his particular vision of the city – to foster his own idea about what, to use a term favoured by the current one, constitutes 'good growth'.[5]

MAYORS' PLANNING POWERS AND RESPONSIBILITIES

Although London's mayors have acquired additional controls over how the city has taken shape since those enshrined in the Greater London Authority Act 1999, their powers remain constrained and designed more to complement than to supersede those of London's thirty-three local authorities.[6] The master document enshrining mayoral planning policies is the spatial development strategy, known as the London Plan. This 'integrated framework' is a detailed blueprint for what could and should be built up or knocked down across Greater London's 606 square-miles and why. Its policies encompass not only buildings – housing, office, retail and industrial – but also parks, streets, squares, transport infrastructure, environmental standards, biodiversity, employment provision, health and social equity and identifying 'opportunity areas' for potential major redevelopment.

As one of seven strategies that mayors are required by law to compile, the London Plan overarches and must be consistent with the other six, which cover transport, housing, economic development, health inequalities, environment and culture. London Plans take around four years to prepare. Prior to publication and coming into effect, they are subject to public consultations and lengthy examinations in public under the auspices of a planning inspector appointed by the national government. Ministers can require mayors to make changes. The Mayor of London can override London boroughs, but national governments can override the mayor.

The London Plan makes demands on the individual development plans of London's local authorities, which must be 'in general conformity' with it.[7] It also retains the general principle that London's boroughs are the first ports of call for people bearing planning applications, be they home owners craving substantial kitchen extensions or property firms with larger ambitions. However, the law does give the mayor mechanisms of control over what boroughs do.[8]

These controls apply to those applications judged to be of 'potential strategic importance' to the capital. Schemes so defined must be referred to the mayor by the local authority to which they've been submitted. If mayors judge them to be at odds with their strategic objectives, they are empowered to 'direct refusal', meaning the authority and the applicant must go away and think again, or even 'act as the planning authority for the purpose of determining the application' if they consider the development 'would have a significant impact on the implementation of the spatial development strategy'. In effect, if a mayor is so moved they can take an application out of a borough's hands and approve or reject it from City Hall instead. The latter power was introduced under the Greater London Authority Act 2007, which also widened the definition of 'potential strategic importance' to cover, among other things, any 'large-scale development' including more than 150 homes compared with 500 before.[9] However, decisions taken by mayors can also be the subject of an appeal to national government.

The Localism Act 2011 gave mayors some further planning scope. They could now set up mayoral development corporations, entities responsible for transforming regeneration areas, including as their planning authority. There are presently two of these: the London Legacy Development Corporation, and the Old Oak and Park Royal Development Corporation. The Localism Act also transferred to the GLA the housing functions previously undertaken through the Homes and Communities Agency, giving mayors full control over the distribution of whatever affordable-housing cash national government has bestowed.

In 2012, the mayor acquired the power to raise his own Community Infrastructure Levy (CIL), a London-wide variation of a measure enabling local authorities to secure financial contributions from property developers that had come into effect nationally in 2010.[10] The mayoral CIL was introduced to help finance the huge new Crossrail rail link and can be charged on developments across the capital.

These are the latest chapters in an uneven history of 'strategic' London planning endeavours, few of which have been delivered in full. This might be said to have begun with the proposals for rebuilding London after the Great Fire of 1666, to which Christopher Wren and John Evelyn were among the illustrious contributors, and which was frustrated entirely.[11] In 1943, the London County Council published the County of London Plan, created by architect John Henry Forshaw and University College London town planning professor, Sir Patrick Abercrombie. This plan, which looked to the capital's post-war future, has been described as 'predicated on the decentralisation of population from central London'.[12] The following year, Abercrombie prepared the Greater London Plan, which addressed the wider metropolitan area.

Expectations that the capital's population would keep falling also underpinned the GLC's 1969 Greater London Development Plan, though it anticipated a shift from inner to outer London too. A revised version of the plan appeared in 1983, giving emphasis to reviving the inner city, but three years later the GLC was abolished and its development proposals abandoned. Regional planning for London became national government responsibility until the creation of the GLA. By then, it was plain that four decades of contraction after the Second World War were over and London's population and economy were rising again. It had become a town of big opportunities and the first boss of City Hall grabbed them with both hands.

KEN LIVINGSTONE: THINKING BIG

The towering totem of London's revival – and of disputes about its character and worth – is, of course, the Shard. The cloud-pricking glass spire by London Bridge Station is celebrated as a bold and imaginative symbol of the capital's 'world city' glories and is derided as a symbol of 'neoliberal' dominion or as an aesthetic affront – too big, too modern or just in the wrong place. The story of its climb from a sketch on a napkin to a London skyline fixture – one Londoners appear to like – illustrates City Hall's insertion into the planning power pyramid, the foundations of which are the capital's local authorities and sitting at the apex is Whitehall.[13]

Planning applications of potential strategic importance were defined for London's local authorities at that time in a town and country planning order, which came into force on 3 July 2000.[14] Along with 'major infrastructure projects' and any seeking to provide more than 500 residential properties, the order encompassed buildings envisaged as rising above particular heights. For most of London, the height threshold was thirty metres, although the City of London was allowed to give consent to buildings up to seventy-five metres high without having to satisfy City Hall, while for prospective buildings 'adjacent to the River Thames' the limit was twenty-five metres. The Shard, the mountainous proposition of architect Renzo Piano and developer Irvine Sellar, clearly met criteria for referral.

Some of the more fraught planning struggles over the past two decades have centred on mayors having public differences of opinion with boroughs. However, in practice the London Plan's prescriptions and the existence of mayoral legal powers to intervene have usually meant that differences between the two spheres of London government are resolved before matters reach that point. And it's important to stress that boroughs aren't always sorry when mayors exert dominion over them – sometimes it has been exactly what they need to get the development they favour past stubborn obstacles of local, sometimes parochial, opposition but without paying a political price.

With the Shard, the main opposition came not from Southwark Council but from English Heritage.[15] This led to the involvement of national government in the form of a public inquiry, which was held in 2003. There were fears that the Shard would spoil the view of St Paul's cathedral from Parliament Hill. But the outcome gave the go-ahead to what became the most spectacular result of Livingstone's enthusiasm for towers.

The Shard was not completed until after Livingstone had left City Hall, having been salvaged from the financial crisis by Qatari investors, but it remains a monument to his time there. 'It is a visitation from a hyperverse where different dimensions apply and also different orders of money,' wrote architecture critic Rowan Moore.[16]

Livingstone has often divided opinion as a politician, sometimes fiercely. His arrival at City Hall made some boroughs and, given his 'Red Ken' reputation, much of the development world nervous. Yet his first London Plan, published in February 2004, sought consensus over important big themes. The mustering of the first plan entailed a new layer of London government forming an identity and finding its feet. Its content was an expression both of Livingstone's widescreen picture of how London should move forward and a recognition of the city's trajectory since the end of the 1980s.

The mayor recruited the advice of architect Richard Rogers and inherited the work of the cross-party, post-GLC London Planning Advisory Committee, two chairs of which, Liberal Democrat Sally Hamwee and Labour's Nicky Gavron, were among the first intake of London Assembly members. Their role is also considered in Chapter 20. Livingstone made Gavron his deputy and his advisor on strategic planning. He would later be accused of giving too much attention to central London, and was derided as 'a Zone 1 mayor', yet the gestating plan embraced the concept of 'polycentrism', recognising the city's array of clusters of output and creativity. There were internal debates about the balance between the plan's ambitions for economic growth, social equality and environmental improvements. The first of these secured high prominence, which observers saw as resulting from the influence of big business.

For some, this was a sell-out. For others, it was welcome confirmation that Livingstone was committed to thinking big. A more nuanced view is that the nebulous notion of 'sustainability' was, in fact, built into the plan with prescriptive clarity – right down to car-parking policies – while its heady 'world city' language was partly pragmatic. That is to say, it was consistent with Livingstone's need for business interests' indulgence of 'progressive' policies, such as his aspiration for half of all new homes in London to be 'affordable', and to secure financial backing from an initially suspicious national government, for whom the plan could be seen as a kind of prospectus. Livingstone, famously, had been elected in 2000 as an independent candidate after Labour effectively imposed a national leadership-friendly candidate. Livingstone's success in securing funds to, for example, vastly enlarge the bus service is seen as flowing from the plan's globalist goals.

The plan was also in tune with strong prevailing themes: the rapid expansion of the service sector; investments in transport, most notably in the London Underground Jubilee Line, which opened in 1999, and extensions to the Docklands Light Railway. Continuing population and employment growth were forecast. Livingstone's plan foresaw accommodating this by enabling building at higher densities – including higher heights – especially around transport interchanges. At the same time, it would leave alone those parts of the Metropolitan Green Belt – land in and around Greater London protected against development in order to control urban growth – that fell into the mayor's territory, along with other preserved green spaces.

The first London Plan also stressed shifting London's centre of gravity eastwards. De-industrialisation had left large areas of relatively cheap, under-used land where dock industries had died, known collectively as the Thames Gateway. The mayor was not the first to spot that part of it, the Lower Lea Valley, spanning parts of Hackney, Tower Hamlets, Waltham Forest and Newham, was ripe for a major makeover. Government planners had been eyeing it for years, though little progress had been made. Following a visit from the British Olympic Association in July 2001 – at the GLA's temporary first home of Romney House on Marsham Street – Livingstone publicly backed London making a bid to host the 2012 Olympic Games and urged Tony Blair, who had been re-elected Prime Minister the previous month, to come on board.[17]

The London Plan must have helped. A draft version, produced in 2002, identified the Lower Lea Valley and adjacent Stratford as 'opportunity areas' and noted that the feasibility of an Olympic bid was being explored. The final version of the plan marked the area out as a games core location. A government-sponsored development corporation was its planning authority, but in 2005, by which time Livingstone had been re-admitted to Labour and then re-elected, the London Development Agency prepared the case for a huge compulsory purchase order. Livingstone's Olympic ambition was shared by Blair's culture secretary Tessa Jowell, and had an outstanding champion in his regeneration advisor Neale Coleman. This mobilisation of national and regional government in pursuit of a common goal was exceptional, and the London mayoralty, still in its infancy, was at the forefront.

In the planning and development world, Livingstone's mayoralties are often looked back on with nostalgia. His attitude and energies were seen as resolutely trained on making the most of opportunities to build, by using such influence and resources he had to help ambitious schemes get off the ground. The later vexed issue of projects' financial viability calculations became central under Livingstone, as in those numbers lay the scope for maximising 'community benefits'. The word 'strategic' is used of him wholeheartedly and approvingly. 'He was engaged, he talked to the industry, he trusted his team to do things, he had a widescreen view of things,' says one major planning consultant.[18]

In May 2007, one year before he was toppled by his Conservative nemesis Boris Johnson, Livingstone told *Prospect* magazine that most of his job as mayor was about putting together 'coalitions of interests around a common agenda'.[19] Hence, 'everybody signed up to Crossrail'. He said, remarkably: 'There isn't a great ideological conflict any more' and that London's business community had become 'almost depoliticised'. He recounted the City Corporation assuring him that they could do great things together. 'I didn't believe a word of it,' Livingstone said. 'But it turned out to be true'.

Livingstone addressed accusations that he had been too friendly with property tycoons: 'You most probably never hear from the developers that I throw out of my office, with their ghastly schemes,' he said. And he stressed the importance of generating sub-market priced homes through 'planning obligations' – developer contributions made as conditions of securing consents written into agreements under Section 106 of the Town and Country Planning Act. Such agreements had become important for raising funds for many things that the public purse would not pay for.[20]

Was there a sense, then, in which 'Red Ken' and international property capitalists were on the same side? 'We accept globalisation and are working with the trend,' Livingstone replied. Years later, one property executive made a succinct distinction between the first mayor and his two successors: 'Ken wanted to get things done.'[21]

BORIS JOHNSON: CONSERVATIVE ALTERNATIVE OR KEN-LITE?

Boris Johnson was lucky in some ways. His inheritance included the increased planning powers under the Greater London Authority Act 2007 and £5 billion to invest in affordable homes in London courtesy of a Labour government.[22] This was to be distributed to housing associations by way of the London board of a national body, the Home and Communities Agency, which Johnson chaired. Yet Johnson's options were also conditioned by large external factors. One was the onset of the world financial crisis, the depth of which was epitomised within six months of his election by the collapse of the investment bank Lehman Brothers, whose London base in Canary Wharf suddenly emptied as employees left clutching their possessions in carboard boxes. Another emanated from closer to home: the squeeze on public spending introduced by the Conservative-led coalition government that was elected in 2010.

Johnson's approach to development looked to accommodate conservatism's ancestral conflict between the urge to let market forces have their way and the desire for everything to stay the same. It also honoured the Tory tradition of seeking ways to help people into home ownership: he wasted no time tilting the balance of 'affordable' supply more in favour of 'low-cost home ownership' as compared with social rent. His first planning advisor was Sir Simon Milton (who went on to become his deputy mayor for policy and planning and his chief of staff), a creative and accomplished steward of central London's complex building and transport terrain.

Johnson's new London Plan, published in July 2011, pulled the threads of his thinking into one place. At its draft stage, Nancy Holman, professor of urban planning at the London School of Economics, contrasted the plan with what had gone before. She concluded that it was not 'a complete retreat' from what Livingstone had achieved but that Johnson's 'abandonment of a centralised strategic vision is an important change'.[23] Holman argued that a key difference in the Johnson London Plan was its flexibility towards the boroughs, suggesting that the second London mayor would be more tolerant of spatial development plans of local authorities reflecting different priorities from those of his own – a more permissive interpretation of 'general conformity', maybe.

This seemed attuned to the political geography that had delivered Johnson to power – a so-called 'doughnut strategy' focused on the mostly Tory-run outer London boroughs, where resistance to development tended to be strongest. Johnson had already appointed an Outer London Commission, to look at the development needs of suburban areas. He now proffered a different approach from Livingstone's, characterising it as 'working with' boroughs as opposed to imposing changes on them. Principles of sustainability, disciplined into precise demands under Livingstone, underwent translation into the looser category 'quality of life', with looser connections to the plan's larger goals too. The term 'world city' was little used. Holman was not alone in spotting the 'odd paradox that Johnson, a Tory, appear[ed] to be less pro-business and development than Livingstone, who was once famously seen as part of the "loony left"'.[24]

The Johnson plan reflected the outlook of a more casual, less detail-minded mayor, instinctively averse to 'interfering' governments, including regional ones, and who knew which side his electoral bread was buttered on. It also placed stress on protecting heritage, including by keeping a 'designated list of strategic views under review' and said that 'tall and large buildings should not have an unacceptably harmful impact on their surroundings'.[25] The plan was also notable for requiring boroughs to incorporate minimum space standards for new dwellings.

By the time the plan was published in 2011, the Tory mayor's lead lieutenant was seasoned former Wandsworth Council leader Sir Edward Lister, who succeeded Milton after the latter's untimely death as Johnson's planning advisor and chief of staff. Lister was widely seen, including by Labour borough leaders, as immensely able and, where housing was concerned, less concerned with affordability than quantity. As far as boroughs or developers were concerned, he was the real boss at City Hall if something complicated needed sorting out.

Two planning struggles illustrate the approach of the Johnson administration. One, an extended failure, was Earl's Court. The mayoralty was solidly behind the massive scheme worked up by kindred (Conservative) spirits who ran Hammersmith and Fulham Council at the time. It entailed Transport for London, a major landowner in the area, forming a joint venture company with the lead developer. The first of a series of such tie-ups, it has become the least successful. Local opposition, the capture of the borough by Labour in 2014, Sadiq Khan's election as mayor in 2016 and, finally, the effects of stamp duty increases on higher-value properties and saturation at the top-end of the housing market together ground it down. There were good arguments for refreshing the famous inner-west London district and for supplying more intermediate affordable homes, but the configuration of the new 'mixed neighbourhood' and the Tory borough politicians' attitude to social housing tenants meant push-back was guaranteed.

During Johnson's second term, a different type of dispute focused on spare land at the Mount Pleasant Royal Mail sorting office site, which straddled the boundary between two Labour-run north London boroughs, Camden and Islington.[26] Together, the two councils were holding out for a better affordable housing yield, while other critics berated the scheme's design. In such situations, mayors can approach boroughs with offers of cooperation while carrying big sticks. The upshot of this dynamic has varied. Planning is a form of regulation, and regulation usually implies constraint. But mayors have also used their 'call in' powers to liberate. This, in his eyes, is what Johnson did, losing patience with the boroughs and determining the application himself, having negotiated terms with the developer that he found acceptable. There were limits to the autonomy he was prepared to let boroughs enjoy if he felt they were holding things up.

What difference had Johnson made by the time he stood down as mayor in 2016? Although accepting of austerity, he used his mayoral platform to make the case for transport infrastructure investment, believing it stimulated development. He was accused of over-indulging property speculators, especially from overseas. But without foreign investors, less 'affordable' housing would have been built along with all the much-criticised 'luxury' flats. In the end, his approach was more of an evolution of Livingstone's than a revolution against it – and skyscrapers were still sprouting when Johnson departed City Hall.

SADIQ KHAN: THE GOALS OF 'GOOD GROWTH'

In May 2016, Labour's Sadiq Khan moved into the eighth floor of City Hall buoyed by pledges to address London's many housing woes, especially the spiralling costs of renting and buying. The capital had never been a cheap place to live, but for private renters and would-be first-time buyers – who are often the same people – and the growing number of homeless households, the term 'crisis' felt fully justified. Much of what passed for a debate about the issues often missed the point, heaping misleading blame on overseas investors and failing to recognise that the alternative to partnering with the private sector to upgrade neighbourhoods and improve housing quality and supply – including of 'affordable' homes of all kinds – could easily be doing nothing much at all.

This was the context in which Khan fought his election campaign, the themes of which were shaped accordingly. He was not averse to aligning himself with oppositional sentiment, legitimate and populist alike. As mayor Khan has become regarded in development circles – and those include some Labour-run boroughs – as far less ambitious, imaginative and accessible than either of his predecessors. Some have found him lacking any real interest in planning issues or pushing towards a widescreen future for the city, in keeping with his strategic role. He is also characterised as the most 'political' mayor so far: more tribal, risk-averse, too mindful of keeping on the right side of public opinion and, during the time of Jeremy Corbyn's leadership, of London Labour Party activists. Some of the more harsh critics from his own side of politics have said he is better at winning elections than shaping a big city with vision and flair.

Yet Khan has had a manifesto to deliver and Londoners' concerns to address. And a more generous view of his administration would be that it has sought to meet these obligations with policies that acknowledge complex realities. Collectively, they can be seen as expressing a practical interventionism which seeks the necessary buy-in from interested parties with assurances of consistency some found lacking in the Johnson years. He has also used his planning powers more often than Johnson: the Conservative mayor directed refusal of applications seven times in eight years, and called in eighteen for his own determination; Khan, in just over four years up to the original end of his 2016–20 term, had directed refusal eleven times and called in twenty-one times.

Khan appointed Jules Pipe, the experienced and respected mayor of Hackney, as his deputy for planning. His first housing deputy, Islington's James Murray, devised a 35 per cent 'threshold' approach to the provision of 'genuinely affordable' new housing through the planning system without grant support (discussed in Chapter 16), and set a long-term, higher, goal of 50 per cent for housing supply overall.[27] This figure was to be reached with the help of TfL land and by the efforts of housing associations – and later boroughs – supported by sums se-cured from national government (Team Khan was pleased by what it received under Theresa May). The effects of investment from overseas were investigated for Khan by London School of Economics housing specialists, who found the impact to be beneficial overall and, indeed, questioned claims that foreigners were buying job lots of 'luxury flats' which they then left as empty investment 'gold bricks'.[28]

Khan's campaign slogan, 'A city for all Londoners', was translated into the planning and development catch-all term 'good growth'. In his foreword to his draft new London Plan, published in December 2017, he said that this meant 'working to re-balance development in London towards more genuinely affordable homes for working Londoners to buy and rent [and] delivering a more socially integrated and sustain-able city'.[29] It was 'not about supporting growth at any cost, which for too long has been the priority, leaving many Londoners feeling ex-cluded and contributing to a lack of community cohesion and social integration'.

The draft new plan also proposed tighter protections on industrial land. For some, this sat uneasily with an overall home-building target of 65,000 a year – far higher than any previous plan. At the same time, the plan showed Khan to be as resolute in office as he had been when seeking it, that the protected Green Belt – which makes up 22 per cent of Greater London, much of it comprised of golf courses and farmland – should remain intact.[30] In this, he was at least as chary of an enduringly explosive political issue as Livingstone and Johnson.[31] But where, it was asked, would all those extra homes go? City Hall's answer was effectively that far more dwellings could and should be built on small sites scattered across the city, especially in its outer fringes. Boroughs were to be told to adopt a 'presumption in favour' of accepting schemes for up to twenty-five new homes. Other promi-nent features of the draft plan proposed steps for protecting London's 'cultural infrastructure', including live music venues and cinemas, and nurturing the night-time economy.

The draft plan took a substantial time to put together and rather less to be pulled apart. First, the government's inspectors urged Khan to drop the small-sites policy on the grounds that it was impractical. They also recommended a Green Belt review. Khan looked set to hold his ground, but later retreated on small sites. However, this wasn't enough for central government, which by this time was being led by the man Khan had succeeded as mayor, Boris Johnson. Johnson's secretary of state for housing, communities and local government, Robert Jenrick, scathingly rejected Khan's draft plan.

In a letter released just as Khan's campaign for what turned out to be the postponed May 2020 mayoral election was getting into gear, Jenrick wrote: 'Your Plan added layers of complexity that will make development more difficult unnecessarily.'[32] Citing 'inconsistencies with national policy' and 'missed opportunities to increase housing delivery' he declared that he was exercising powers under the 1999 Act 'to direct that you cannot publish the London Plan until you have incorporated the Directions I have set out'. The mayor was told he should support ambitious boroughs, though unambitious ones were not mentioned. He was also required to undertake 'a programme of work … to kick-start stalled strategic sites'.

With the approach to planning of London's second Labour mayor not to the liking of the national administration headed by his predecessor, Whitehall has not hesitated to impose its will on City Hall. And so the remaining strict limits of Tony Blair's devolution of planning powers to London regional government were confirmed.

CONCLUSION

Planning London can often seem a contradiction in terms. Slippery combinations of national government attitudes, London government rivalries and the sheer complexity of the city have long conspired to create the impression – and, to a degree, the reality – that no one is ever really in charge. How much difference have twenty years of London mayors made? They and their London Plans have certainly had some impact. They also make precursors look incredibly dated: the 1944 Greater London Plan, with its assumption of post-war shrinkage and dispersal; the GLC's 1969 Greater London Development Plan took these as read and proposed a new 'motorway box' network, the very opposite of sustainable travel. But these serve as a reminder, were one needed in 2020, of how suddenly things can change.

15

MAYORS AT MIPIM

ROBERT GORDON CLARK
AND NICK MCKEOGH

THE ROLE OF SELLING LONDON

I t may not be in the formal job description, but one of the Mayor of London's most important roles is to be a super-salesperson for the city.

Of course the Lord Mayor of the City of London has been doing this, for the financial services and Square Mile, for many years (if not centuries).

Meanwhile, since 2000 Ken Livingstone, Boris Johnson and, more recently, Sadiq Khan have all done this job for the whole of London, with varying degrees of enthusiasm.

One of the key weeks of the year for promoting cities to attract inward investment is in mid-March in the French resort of Cannes.

The event is MIPIM, which stands for *Le Marché International des Professionnels de L'immobilier*, which translates as 'The International Market for Real Estate Professionals'.

Started in 1991, 2021 will be the thirtieth anniversary of the event, which was interrupted of course by Covid-19 in 2020.

To many people the event appears either mad (20,000 property people and politicians piling into a small town on the Mediterranean where the three-day event is held in an old multi-storey car park), or corrupt (to be fair, photos of politicians swilling champagne on luxury yachts isn't a great look).

The truth is more nuanced.

MIPIM is the global shop front for cities and regions marketing themselves to attract mobile inward investment.

For the first decade that MIPIM was running London had no mayor and only from 1994 any proper representation. Those early years saw the City of London at one end of the exhibition and the London Docklands Development Corporation at the other.

Pipers, the architectural model makers, persuaded the City, Docklands, Canary Wharf, British Land and others to join forces, arguing that London's proposal and message to the world had to be united. The 'London stand' started in earnest in 1998 and set the benchmark for other cities which soon copied their approach.

KEN: MAN OF DETAIL, THE EXPERT'S EXPERT

The arrival in 2000 of the GLA, with the Mayor of London and the London Development Agency, provided a new focus for promoting London.

Ken Livingstone got this straight away. He attended his first MIPIM in 2002 and kept coming back each year until 2007. Ken's technique with the development industry was both amusing and effective.

He never lost his socialist tendencies from his old GLC days, and so saw the industry as a way to deliver much of this agenda – 50 per cent affordable housing, community facilities and more.

His line was: 'I will sup with the devil, I will tax you, you will like it and we will get along if you give me what I want.'

Legend has it that he cut the final deal with the late Irvine Sellar to back the Shard, over a glass of wine on the beach in Cannes.

His speeches on the London stand were always popular. But he also appealed to fellow city mayors from across Europe. They would arrange to meet him privately to take advice from him, whether on congestion charging or how to promote their city.

But Ken was more than just good at the speeches and networking.

His tours of the London stand, which featured models and schematics of perhaps 100 different London projects, were marked by a detailed knowledge of many of them.

His understanding of the critical interconnection between transport and development was key too and he did much to keep alive hopes of delivering Crossrail during this mayoralty.

And of course his campaigning played well as London geared up to bid for the 2012 Olympics. Paris was the main competitor to London – and many thought that Paris would win in 2005. Certainly that was the view of the Paris stand at MIPIM in March that year.

But Ken's personal commitment to the bid, the focus on regenerating east London and the super sales technique of the London Organising Committee of the Olympic and Paralympic Games (Seb Coe and the late Mike Lee) helped give London that edge.

BORIS: CROWD PLEASER, CELEBRATORY MAYOR AND SELFIE GENERATOR

Boris's mayoral victory in May 2008 provided him with the perfect first international PR event: accepting the flag in Beijing at the end of the 2008 Olympics in front of a global TV audience of billions.

Boris became a rapid convert to MIPIM too, recognising that in the run-up to the Olympics it was essential to maximise the opportunities to attract investment to London.

He came to MIPIM in 2009 and made an immediate impact as the ultimate mayoral crowd-pleaser.

His deputy mayor, the late Sir Simon Milton who, while running

Westminster City Council had no time for MIPIM, realised the benefits too and became a fan of the event.

And Boris was very popular with the organisers of MIPIM, Reed MIDEM, as he always guaranteed a good crowd at their 'head-to-head mayoral events'. On one occasion a crowd of 500 sat and waited patiently for an hour for a late Boris to hear him speak and he promptly teased the mayors of Berlin and Paris, claiming London as the sixth largest French city.

And as we found in London, people loved having selfies taken with him, whether they were major developers, other politicians or simply residents of Cannes.

In Boris's second term (2012–16), post-Olympics, the message was all about legacy and in 2014 he started to really push the need for more affordable housing.

But he still had time for some fun with quips like 'MIPIM stands for making important property investment for millions of people' or 'meet me in the pool in a minute' and for demonstrating that a 'Hermes scarf was cheaper in Bond Street than the Champs-Elysees'.

AND SADIQ?

And now we have Sadiq Khan, who sadly has not been to MIPIM since becoming mayor, despite his 2016 manifesto stating he would be the 'most pro-business mayor yet' and a 'ceaseless advocate for investment in London, and a champion for the interest of our industries, at home and abroad'.

To be fair his agenda was skewered first by Brexit, then by various atrocities on London's streets and more recently by Covid-19.

And while Sadiq has many talents, playing to the political and business gallery on the shores of the Mediterranean is not something many Londoners can imagine him doing or enjoying. The role has been left to deputy mayors James Murray and Jules Pipe, which is simply not the same as having the directly elected mayor banging the drum.

But with the future of events like MIPIM hanging in the balance, it may be the case that Sadiq is not needed anyway.

However, the role of selling London overseas remains a vital one, and whether it's MIPIM or a trade delegation trip to India, let's hope the next mayor does sell London hard. We will need it.

16

HOUSING

KATH SCANLON

INTRODUCTION

Housing has risen steadily up London's political agenda over the twenty years of the GLA. A poll conducted in the run-up to the last mayoral election in 2016 found it to be the issue that was at the top of the list, with 56 per cent of those surveyed saying it was one of the biggest issues facing London.[1] But 'housing' as an issue encompasses a huge range of concerns. The specific topics of debate have evolved, reflecting the controversies and political configurations of the day. In 2000 the hot topics included key worker housing, the poor condition of some council housing and the effects of the right to buy scheme. Today we are concerned with the lack of security for private tenants, the politics of estate regeneration, homelessness and temporary accommodation.

Whatever else is on the agenda, affordability has been a constant issue. There are two underlying reasons for this. First, the continued strong growth in the number of households living in London has not been matched by a commensurate growth in the number of homes. This shortfall, plus London's economic strength, has contributed to a steady increase in house prices from (coincidentally) about the time the GLA was created, except during the downturn of 2008 to 2009 (see Figure 1).

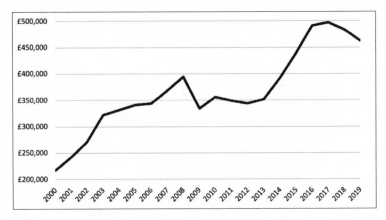

Figure 1. Average house prices in London after adjusting for inflation, 2000 to 2019

Source: 'Housing in London: 2019', Greater London Authority, September 2019

Second, there has been a significant shift in the tenure makeup of London's housing, with falls in owner-occupation and especially social renting, and a huge rise in private renting (see Figure 2). Many households on low and even middle incomes now face real difficulties – they can't afford to buy and can't get (and may not want) a social tenancy. Increasingly Londoners can expect to spend years or indeed their whole adult lives renting privately on precarious short leases.

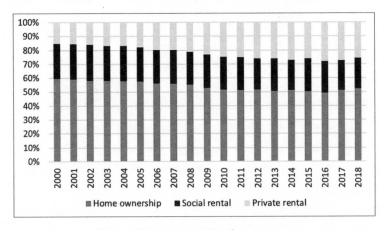

Figure 2. Housing tenure in London since 2000

Source: 'Housing in London: 2019', Greater London Authority, September 2019

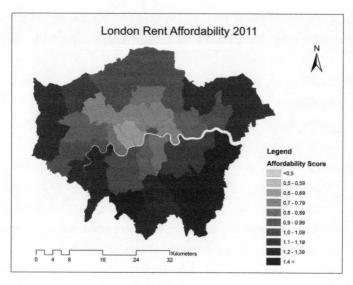

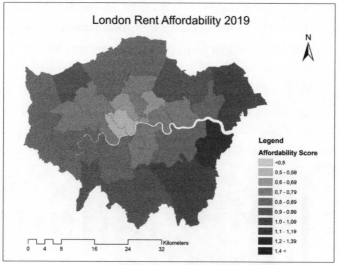

Figures 3 and 4. Affordability in London's private rented sector, 2011 and 2019

Source: LSE London calculations based on Valuation Office Agency rents data and
'Household Income Estimates for Small Areas', Greater London Authority

Mapping the relationship between private rents and household incomes
by borough (see Figures 3 and 4) shows clearly how affordability changed
between 2011 and 2019.[2] Using the GLA's definition of 'affordability'

(households should pay at most 40 per cent of their income on rent), we calculated borough-level rental affordability scores, as follows:

Affordability score =
(borough annual median income x0.4) ÷ borough median annual rent
for two-bed flat[3]

Boroughs with high scores are more affordable than those with low scores. Most of inner-north London was unaffordable in 2011 on this measure, while most of outer London, especially south of the river, was affordable. By 2019 the situation had worsened in every borough, with only three authorities classified as being affordable.

Given Londoners' concern with housing, they quite reasonably expect the mayor to do something about it. All three mayors have responded by promising to do quite a lot. Whether they have achieved much – given the constraints within which they operate – is another question.

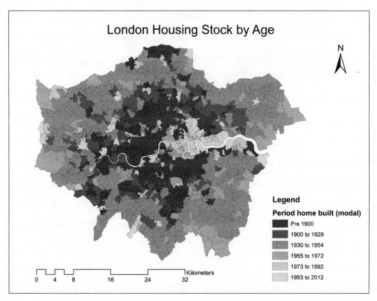

Figure 5. London housing stock by age

Source: 'Dwellings by Property Build Period and Type', Valuation Office Agency

The effects of policy change are felt most in the relatively few areas under active development, while much of the existing housing stock is little affected. In inner and central London much of the housing was built 100 years ago or more (see Figure 5); only in Docklands and parts of east London does newer housing predominate. This pattern of new development has been driven by the reality of land supply rather than by demand: potential home buyers and tenants were not demonstrably keen in 2000 to move *en masse* to brownfield areas of east London, and those living in the surrounding neighbourhoods were not calling for the construction of thousands of new homes.

MAYORAL POWERS

The suite of mayoral powers did not initially cover housing. In decades past, council housing was the source of many intra-London policy skirmishes. Boroughs operated their own stocks of council housing, but the GLC also developed major new estates to serve the capital as a whole and the location of these estates was often contentious. Partly because of this history, the Greater London Authority Act 1999 gave the mayor little power in this area.

In 2007 the mayor's remit was expanded and housing became one of the seven statutory strategies, but even now the mayor's powers in this area remain limited. The mayor sets targets for the number of new homes to be built in the capital but has relatively little control over the amount that actually gets built. And public discussion about housing issues often focuses on cost – but here again the mayor can influence only a small part of the market, as they have no direct powers over private-sector rents or house prices.

The mayor has three main policy and resource levers over housing. The main one is the planning system. Through the London Plan the mayor sets the regional framework for residential development in the capital (though boroughs are the local planning authorities), identifies major development areas and sets targets for the number of new homes for each borough and now for the proportion of affordable homes within that. The plan also influences the built form of new housing, through guidance on things like density, floor area, storage space and aspect. The mayor can also 'call in' the planning applications for major development schemes if they disagree with the decision of the borough, as outlined in Chapter 14.

Within London the mayor also controls a sizeable affordable housing budget. Since the Localism Act 2011 the mayor has controlled the London element of the Homes and Communities Agency, which makes funding available for affordable homes to boroughs, housing associations and developers. This was a significant devolution of power from central government, as the London region accounted for 40 per cent of the national housing investment budget when this decision was taken. The GLA's current affordable homes programme, which ends next year, had a five-year budget of £3.25 billion.[4]

Finally, the mayor controls a large amount of land owned by the GLA and its sister organisations, particularly Transport for London. Land ownership is hugely powerful: obviously new housing has to be built somewhere, and unsurprisingly TfL land tends to be extremely well-located for public transport. In addition, the cost of land is by far the biggest component of the cost of new housing. Putting in public land at low or even no cost can be key to unlocking genuinely affordable homes – but there are clear trade-offs in terms of revenues foregone for the landowner. The GLA also exercises control through its mayoral development corporations, as outlined in Chapter 12.

But the mayor doesn't determine what gets developed and how fast – this is a decision for developers, which are mostly private profit-making companies. The mayor has an influence over the flow of new affordable housing, but almost none over the existing affordable stock, which is in the hands of boroughs and housing associations. And of course the annual production of new homes represents a small fraction of London's housing stock. There are 3.56 million homes in London, while annual construction of new homes did not approach 1 per cent of that figure in any of the six years to 2018 (see Figure 6).[5]

In decades past, London's then small private rented sector provided relatively temporary homes for young single people, corporate transfers and migrants. But with owner occupation and social housing now increasingly out of reach, many people who would prefer a permanent home, including families with small children, are renting for long periods. This has brought pressure for longer leases and rent controls. However, unlike his counterparts in many other countries, the mayor has little control over the private rented sector: enforcement of standards is carried out by boroughs and rules on tenancy length and rent levels are set by national government.

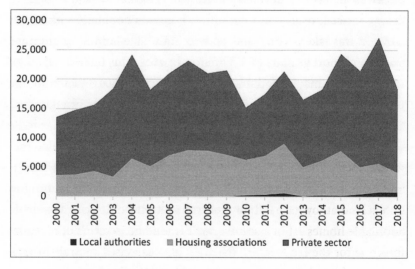

Figure 6. Annual construction of new homes by type of developer, 2000–2019

Source: 'Housing in London: 2019', Greater London Authority, September 2019

One of the challenges in looking at housing policy is that changes often have discernible effects only in the long term, while electoral politics are about the short term. The following section sets out the main housing policies of the three mayors to date. But while it is straightforward to date policy documents and plans, it is much more difficult to neatly categorise new homes as 'Livingstone era' or 'Khan vintage'. Mayoral terms run for four years, but major developments can take much longer to build out (e.g. the 10,000 homes at Barking Riverside, where construction began in 2010, are expected to be complete in 2031).

POLICIES OF THE MAYORS

KEN LIVINGSTONE 2000–2008

At the start of Livingstone's mayoralty, many of the documents and policies guiding London's housing still reflected the post-war policy of dispersing homes and businesses from the capital to what were then seen as more salubrious and less congested parts of the country. In fact when Livingstone took office, London's population had been growing for fifteen years and was forecast to continue to increase from 7.3 million in 2003 to 8.7 million in 2026; this turned out to be an underestimate, as London's population had reached 8.96 million by 2019.[6] Under Livingstone's mayoralty the policies were brought into line with what was happening on the ground.

Just after his election, Ken Livingstone told me and a fellow researcher that '[transport is] the only area where I've got real power, in everything else it's marginal'.[7] Our research at the time found that his operational agenda initially centred on transport, while affordable housing formed part of a secondary, 'big tent' agenda.[8] Under Livingstone's successors, transport schemes (particularly Crossrail) would come to be seen as important enablers of housing policy.

The GLA's first housing targets were announced in 'Towards the London Plan', which called for 23,000 new homes per annum. The key question for Livingstone, as for his successors, was what proportion of these new homes should be technically 'affordable' (leaving aside for now what 'affordable' means). Housing-needs surveys found that the greatest need was not for market-priced or luxury homes, but for housing that lower-income households could access. Livingstone's goal was to provide the maximum amount of affordable housing possible given the constraints of the overall framework, set in policy terms by central government and by the workings of the market. When Livingstone took office the target had been 25 per cent; he upped it to 50 per cent overall. There was a notional split within this envelope of 35 per cent social rented (defined as costing 30 per cent of net household income or less) and 15 per cent intermediate. The size of the affordable housing target, the definition of 'affordability' within it, and the practicalities of achieving it (the viability debate) have been constant elements of the London housing policy debate ever since.

In 2000 the Housing Corporation funded social housing with grants that by current standards are unthinkably generous. Even so, the amount of affordable housing that Livingstone sought required more than just government grants: developers also had to make so-called 'planning contributions', which was effectively a hypothecated tax. Section 106 of the Town and Country Planning Act 1990 allowed local planning authorities to require developers to make contributions to neighbourhood facilities as a condition of receiving planning permission. These S106 contributions were originally intended to rectify or address those consequences of development that would otherwise make new schemes unacceptable. This was interpreted very widely, and in fact local authorities could use the resources to improve local transport, build schools, provide job training or refurbish historic buildings. In London, though, the negotiations generally focused on one thing: how much affordable housing could be provided without making the scheme 'unviable'. In a 2007 interview, Livingstone said approvingly,

In the old days, they would have gone into the GLC and no doubt paid a big backhander to some planning officer. Now they come in and they pay a big backhander to the city in the form of a Section 106. I think that's an improvement. And I can get more affordable housing out of property developers than I can out of the govern-ment, which hasn't funded any.[9]

Under Livingstone's tenure the shape of new homes in London changed. Glass-walled towers topped with penthouse apartments, formerly seen as the kind of architectural bling more suitable to Manhattan, began to appear along the Thames and around transport nodes, even in suburban areas. This also reflected Livingstone's decision to remove the height limits that had hitherto kept most new buildings below the height of St Paul's Cathedral. The main thrust of Livingstone's first London Plan was to maintain and enhance the capital's world city status, and he felt that to be taken seriously as a global city, London needed some skyscrapers. In a 2001 op-ed, Livingstone said that discussions about tall buildings were:

An argument about whether London stays as a world city capable of delivering the employment, investment, infrastructure, housing and office space that are needed to compete with New York, Tokyo, Frank-furt or Berlin ... I do think that a variety of interesting and beautiful tall buildings would enhance the whole of London's skyline.[10]

Livingstone was also influenced by Richard Rogers's views as ex-pressed in *Towards an Urban Renaissance*.[11] This report espoused the compact city approach, which positively encouraged density in the right places rather than seeing it as being a synonym for pernicious overcrowding. Livingstone emphasised that density was central to his vision for London:

I made it clear throughout my campaign, in all the debates with other candidates, that I was in favour of higher densities and higher buildings in London. It was not a minor issue. Once Londoners re-alise, by the time of the next election, that the mayor is a crucial factor in determining the way in which the look of London evolves, this will be much more of a factor in the debates in the next and subsequent mayoral elections.[12]

The density policy was expressed systematically in the density matrix of the 2004 London Plan, which set out permissible density ranges for residential developments in various types of location. In practice many new schemes exceeded the maximum indicative densities (driven by increasing land values, which in turn led to higher densities, thus increasing land values yet more), even after recommended densities were raised, and the 2019 draft plan omitted the density matrix altogether.

While Livingstone could set out his vision for boroughs and developers through the London Plan, he had very little power himself to generate new housing. The GLC had been a major social landlord, having inherited more than 200,000 homes from its predecessor the London County Council, and building many estates of its own.[13] However, the GLA had no direct responsibility for providing housing: the GLC's stock had been dispersed to the boroughs and the funding responsibilities were initially kept by the secretary of state and the Housing Corporation. Indeed, the original Greater London Authority Act expressly forbade any direct housing expenditure by the mayor.

This changed in 2007 when the mayor was given responsibility for the London Housing Strategy, which was previously written by the Government Office for London. This document was to guide the investment decisions of the new Homes and Communities Agency, which replaced the Housing Corporation as grant funder for new affordable housing. Within London the mayor was to chair the Homes and Communities Agency board, thus giving him power over investment decisions in the capital. This change happened shortly before the end of Livingstone's mayoral tenure so he could not meaningfully influence funding decisions; that was left to his successor Boris Johnson. This was a disappointment to Livingstone, who said, 'The tragedy is, when Tony Blair created the office of London mayor, there was a clause that said the mayor will have no responsibility or power over housing … It took my entire mayoralty to get Tony Blair to lift that … That restriction was lifted just as I lost to Boris.[14]'

TRANSPORT-ORIENTED DEVELOPMENT: AN EXAMPLE

Hale Village is an example of a recent major development around a transport node. This large 'urban village', with over 1,200 residential units, is situated immediately to the east of Tottenham Hale Station and next to the River Lea Navigation. Given its transport accessibility – the station is on the Victoria Line and the train line to Stansted Airport – and stock of former industrial land, the neighbourhood was an obvious target for densification. This was historically an industrial area, made up of factories along the river. Local housing was low-rise: a mixture of council estates and small Edwardian and Victorian terraced houses.

A planning application was submitted to the borough of Haringey in 2005 and approved in 2007 (during Livingstone's time as mayor) and the first homes were occupied in 2013 (during the Johnson period). Hale Village is the first of what will be six privately developed regeneration sites, which together will make up a new, high-density district centre. The mixed-use scheme is on a 4.9-acre site once occupied by a GLC depot. A design code by the architects BDP governs the entire scheme, but the various blocks, each of which is single tenure, were designed by different architects. Local master developer Lee Valley Estates worked with partners including Bellway Homes and Unite student accommodation. With its 'green' features, including a biomass energy system and green roofs, Hale Village claims to represent a 'new generation of eco-district'.

After the Grenfell Tower fire it became apparent that

potentially flammable cladding had been used on some of the blocks in the development, which rendered the flats un-mortgageable and led to a dispute between residents and developers about who should pay for its replacement.[15]

BORIS JOHNSON 2008-16

In the run-up to the May 2008 election, both Livingstone and Johnson published housing manifestos. Livingstone's was straightforwardly entitled 'Why London Needs a 50 per cent Affordable Housing Policy', while Johnson's contribution, 'Building a Better London', focused on first-time buyers and promised that he would not allow 'garden grabbing' or development on the Green Belt.[16] The expectation was that as a Tory mayor on the heels of a left-wing Labour mayor, Johnson would up-end housing policy and focus on supporting owner-occupation, looking to appeal to 'Bromley Man' rather than to 'Islington Woman'. In 2008, Johnson talked about the need for family-sized homes, stating: 'I am not about building homes for hobbits ... they need to be human-sized.'[17] In fact, much of Johnson's housing policy was an extension of Livingstone's approach, as he accepted – at least implicitly – the density implications of aiming to meet London's housing needs within the city's own boundaries.

The central housing questions for Johnson, as for Livingstone, were two-fold: how many new homes should be built? And what proportion should be affordable? The Johnson plan had a more ambitious target for the annual number of new homes than the Livingstone plan it replaced (32,210 versus 23,000). Livingstone had aimed for 50 per cent of new housing to be affordable. Johnson replaced this percentage target with a number for each London borough. These were not so far from the targets they replaced – the main difference was the way 'affordable' was defined. Livingstone had emphasised the production of homes at social rents, which are accessible to low-income households (social rents in London average about 25 per cent of private sector rents for similar homes). Johnson adopted a rather different definition of 'affordability', in line with that of the coalition government, which included shared-ownership properties and homes renting for up to 80 per cent of market levels in the definition of 'affordable'. These homes were meant not for the lowest-income households but rather for middle-income and key worker households who would otherwise struggle to afford to live in London.

Although the Conservatives were in power in Westminster through most of Johnson's tenure, the mayor hit out against national housing policy changes that were detrimental to London. Of the 2010 housing benefit cuts, which were expected to hit London hard, Johnson said: 'What we will not see and we will not accept any kind of Kosovo-style social cleansing of London. On my watch, you are not going to see thousands of families evicted from the place where they have been living and have put down roots.'[18]

In housing, as in other policy areas, Johnson delegated much authority to his aides – in this case deputy mayor for policy planning, Edward Lister, and deputy mayor for housing and land, Rick Blakeway. There was a perception that the Johnson administration was permissive, and the mayor was criticised for approving high-profile major schemes with little or no housing such as the redevelopment of Millbank Tower. In other cases, though, he sought to achieve the maximum reasonable percentage of affordable housing.

From 2012 Johnson had power over Homes and Communities Agency affordable-housing funds for the London region, although much of the money for that and subsequent years had already been committed. Because planning and grant-making powers had not been designed together it could be difficult to coordinate investments with strategy, as the grant-making depended on developers and housing associations applying for funds.

In spatial terms, London's main development focus had for some years been the Thames Gateway, an enormous area spanning both sides of the Thames and reaching eastwards beyond London's boundary. The awarding of the 2012 Olympic Games to London moved the development focus away from the banks of the river itself towards Stratford. The original masterplan for the Olympic athletes' village was described by an official as a series of 'high-rise and fairly bland' blocks that 'could have been anywhere'.[19] Johnson backed a rethink which produced a design for a series of landscaped pedestrian routes flanked by medium-rise courtyard blocks, in a new London vernacular style. These were outwardly similar in appearance but the exteriors were each designed by a different prominent architect. The athletes' village was repurposed after the games and transformed into a pioneering rental-only scheme. When the games ended the mayor assumed control of the successor organisation that became the London Legacy Development Corporation.

The government's housing zone initiative was piloted in London under Johnson. The aim of the scheme was to accelerate development on large-scale (sometimes multi-site) developments, many of which had been stalled because of difficulties in land assembly, viability or agreeing priorities. Local authorities were invited to identify and assemble developable brownfield land, and partner with a developer to build new homes. The idea was to bring together all the elements of placemaking – not only housing but also investment in enabling infrastructure like stations and bridges, as well as new schools and community amenities – in the service of site-specific visions.[20] Mayoral development orders, created in 2015, allow the mayor to remove planning obstacles in these areas but the power has been used only once, to create the Old Oak and Park Royal Development Corporation in 2015.

The initiative was structured as a competition, with bids received from borough-led partnerships. Nine zones were designated in the first round; currently there are thirty including Meridian Water (a former industrial area next to the river Lea in Enfield), the Old Kent Road (an inner London road lined with big-box retail) and the area around Wembley stadium. Housing zones attract funding in the form of grants and loans from the GLA and central government, which are intended to leverage much larger amounts into these developments. There has been no formal evaluation of the housing zones programme, and given the scale of these sites a definitive judgement will not be possible for some time.

SADIQ KHAN 2016-

Sadiq Khan's 2018 housing strategy officially described the London housing situation as being 'crisis'. He set out five main goals:

- building homes for Londoners;
- delivering genuinely affordable homes;
- high-quality homes and inclusive neighbourhoods;
- a fairer deal for private renters and leaseholders; and
- tackling homelessness and helping rough sleepers.[21]

Using the term 'genuinely affordable' to contrast with Johnson's merely 'affordable', Khan set a strategic target for 50 per cent of new homes. He emphasised the need for homes at low social (or quasi-social) rents rather than more costly housing for the intermediate market. This is a political and financial balancing act: a given amount of subsidy (either through grants or income from Section 106) will produce a small amount of social housing or a larger amount of intermediate housing. Some housing advocates say the need for low-cost housing in London is so great that *all* affordable homes should be social, but many middle-income households also face major affordability problems.

ESTATE REGENERATION

Across London, from the city centre to the suburban hinterland, the process of 'estate regeneration' has replaced former local authority social housing estates with clusters of gleaming high-rises built by private developers. The process is win-win, say councils: existing residents get better homes, the new blocks address London's housing needs as they have more homes than the estates they replaced, and boroughs already own the land so costs are reduced. But local campaigners and housing advocates say that estate regeneration destroys communities. They observe that the new mixed-tenure schemes have far fewer low-cost homes than the council estates did, that local people are moved out – often for years – during the development process, and that few can afford to return when the schemes are complete. Bitter and long-lasting controversy has surrounded high-profile schemes, such as the regeneration of south London's Heygate Estate, with Southwark Council accused of colluding with developers in gentrification and 'social cleansing'.[22]

Although estate-regeneration schemes are instituted by boroughs, not the GLA, most of them are large enough (over 150 units) to be subject to call-in, and/or receive grant funding from money that the mayor controls. In 2018 Khan brought in a new rule requiring approval from existing residents before major estate regeneration schemes involving any demolition of social homes can receive City Hall funding, and stipulating that any social housing lost should be replaced like-for-like.

Khan's solution was to subdivide the overall target for affordable housing into at least 30 per cent social (or quasi-social), at least 30 per cent intermediate and the remainder (up to 40 per cent) for the borough to determine.[23]

Affordable-housing contributions are not hard-and-fast requirements; developers and local planning authorities (in London's case boroughs) negotiate them individually for each scheme. Planning authorities aim to get the highest proportion of affordable housing, while developers try to minimise the effect of developer contributions on profitability. The discussions centre around 'viability' calculations, for which the opposing sides often engage outside experts. For major schemes these negotiations often take months and sometimes years, slowing development and arguably reducing investment in new housing.[24] To speed things up Khan introduced a 'threshold' approach, under which planning applications that provided for at least 35 per cent affordable housing (50 per cent on public land) would not have to undergo detailed viability scrutiny – a significant carrot. Developers and landowners have reportedly responded positively to this.

The threshold of 50 per cent affordable housing applies to land owned by boroughs, the NHS, the GLA itself and TfL. Most TfL land is by definition well-located for public transport and thus ideal for what is known in the United States as 'transport-oriented development', which means high-density residential development near transport nodes, which aims to reduce car use. As chair, Khan can direct TfL on how to use its land and made it clear early in his mayoralty that his priority was affordable housing. TfL has partnered with several major developers to bring forward an ambitious programme of residential building, including some schemes that are all-affordable.[25] Crossrail has led to a boom in building around the future stations – some new, some expansions of existing ones.

There is however a major tension between producing affordable housing and maximising land value. Since 2015, the government has required TfL to be self-financing, so the organisation must realise assets, including through land sales, to keep fares down. Land value is a function of what can be built on a site: the possibility of intensive residential use confers high value, while a requirement for developer contributions (including affordable housing) reduces that value.

Densities have continued to increase under Khan. The 2004 housing capacity study had identified capacity for 30,000 homes per year in London, but fifteen years later the city was looking to produce houses at more than twice that rate.[26] The assumption of the London Plan has always been that the capital will meet its own housing needs, and it is a political given that it must do so without impinging on the Green Belt – in the 2016 mayoral election campaign all six major candidates had ruled out development there. These seemingly unbreakable constraints, combined with local antipathy to small-scale interventions, make higher densities inevitable. Khan has not advocated high-density living as a good thing *per se* but, like his predecessors, he has been trapped by the ruthless logic of the maths.

The 2017 Grenfell Tower fire, in which seventy-two people died, refocused attention on the condition of the capital's existing high-density housing, especially high-rise council blocks built in the 1960s and 1970s. The fire was started by a malfunctioning refrigerator on the fourth floor of a 24-storey block in Kensington and Chelsea. Flames spread rapidly up the sides of the building in the gap between the walls and the recently installed external cladding. Investigations later showed that the cladding was not approved for use on tall buildings and was the main reason for the fire spreading. In the aftermath of the fire Khan ordered an inquiry; on the basis of its findings he issued a number of recommendations for the London Fire Brigade about equipment and evacuation procedures. He also made recommendations to central government about building regulations, and to owners and managers of high-rise blocks.[27]

The cost and insecurity of private renting have become significant political issues. Families are living for longer periods in rented homes, young professionals unable to afford owner-occupation press for more secure tenancies through groups like Generation Rent, while boroughs needing temporary accommodation for homeless households must put them in expensive but often poor-quality private rented sector units. In a speech in March 2020, before the mayoral election was cancelled, Khan stated:

I am making the mayoral election on 7 May a referendum on rent controls – showing Londoners that I will stand up for renters. The

Prime Minister will have to give us the powers we need, because if he refuses to do so he will be denying the express democratic will of millions of Londoners.[28]

Khan has been lobbying for the power to introduce rent controls in London and has suggested a London rent model that could require landlords to reduce existing rents, going further than the models operating in other world cities.[29] Polling suggests that this would appeal to most Londoners but the initiative has no realistic chance of succeeding under the current government.

CONCLUSION

In housing it can be difficult to attribute success or failure to specific policies, particularly when looking at the rate of construction of new housing. This is partly because most of the mayor's policy levers are elements of the planning system, whose processes are notoriously slow. Policies announced in mayoral manifestos can take years to emerge as legally binding documents – for example, Boris Johnson took office in 2008 but the final version of his London Plan was not in place until July 2012. And even after planning permission is granted, the construction process on large sites can take more than a decade. As the GLA's most recent annual monitoring report noted: 'It will take several years before most of the referable planning permissions granted under the current administration make it through to completion.'[30]

The main metrics of housing policy success over the last two decades have been the numbers of new homes built and the proportion of affordable housing achieved. None of the three mayors has achieved their goals, partly because they have set them implausibly high for political reasons. Numerical targets for new homes and affordable housing are meant to reflect planners' objective assessments of housing needs and the amount of land available – but these in turn depend on the assumptions fed into them, which reflect the political imperative to be seen to build more housing.

Although housing production has increased over the last twenty years, mayoral housing targets have increased even more. The GLA's annual London Plan monitoring reports, which show what has actually been accomplished against plan targets, receive little public and media attention compared to the plan itself. But they starkly highlight the gap between the plans (which are in the mayor's hands) and action (which mostly is not). In only a few of the last twenty years has housing production – in terms of total units or affordable homes – reached official targets; in most years there has been a large shortfall. In 2017/18, the latest year for which the data is available, the official target (expressed as a multi-year average) was 42,010 net additional completions, but actual production fell far short of that at 32,083.[31] For affordable housing the picture was much worse: actual production was 4,703 new units against a target of 17,000. The targets have since been raised (and the current housing minister told Sadiq Khan in January 2020 that it should be higher still), but some time ago the targets crossed the line from aspirational and achievable to hopelessly unrealistic.

Housing policy is inextricably intertwined with economic development and transport policy. The city's future economic growth will affect its population, which will in turn affect housing need. If London continues on the trajectory set since 2000, transport investments such as Crossrail will continue to open up new areas to transport-oriented development and TfL land will contribute significant amounts of affordable housing. On the other hand, 2020 may be the year that the policy of 'good growth' starts to morph into 'right-sizing the city'.

17

MAYORS, MINISTERS AND LOCAL AUTHORITIES

TIM WILLIAMS

I know that we are meant to live life going forward then understand it afterwards by looking backwards, but in terms of my London experiences my understanding of them is still a work in progress. So here are four scenes where I found myself in the middle of the scrappy tripartite relationship between the Mayor of London, the UK government and London's local authorities.

SCENE 1: 2005-6:

During this time I was special advisor to Labour's communities and local government minister David Miliband. I had been given the job of going around the various government departments seeking to put a package of devolutionary measures in place to give London government more powers, as eventually enacted in the Greater London Authority Act 2007. I was and am a convinced city devolutionist, and I went about my task in my usual bright-eyed and bushy-tailed manner.

It did not go well. This was partly for high-brow reasons to do with a socialist preference for equality and efficiency and thus centralisation, rather than local variation and thus devolution. But it was also down to low-brow reasons to do with political and personal animus. My favourite from the latter camp is this pithy aperçu from a very senior minister who reminded me that Ken Livingstone had stood against the Labour Party in the mayoral election of 2000. While he had been re-admitted in 2004, the memory of betrayal was strong and Livingstone was still seen as a 'class enemy' by many: 'Tell David if he thinks I'm going to give that f****** c*** an extra paperclip to f****** play with he's off his f****** rocker.'

I think it's fair to say that these lingering hostilities made our devo-lutionary effort less comprehensive than we had hoped. We did make some progress on planning, *viz.* powers we had within our own de-partment and therefore had capacity to devolve. However, even within the department, our love of devolution was tempered somewhat by distrust of the aforementioned 'class enemy'.

SCENE 2: 2007

After David Miliband moved on, I became special advisor to the planning minister, the brave and characterful Yvette Cooper. The 2007 Act allowed for the mayor to act as planning decision-maker for applications of strategic importance, and we were preparing a planning order to define what such strategic applications might be.

We were a bit worried that some officials were a tad gung-ho on the devolutionary front, and were planning to hand almost all large applications to the mayor. Our concerns were focused on that other key part of London governance, the City of London Corporation. We needed to protect the City against the 'class enemy' Ken Livingstone (who was still viewed with suspicion) in case he took that socialism stuff a bit too seriously. I mean, by all means give the capitalists a kicking – you first, comrade, then me – but please don't muck up the only economic engine making the country a profit, enabling us to distribute to the bits that, well, don't make a profit.

So we were happy to give Livingstone more powers over housing schemes across the capital, but not to let a neo-Marxist from Neasden and his *gauchiste* coterie in City Hall flood London's financial epicentre with houses rather than offices, and thereby killing the goose that laid the golden eggs, and raising awkward questions of democracy in a local authority where businesses as well as residents had the vote. The result was that the City Corporation kept most of its planning powers (to a much higher threshold than other boroughs) with the mayor only able to intervene on the very biggest buildings – those that were over 150 metres tall or providing more than 100,000 square-metres of space.

I must add that our perception of Ken's commitment to hard-left policies was in error and he seems to have been as committed to meeting the office needs of the global elite as any New Labour Mandelsonian would have wished. Also, I'm not now sure who to blame for some of the poorer buildings erected in the City area since we did the deal, but possibly the correct answer is 'us'.

SCENE 3: 2008–10

The 'class enemy' in City Hall loses to Boris Johnson, another foe – though as he was a Tory rather than an aberrant sometime member of our own party, Boris was better understood as an 'opponent' rather than as an 'enemy'. I can't help thinking we treated him as the former and thus relations were cool but not embittered.

I was seeing this from a few different angles in the period to 2010 when I worked as a specialist advisor to various housing and planning ministers and sometimes the east London boroughs. Certainly Boris treated the government more politely and had rather a warm relationship with the London boroughs particularly in the east – who I knew well as former CEO of the Thames Gateway London Partnership – where planning for the Olympics and the legacy went more smoothly than I think it would have if Ken had remained in place.

Given my experience of the difficult birthing of limited devolution to Ken in 2005 to 2006 it was remarkable how even though – or even because – Boris was now the mayor, the completely new Homes and Communities Agency found itself more or less hiving off its operations in the capital to the mayor, with the relationship between serious devolutionist Bob (now Lord) Kerslake, who was heading the new agency, serious housing expert David Lunts, the mayor's director of housing and land, and serious operator and advisor to all three mayors Neale Coleman being key.

Lesson for class theorists: the great man (or woman) view of history adds something real to dialectical materialism – people matter. And the deal that these people brokered devolved housing investment to London – after the financial crisis, when it was most needed both to save the private housing sector and to enable serious numbers of social units to be built.

SCENE 4: 2011–12

While it is true to say that without deputy Prime Minister John Prescott there would have been no Channel Tunnel rail link, thus no Stratford International Station, thus no Olympic Park in east London, without London government working closely with the Blair/Brown government there would have been no London 2012 and none of the best legacy work done for any Olympics. The boroughs get forgotten, but it was also the partnership between host boroughs (who I advised) and the mayoral bodies, such as the London Development Agency, which enabled the successful bid and then implementation. Ken Livingstone supported and backed the necessary risk-taking by his officials – some of whom got whacked immorally after he had gone, on the well-established principle in government that 'no good deed goes unpunished'.

But perhaps more importantly than the man was the mayoralty itself. The model delivered for London, albeit in a cranky and sometimes abusive relationship with the government on the one hand, and the boroughs on the other. Whatever its faults or the character of specific mayors, twenty years on, nobody doubts that London is a lot classier than it would have been without a return to devolved government.

18

CIVIC LEADERSHIP

TIM DONOVAN

When the mayoralty was established in 2000, London had been without a voice for nearly a decade and a half. Alongside newly devolved powers came an opportunity to shout loudly again for the capital, and carve out a distinctive civic leadership role. This role was not – and could not – be defined exactly, but over two decades it has come to mean many things. Mayors have articulated responses to crisis and to celebration, reached out to central government and local government, spoken to and for business, unions, London's many different communities, and have sought an international identity, both in competition and in solidarity with other global cities.

How much has this been down to personality and how much to powers? In both Ken Livingstone and Boris Johnson we have seen huge, unique, political figures. In Livingstone there remains widespread regard, even among staunch Tory opponents, for the strength and shape of the template he set – from which his successors have not deviated. In Sadiq Khan, there is a prevailing view that this is a work in progress. As well as reaching out to different sectors and communities, these mayors have sought to shape the profile of their city and promote it (as well as themselves) with sometimes spectacular results.

DOING THE BUSINESS

Mayoral credibility has depended to a large degree on the confidence of employers and other economic actors across the capital city. While broadly welcoming the creation of an elected mayor to re-energise the capital, many in the business community were fearful of the prospect of 'Red Ken' becoming that figure. For a while there were thoughts of mounting a campaign against him.

But once he arrived at City Hall fears soon dissipated. Many were impressed by Livingstone's acumen and leadership. 'He had the strategic brain of a FTSE-100 CEO,' recalls one leading business figure.[1] 'He knew how to get things done and which levers to pull.' Some in the City of London Corporation – which speaks for London's financial sector – were concerned there might be incursions into their sphere of influence. The very title of 'Mayor of London' caused unease in the City because they thought it would confuse and detract from their own Lord Mayor.

It soon became clear that Livingstone had no intention of interfering, and was relaxed about the wealth creation and innovation of the Square Mile. He praised the de-regulation resulting from the financial sector's Big Bang, unleashed by Margaret Thatcher, and he liked to boast that London had overtaken New York as the world's pre-eminent financial centre.[2] He enjoyed warm relations with City of London officials, appointing one top corporation figure, Dame Judith Mayhew, to his first mayoral advisory board, and establishing effective links with one of her successors, Sir Michael Snyder. Snyder was one of the few public figures to back Livingstone over the congestion charge and shared information from the 'ring of steel' vehicle recognition technology put in place to shield the City from IRA attacks.

Between them, business people and Livingstone also unlocked the funding arrangements for Crossrail that finally persuaded Gordon Brown to sign off on the project. 'Ken would always say it was important we were seen to be driving this. That government would listen to us more,' says one figure who was closely involved.[3] Leadership was knowing when to let others be seen to be leading. Livingstone was at no stage seen as an impediment to the capital's economic health – even if few found palatable what they imagined were still the underlying politics of the mayor and his key advisors from the left, John Ross and Redmond O'Neill.

FOLLOW THAT

Unexpectedly, it was Johnson who caused more concern for the City in his early days as mayor. He and his economic advisor, former think tanker and journalist Anthony Browne, looked across the river from City Hall to the Square Mile and wondered whether creating alliances there could prove a potential source of enhanced mayoral power and influence. Some corporation figures were alarmed at what they thought was the intention to drag them into a political plan to pick fights with Gordon Brown's government, in the 'defence' of City interests. But there was ultimately no appetite to disturb the broadly constructive relationship which had been established between the Labour government and City Hall, thanks to a large degree to City minister Ed Balls.

As he campaigned to be mayor, Johnson had been on a steep learning curve. 'He really didn't have a clue how the capital was run,' says one business figure who was consulted at the time.[4] Johnson sought to create the impression that a new era of private sector efficiency was dawning at City Hall. Designed to impress the business community, Sir Tim Parker was brought in from the world of boardroom takeovers to become the mayor's first deputy. But the revolution proved short-lived and ended in tears. Instead, Johnson discovered that perfectly competent administrators – such as Sir Simon Milton, leader of Westminster Council, and then Sir Edward Lister from Wandsworth – could be drawn from London's municipal talent pool. Johnson's successor Khan has not been able to draw on quite the same calibre of long-standing local government figures, who know which doors to push open, and which calls to make. If Johnson's detached 'chairman of the board' mayoral style was criticised by his opponents as reflecting his lack of engagement with detail, business figures seemed to have less of a problem with the notion of delegating the heavy-lifting required at the top of government to top-notch executives.

CRISIS, WHAT CRISIS?

When the economy deteriorated during the financial crisis in 2008 to 2009, Johnson came to define himself as just about the only politician 'prepared to stand up for the banks'.[5] Here he was, ready to lift morale, cheerlead for the City and protect London's citizens from the hardship of austerity. Johnson had particularly strong links to Barclays, appointing the bank's chief executive Bob Diamond to head up his new mayor's charity fund, although relatively quickly the latter had to stand down to focus on the financial crisis.

Johnson asked Barclays chairman Marcus Agius to sponsor the capital's bike-hire scheme, an idea that was first developed by Livingstone. Annual sponsorship contributions of £5 million or less from this global banking giant attracted some criticism – the scheme never became self-financing, as promised by Johnson – and eventually Barclays withdrew support, to be replaced by the red livery of rivals Santander in 2015. Some of Johnson's early infrastructure decisions also disappointed business leaders who were concerned about getting their workforces in and out of work each day. He cancelled a new road bridge linking Newham to Bexley via Greenwich, which was ready with the necessary finances sorted by Livingstone and Brown but widely opposed in the Tory-voting boroughs of Bexley and Bromley. He risked angering business with a segregated cycle-lane system which became one of the defining features of his mayoralty. Cycling increased and the number of deaths and serious injuries eventually came down. But some of the bike lanes infuriated many in the City and Canary Wharf due to their effects on congestion, even though the corporation wanted to pursue its own restrictions on vehicular traffic with vigour.

ALL IN THE DETAIL

What business people did find was that while his attention-span was often limited, Johnson learned quickly. He absorbed key arguments, got to the heart of issues fast, and once decided on a course pursued it enthusiastically – even if, as one observer claims, he did tend 'to agree with the last person he was in the room with.'[6] Lots of hopes were raised. Some insist it was a major achievement for Johnson to convince David Cameron and George Osborne not to renege on Crossrail and the Tube upgrade programme. Others say that this was 'well overdone' – there was no real chance of them pulling the plug on such nationally vital infrastructure.

One thing that business people did notice was that Johnson's interest in the job fell off sharply in his second term, and it became more difficult to engage the mayor's office. During this time he was content that there was time enough to author a biography of Sir Winston Churchill – he was allowed to use a quiet spot in the Museum of London in the Barbican to write. Some of those who attended meetings with him during this period claim that he appeared to attempt to adopt the persona of his political hero: 'He was doing this Churchill thing. All gravitas and seriousness. Like he wanted to re-invent himself as a leader. Maybe it wasn't conscious but it was irritating.'[7]

I AM YOUR FRIEND

Sadiq Khan's promise to the capital's wealth creators and job providers was that he would be 'the most business-friendly' mayor there's been.[8] This simultaneously showed how important it was to reach out and, arguably, how low the bar had been set. The main basis for Khan's pledge appeared to be that he had more experience of running a business than his predecessors. That, of course, was not hard, given that neither had any.

Once a partner in a south London law firm, Khan felt that he could better identify with the concerns and insights of the capital's commercial sector. So far, though, it has been difficult to pick up much more than a general ambivalence towards the mayor among the business community: 'I think his political positioning is great. He's a good campaigner. But I am not sure he has a delivery strategy or really knows how to do stuff,' says one close observer.[9] Another states that Khan is running City Hall in a way that is 'cautious, tightly managed and closed-off'.[10] There is a complaint that business leaders can't get much access to him: 'Unless you hear on a broad issue what people's views are, you are cutting yourself off from the best advice which will give you the best answers.'

However, that campaigning instinct has helped in a big way. During a term dominated by Brexit, Khan's strong Remain stance has been warmly welcomed by a business constituency which, to a large degree, felt betrayed by Johnson in the run-up to the referendum. Some claim that Johnson told them directly that he didn't want to leave the European Union. 'It'll be OK,' he'd say. That he then opted to campaign for Leave – and while still mayor of a city so opposed to leaving the EU – felt like an insult.[11] Others say that they could detect something was up with Johnson during the last year of his mayoralty – and wondered whether he could be counted on to keep the UK in the EU. One business figure recalls a lunch near City Hall in December 2015, just months before the EU referendum. When the chat turned to Brexit, the mood changed: 'He seemed to get a bit flustered and left soon afterwards. He didn't want to be pinned down.'[12]

The issue of Europe has continued to pervade the London mayoralty. With his London is Open campaign, Khan has positioned himself vociferously as a champion of the city's economic and cultural internationalism. Claiming that he's speaking for a city which gave him a big mandate for his stance, he's been unambiguously in favour of immigration and freedom of movement, unconstrained by the contrivances of the position Labour felt it had to adopt nationally. With the UK now departed from the EU, it is not clear how Khan plans to shift his thinking to reflect post-Brexit realities. With a Europhile, metropolitan London lawyer now leading the Labour Party nationally in Keir Starmer, it's also not immediately apparent how Khan – already seen as notorious for his preoccupation with political positioning – is going to stay distinctive.

GOOD RELATIONS?

On 11 March 2014, Boris Johnson was on the French Riviera, mingling with investors and financiers at the MIPIM international property fair in Cannes. He was preparing to make a keynote speech on housing, when his advisors hurried him into a side room. News had come from London that Bob Crow, leader of the National Union of Rail, Maritime and Transport Workers (RMT), the biggest Tube union, had died of a heart attack. To the television cameras, the mayor's words were warm, praising Crow as a man of strong principle, who impressed with 'his indefatigable defence of what he thought of as his members' views and interests'.[13]

London's transport bosses genuinely felt the same about Crow, a towering force of a man whom they respected, and liked a lot too. But these were qualities that the mayor had seen only from afar. Apart from one occasion when they were fellow guests on a BBC debate programme, the pair had not met.[14] They did speak one other time – when the producers of LBC's regular radio phone-in with Johnson put through a caller called 'Bob from Woodford Green'.[15] But during his mayoralty Johnson was resolute in not meeting senior figures from any of the major unions, even informally.

Critics said that it was short-sighted not to try to create some level of personal chemistry. Some think Johnson saw it as fundamental to the tough-talking image that he wanted to project, built on a key manifesto promise to broker a no-strike deal. However, other insiders say Johnson was more than happy to meet with Crow, but it was London's senior transport bosses who warned against it, formally or informally, fearing the union-spun 'agreements' and 'pledges' that might arise from free-flowing Johnsonian chats, and believing it would compromise them in future. As one former Transport for London official reflects, 'The moment Crow had met the mayor once, he'd think he could go straight to him next time, cutting us out of the loop.'[16]

As you'd expect between left-wing unions and a Conservative mayor, industrial relations proved to be tricky. Although a generous pay and conditions deal brought the guarantee of peace during the Olympics, the number of strikes during Johnson's tenure was double that under Livingstone. Disruption to the transport network increased as Johnson's mayoralty progressed. According to a freedom of information request by the BBC, in Johnson's first term 12,523 shifts were lost to strike action, rising to 19,689 working days lost during his second term. Khan's pledge to ensure 'zero strike days' has not been fulfilled, but he has met union leaders and tried to keep things cordial. So far there have been 3,824 shifts lost to strike days – with none at all during 2019.[17]

Not that Livingstone enjoyed universally sunny relations with the transport unions. Insiders say he knew that whenever he conceded something with the unions, they would come back for more. He needed to be robust to achieve the transport revolution he wanted. He went in hard against the RMT when they threatened to strike on the eve of the 2004 mayoral election, urging workers to cross picket lines when they renewed the threat a month later. This prompted Crow to resign from the TfL board. Abruptly halting a heated meeting in his office at City Hall, Livingstone showed Crow the door, shouting after him: 'You're a fucking anarchist.'[18] However, there was notably successful cooperation over projects like upgrading the east London line, removing it from the Underground and making it part of what has become London Overground. It is said that Crow agreed to driver-only trains and no guards over dinner with TfL boss Hendy, on the basis of assurances of expanding jobs overall on the network.[19]

MAYOR FOR ALL LONDONERS?

If Livingstone saw the period between the abolition of the Greater London Council and the creation of the mayoralty as a 'rude interruption', how had his thinking on London's cultural, ethnic and religious diversity developed during those years in the cold? His mayoralty saw cultural events flourish. He established the New Year's Eve fireworks event, based around the London Eye, now embedded in the national broadcasters' festive schedules. There was a revival of the 'Thames Festival' too. He created a promotional agency, Visit London, which underlined the economic heft from tourism. He instigated an annual anti-racist festival – first called 'Respect', then 'Rise' – and the Liberty disability arts festival. During this time the St Patrick's Day and Pride celebrations gained considerably from an injection of mayoral energy which made them even bigger.

A significant factor was that Trafalgar Square – along with Parliament Square – came under the control of the Greater London Authority and became an important venue for cultural and religious celebration rather than just protest. The festivals of Eid, Diwali and Vaisakhi packed out the square, which became a place for all Londoners. A re-design which pedestrianised the road to the north and a competition to find occupants for the vacant fourth plinth injected new life into a space that had been dedicated to dead men, although Livingstone was unsuccessful in his bid to remove two historical figures that 'no one had ever heard of'. This pre-figured the anger and debate over statues which grew out of the Black Lives Matter protests in the summer of 2020, which has placed Khan – who set up a commission to review statues in the capital – against his predecessor (and Churchill biographer, remember) Johnson, who warned against the 'photo-shopping' of history.[20]

As mayor, Johnson made a particular fuss of St George's Day, claiming that it had been neglected by Livingstone. He otherwise added little to the cultural legacy that he inherited – moving or discontinuing some events, while he focused mainly on the Olympics. Khan has wanted to revive the notion of arts and culture as a driver of civic pride. Since 2016, innovations introduced have included the 'London Borough of Culture', a Night Czar, campaigns to protect grassroots music venues, and, in Millicent Fawcett, the first statue of a woman in Parliament Square, to mark the centenary of women getting the vote. A chapter on culture even found its way into the London Plan.

Competing identities can bring tensions and resentment. One criticism of Livingstone by his opponents was that he made assumptions about which way different communities were inclined to vote *en masse* and didn't progress to more nuanced, modern notions of diversity.[21] There was, of course, controversy. When he invited renowned Islamic scholar Dr Yusuf al-Qaradawi to speak at City Hall, the objection was not just to Livingstone using the mayoralty as a platform for his geo-political thinking but that he was hosting a figure who didn't reject the scriptural permission to stone gay men.[22] Gay and lesbian organisations didn't contend that Livingstone himself was homophobic, but had it really been worth the deep insult felt by one community arising from this attempt to reach out to another?

Livingstone's reputation was sullied, long after leaving City Hall, by the antisemitism row over comments he made about Hitler's support for Zionism.[23] Few who know him well – political friend and foe – believe he is antisemitic or indeed that he displayed this as mayor. But did he, at best, discount the capital's Jewish community? *Guardian* journalist Jonathan Freedland had been supportive of Livingstone and was one of the few media figures invited as a guest to the Queen's formal opening of City Hall. So when Freedland wrote in 2012 that he couldn't support his mayoral comeback attempt – on the grounds of his casual indifference to the sensitivities of the capital's Jewish community – it was a damaging intervention.[24]

By contrast, in the middle of the 2016 mayoral campaign, Khan was one of the first Labour figures to call for Livingstone's expulsion from the party. Becoming the first Muslim mayor of a major Western city, he opted to do one of his first interviews with the *Jewish Chronicle* – and has since done others. How important Khan's faith is to Londoners is a hard question to gauge. Has there perhaps been more scrutiny of – as well as poignancy to – his public responses to incidents of terror in the capital? After the London Bridge attack in 2017, for instance, he said terrorists 'do not commit these disgusting acts in my name as a Muslim'.[25]

TIMES OF CRISIS AND CELEBRATION

There had been occasions when London had sent collective condolences to other cities, but it was five years before the mayoralty was tested by crisis. In July 2005, Olympic triumph and terrorist tragedy became entwined in forty-eight hours of euphoria and mayhem, as Neale Coleman describes in Chapter 19. This attack proved to be an examination not just of the resilience of the city itself, but also of the qualities of the politician elected to speak for it. At the time, and again rightly when recalled on the tenth anniversary in 2015, Livingstone's response was widely praised. Here was an evocative blend of the language of shared defiance and geo-political awareness, with a sense of the unfolding practical response from the emergency services, working closer than ever as part of devolved city government.

Whatever the exact protocols around communication in response to acts of terror in the capital, which are built primarily around the Prime Minister and the country's most senior police officer, the Metropolitan Police Commissioner, it is to the mayor that Londoners now look for reassurance, and for signals on the way forward. It is easy to exaggerate the degree to which crises bring out a sense of civic pride and cohesion, but it is still possible to assert that the mayor has become a crucial agent around which identity, solidarity and defiance can co-alesce, and build. It is now certainly an essential part of the mayoral job specification: that the candidate must be able to capture tone and mood, and articulate Londoners' collective pain and pleasure.

Johnson fortunately never had to find the right words to respond to terror in eight years in the job, although he was severely tested by the 2011 riots, returning late from holiday and being booed in the street.[26] Instead, he benefited from his articulation of the Olympic pomp and spoils, from flag-carrying in Beijing in 2008 to the golden haul of medals in an unforgettable August 2012 in Stratford. It was a perfect stage for him. And bar the odd team coach getting lost, the city he led delivered an Olympics that meant predictions of infrastructure failure were proved wrong. By contrast, in his first term alone, Khan has had to respond to several terror attacks, coronavirus and the fire at Grenfell Tower. In the latter case, while others were criticised over their response in the immediate aftermath, Khan seemed sure-footed and able to articulate – for the bereaved – the desperate need for answers. Few can argue with the effort that he makes to strike the correct note. In August 2016, he interrupted a holiday to come home after one incident where an American woman was stabbed to death in the street which, it turned out, was not terror-related. Following a series of attacks in European cities and Manchester in 2017, he has not missed a chance to stress the importance of civic fraternity and international solidarity. It is cities which, by restraint, defeat terror and hold communities together.

CONTROVERSY

London has experienced external crises of the kind considered above, but there have also been controversies that mayors have brought on themselves. And for one short moment over these two decades, an incident effectively meant that London briefly had no mayor in office. Questions of democracy, freedom of speech and when a mayor is or is not 'on duty' arose after an agreeable party at City Hall (to celebrate the career of the UK's first openly gay MP, Chris Smith) turned sour in early 2005. Door-stepped by an *Evening Standard* journalist as he left the party, Livingstone aimed a few barbs his way, including likening him to a concentration camp guard. Because the reporter was Jewish, and working for Livingstone's arch-enemies at Associated Newspapers, a perfect storm was triggered.

It wasn't just that the mayor would not apologise. He went on the attack, insisting he would take no lectures from a newspaper group which once appeased the Nazis. (To make matters even more complicated, the *Standard* actually belonged to an anti-Nazi proprietor in the 1930s.) He ignored pleas from Prime Minister Tony Blair and Olympics minister Tessa Jowell to say 'sorry', as an International Olympic Association delegation rode into town for a final look at London's plans before the crucial decision on the winning venue later in the year. Was he jeopardising the bid, or showing just the kind of inner steel which was needed to deliver the Olympics?

His conduct was made the subject of a hearing by the obscure (and short-lived) Adjudication Panel For England, which found that Livingstone had brought the mayoralty into disrepute and suspended him for a month. An appeal court judge overturned the suspension, finding that while he could have avoided the political struggle with an apology, Livingstone wasn't 'on duty' at the time of the incident and, anyway, implicit in his right to freedom of speech was a right to be offensive. Livingstone hailed it as a victory for democracy. Many felt that it had been a grubby affair.[27]

Livingstone showed a similar obstinacy towards the end of his second term, in a manner potentially more costly to him this time, when the *Evening Standard* made claims about inappropriate grants for certain organisations by the London Development Agency.[28] A subsequent inquiry found no individual wrongdoing. But at the time, some of Livingstone's closest advisors thought that he should have risen statesman-like above the fray, taking the heat out of the situation and reducing the political risk with an earlier suspension (if only for strategic reasons and without prejudice) of his policing deputy Lee Jasper, who was the main protagonist in the affair.

While some saw the newspaper's campaigning as partisan and relentless, had Livingstone's judgement been exposed? It did underline for some what they claimed was Livingstone's sectional, divisive approach to London's electorate, where support among minority communities in general, and a growing Muslim population in particular, was actively courted. Livingstone always rejected any suggestions of antisemitism, but he has been a strong critic of Israel. Years after he had left City Hall, casual and injudicious language around the issue set off a chain of events which has left Livingstone, well before time, isolated from mainstream political discourse.[29]

SORRY IS THE HARDEST WORD

Here was what has proved to be part of a common theme. Two decades of mayoral defiance, bullishness towards the media and a refusal to say sorry. Whether or not this has been exacerbated by the sense of power imbued by a mandate to represent 5 million people, examples of tactical retreat through qualified or limited apology have not yet found their way into the mayoral playbook. The nature of the job, or of the people so far drawn to it?

Johnson had more reason than most to empathise with those who discovered during his mayoralty that their phones had been hacked by tabloid newspapers. He had been a victim himself, according to his deputy mayor Kit Malthouse.[30] Whether it was because he was also a journalist, or didn't want to alienate the supportive Murdoch publications, Johnson never pushed the Metropolitan Police hard to uncover the extent of the problem and dismissed the scandal in its early stages as 'codswallop'.[31] As more details emerged, no apology was forthcoming.

Neither were there words of regret when he was tardy getting back from a holiday in the Rockies to take control of the capital that was beset by rioting in 2011, and the police apparently in strategic disarray. Implementing Coalition-led cuts, as mayor he managed to avoid apologising for austerity. He also felt no compulsion to apologise for the excesses of the banks when the financial sector crash occurred in 2008 to 2009, but instead chose to present himself as their courageous defender.

Faced by rising violent crime, Sadiq Khan has sought to swerve the need for *mea culpas* on the speed and effectiveness of his early response, through regular attacks over the lack of funding. Khan often seeks to blame the government for things that are not right. In the view of one long-standing former City Hall official, 'You don't win all the friends you need by saying, constantly, the government should be doing this or that. It gets on people's nerves and they react against it.'[32] It will be more problematic for Khan to get away with this approach on housing, an issue where there has been under-delivery in relation to need during the periods in office of all three mayors. It is difficult for Khan to absolve himself of responsibility given he accepted a record amount from the government to build more affordable homes. On the other hand, Khan has so far avoided the kind of embarrassment which regularly beset Johnson over his choice of advisors, who in the early days came and went with alarming regularity. However, he faces a different problem: whether or not his appointees have the capacity to deliver policy outcomes.

NATIONAL PLATFORM AND STEPPING STONE

There are considerable limitations to the mayor's powers. This has been a frustration to all of the holders of the office. But alongside those limitations has lain an enormous opportunity not only to advocate for the city, but also to use the legitimacy of the office to act on the public mood. City Hall has proved to be a fine platform and pulpit.

It is now impossible to see someone succeed in the role without top communication skills and strategies, a huge degree of confidence and self-belief and, perhaps most of all, an eye for an opportunity. The fact that two of the three incumbents so far are, or have been, seen as being on a journey, a stepping stone, to greater things on the national stage (Livingstone was clear it was his last and only ambition) is less important than the fact that a mayoralty in our capital city has created a tier of sub-national government which genuinely commands attention and can shift the national discourse. Powers may or may not catch up with this visibility in due course.

What has also happened, inevitably, is that all three office holders have used the position to fight their own personal political battles, often under the guise of standing up for the interests of Londoners. This has nevertheless arguably benefited London by elevating debate about its infrastructure needs and economic contribution to a national level. But it was civic leadership which raised the profile of the city as well as the individual in public consciousness. In Livingstone and Johnson especially, the job seemed tailor-made for their talents.

But what was the intention? Did those in the Blair administration, who painstakingly drew up the legal clauses which brought into life the Greater London Authority and its fellow service bodies, imagine what was to come and to what purposes this platform might be put? The opportunity to pursue personal agendas was inherently interwoven with the duty to provide London with civic leadership.

HERE AND ABROAD

It has therefore proved impossible for all three holders of the office to confine themselves to affairs of the capital, and the combination of circumstances and the eye for an opportunity has thrust them into the international spotlight. On this at least, it would be fair to say, the current mayor has trumped the lot. As the President of the United States touched down at Stansted airport at the beginning of his official visit in June 2019, a couple of tweets landed with him:

> @Sadiq Khan, who by all accounts has done a terrible job as Mayor of London, has been foolishly 'nasty' to the visiting President of the United States, by far the most important ally of the United Kingdom. He is a stone cold loser who should focus on crime in London, not me...
>
> Kahn [sic] reminds me very much of our very dumb and incompetent Mayor of NYC, de Blasio, who has also done a terrible job – only half his height. In any event, I look forward to being a great friend to the United Kingdom, and am looking very much forward to my visit.[33]

Forget zip wires, wasn't this hitting the political jackpot? It was the latest in a salvo between the President and the mayor. Khan had first condemned Trump for floating a discriminatory temporary travel ban for Muslims coming into the US.[34] Trump criticised Khan for doing a 'bad job' of protecting London from terrorism and failing to get on top of violent crime. There were rival 'blimps' of each raised over Whitehall. You can't argue that it's a notable PR triumph when the most powerful politician on the planet, however unusual, not only knows who you are but can be bothered to try to attack you.

Khan had, of course, already come to fairly widespread attention as the first Muslim elected to lead a Western capital. But the spat fitted with Khan's aspirations. With his celebrity appeal and journalistic background, Johnson could always command national media attention. Khan has geared his press operation to aim as high. The mayoral Twitter feed never rests, a presence that has been magnified during the coronavirus crisis. There is a premium placed on broadcast appearances on *The Andrew Marr Show*, other breakfast TV programmes and *Today* on Radio 4, and much time dedicated to attempting to place stories and comment pieces in national newspapers.

Unmistakably, Livingstone, Johnson and Khan have all seen themselves as international players. Eloquent in his belief that it is cities that drive progress, Livingstone was the prime force behind an initiative to bring major conurbations together in the pursuit of solutions to climate change. The C20 – now expanded to C40 – pooled its urban spending power to drive innovation. It was detail that Livingstone loved. When Johnson defeated him, with what some claimed was a record of scepticism on climate change, London quietly lost its position leading the organisation. In 2009, at its annual international conference in South Korea – attended by Bill Clinton – Johnson was sidelined and sloped off for a sight-seeing trip to the demilitarised zone at the thirty-eighth parallel.

FOREIGN TRAVELS

In the pursuit of international attention, Livingstone was no less well-travelled than his Tory nemesis. Arriving in China to drum up investment in London in 2006, he used a photo-op at the Olympic countdown clock at Tiananmen Square to attempt comparisons between the notorious massacre and London's poll tax riots.[35] The ensuing fuss was all orchestrated by the media, he argued. Some observers thought that this was just the kind of refusal to offer an unequivocal condemnation of the massacre that would get him noticed and impress the Communist Party top brass who hosted him. As the five-day promotional trip progressed, on which City Hall had spent heavily, advisor John Ross eagerly showed off a folder of hundreds of Chinese newspaper cuttings, as Livingstone posed for photographs – against the Shanghai skyline – alongside pop group Girls Aloud, and the winner of the Chinese equivalent of *The X Factor*.

Under Livingstone, London did its own trade deal with an unlikely partner. Venezuela's Hugo Chávez offered discounted oil for London's bus fleet in return for TfL officials providing advice on tackling the traffic problems in Caracas. Sir Peter Hendy, transport commissioner, was dispatched to make headway, taking a helicopter trip to survey the sprawling Latin American capital. Livingstone arranged a trip to seal the bonds of friendship but only got as far as Cuba before Chávez revealed he was too busy electioneering to see him. Livingstone was not successful either in seeing an ailing Castro, so confined himself to reading a biography of former Vietnamese premier Ho Chi Minh in the gardens of Havana's National Hotel, as the press back in London gleefully recounted the mayor's failure to meet the hero of the left.

It was during the 2012 Olympic Games that Johnson took international (self-) promotion to new dizzying heights when he was 'accidentally' suspended on a zipwire in Victoria Park in east London. Some blamed his weight and his own version of the incident was that there had been a technical malfunction. However, another suggestion was that he'd come to a halt because – going against the guidance of the operators – he'd stretched out his arms, waving little union flags, rather than folding them across his chest. Investigating afterwards, Tower Hamlets Council's environmental health team found nothing wrong with the equipment. Could getting stuck have been part of the plan?

Similar suspicions arose three years later in Japan. A demonstration of street rugby in Tokyo was coming to an end and Johnson turned to begin the last run of the session. With two UK photographers well-known to Johnson ideally positioned, a ten-year-old boy called Toki was sent flying to the ground. How could journalists ever prove this was deliberate? Yet the desired effect was achieved. An international trip of otherwise minimal consequence was eclipsed by a video going viral – and London (or definitely its mayor) duly promoted across the globe.[36]

Khan has followed on the path of international promotion, with less dramatic results, visiting the US, India and Pakistan. But most of his focus has been on post-referendum Europe, ever hopeful that his noisy Europhile stance will give him access to government ministers, not just his mayoral counterparts. He has managed, so far, no mayoral 'gaffe' to propel him on to the front of newspapers around the globe.

WHAT NEXT?

Coronavirus has led to the postponement of the mayoral election from 2020 to 2021 – and thus delayed the key official reckoning of Sadiq Khan's progress since 2016. But can his perpetual 'campaign' style prevent, for long, a cooler assessment of how he is doing? His pugilistic approach raises an important question in a country where mayors rely heavily on central government for their resources. Do you do better for your city if you reach out, make friends and play things calmly with your political foes in government, because they control the money?

Given Livingstone, though elected as an independent, remained broadly Labour in outlook, up to Khan's election in 2016 there had been only Johnson's two years between 2008 and 2010 when mayor and government came from opposing sides and by this time the Labour government was in retreat. Does political alignment, or political shaming, lead to a better deal for the capital? This isn't straightforward. Brown's largesse towards London ended up benefiting a Conservative not a Labour mayor. It was investment nonetheless. A fair amount of Cameron/Osborne *schadenfreude* greeted the early farces of Johnson's reign and there was importance in trying to keep him on a tight financial leash. Over Brexit, of course, he could not be kept quiet.

Irrespective of the direct powers or limitations of the office, a few mayoral 'essentials' have become clear: rhetorical flair; a nose for anticipating trouble, and staying ahead of it; a boxer's instinct to turn defence into attack; energy and resilience; and the ability to get the light and the shade right tonally. All three incumbents have been able to speak convincingly *for* the city. But these characteristics only take you so far. Does it feel at this point – two decades in – that force of personality brought to civic leadership can make a big difference, but the impediments are now all too apparent? How do we move from here to real change and delivery?

19

6/7 TO 7/7

NEALE COLEMAN

The period leading up to July 2005 had been one of intense hard work and focus. We had spent huge time and effort developing an uplifting, optimistic, but ultimately deliverable bid that could win the 2012 Olympic Games for London and transform the capital's East End. As we travelled to Singapore, several days before the announcement of the winning hosts on the 6 July, we had no idea what an intensely emotional, significant two-day period it was to prove to be.

Nearly everyone assumed that Paris was going to win. Only those of us really close to the action, those who knew about the work that the London 2012 team had done, thought we had a good chance. We were optimistic, but we knew it was going to be close.

Keith Mills and the London 2012 team were astonishing. We were amazingly well-prepped and rehearsed. Everything was extremely tight and well-organised. It was an incredible place to be, a once-in-a-lifetime moment.

The team was entitled to bring a certain number of people in the delegation, and we decided to use this to bring a group of schoolkids from east London with us. They were terrific. But it was also a brilliant touch, which differentiated us from Paris.

We also had Denise Lewis, Seb Coe, David and Victoria Beckham, all in these matching Jeff Banks beige suits alongside us. Ken Livingstone wore his repeatedly afterwards. Beckham was so good. He was from east London, which was important, and he put a huge amount into whatever we asked of him.

Tony Blair also arrived around the same time as the London mayoral team, with his entourage. Every morning we would meet at 7 a.m., and go through our plans – who was Blair seeing? Who were the other delegates seeing? It was an astonishing operation, working in as many of the International Olympic Committee delegates as possible.

French President Jacques Chirac didn't bother showing up until just before the event. You could feel that things were beginning to go our way. It seemed like the French thought that they were a shoo-in, while we were really working hard.

The main task that we were given was to get the Russians on side. Everyone assumed that they would vote for Paris, but Ken had strong contacts there. Yury Luzhkov, the Mayor of Moscow, was heading their delegation. The day before the vote, we had this extraordinary meeting in Luzhkov's hotel suite, where we signed off on the notion that they would vote for London in the final round, and that in any future Moscow bid, the British IOC delegation would be sympathetic to the Russians. Ken had delivered.

Seb Coe was important too. He was a double Olympic gold medallist, which helped. But I also think that Seb convinced a lot of Madrid votes to switch to London, should Madrid be knocked out, through his connections.

I remember the night before the vote, at about 11 p.m., we were drinking in a bar somewhere in Singapore, with a Norwegian speed skater who happened to have an IOC vote. To this day I have no idea if this did any good. But we were pulling out all the stops. There was this incredible atmosphere to the whole thing. Singapore is a strange, vibrant, fascinating place.

The day of the vote had arrived. We watched the other presentations nervously. But our presentation was sensational. It sold London powerfully. By the end, people had been moved to tears, because it was such a wonderful story about London. It was about youth, legacy and change. It was about having a broader purpose for the games. And we meant it. I'm sure that there were things that could have been done better, but we sought to deliver that change for Stratford, and I think we broadly did.

Our wonderful group of young people were all from Newham, but they had connections to every corner of the world – which is not atypical of Newham or London generally. We sold London as a place of diversity and culture and youth. The Paris bid, by contrast, was stiff and dry, based mostly on the idea that the city was completely prepared as they had all the venues already. We were streets ahead of them.

I was told subsequently – and I will never know if this is true or not – that there were actually three or four delegates who voted for us on the quality of the presentation alone. You don't expect anyone to do that, really, because there is so much pre-negotiation and politics. But our presentation was special.

Then came the voting. Moscow went out, New York went out, and we were sitting there drinking water nervously, because there was little else that we could do. Only Madrid, Paris and London remained, and everything became incredibly tense. We thought that we would lose if we came up against Madrid, because of the various voting blocks. And then Madrid went out, which was a huge relief.

At this stage, the London and Paris teams entered a new room for the announcement. The IOC people were at the front. And this huge phalanx of photographers were camped out in front of the French delegation, on the Paris side of the room. 'Oh God, we've lost', I thought.

But then the announcement came: 'The 2012 Olympic Games are awarded to the city of … London.' And we just went berserk. It was an astonishing, unbelievable emotional moment. The only comparable moment I can think of was being behind the goal at Anfield when Arsenal midfielder Michael Thomas scored the last-minute goal to beat Liverpool to the championship on the final game of the season in 1989. It was incredible.

Once we had settled down a bit, we wandered over to see the French, and they looked so incredibly angry. I think they had been convinced that the Olympics were theirs.

Then we went off to this astonishing party down by the waterfront in Singapore with live music. I will always remember this astonishing scene of Ken Livingstone and Princess Anne jiving together on the stage, it was an extraordinary moment.

The next day, I remember getting up, and most of us were pretty hungover. Singapore is seven hours ahead of the UK, so there was a delay before London woke up. We started planning our triumphant arrival back to London. We intended to take a helicopter out to Stratford where we were expecting a highly celebratory mood and a big moment.

I remember being in the hotel pool with Tony Winterbottom of the LDA. We were saying: this is great, but now we've got to actually do this bloody thing! We've got to hold the Olympics! What are we going to do next?

But then word began to filter through that there was a problem in London, an issue on the Underground, which we initially thought had been some sort of power surge. We were thinking about how embarrassing this was, the day after we had won the bid, after saying how wonderful our transport system was. But then, over the period of about an hour, some of us got the news that it had been a terror attack. I can't recall such a rapid and powerful change of mood, from high to low, in my life.

We didn't get the full news straight away. But as the details began to emerge we tried to get a secure phone line to London. Ken had been out shopping to buy some gifts for his family, and we caught him when he got back, gave him the outline, and then we got him on a secure line and he spoke to the Met commissioner. After that he went and had a swim in the pool at the hotel. He composed the speech that he was going to give in his head, in the pool, while he was swimming. He didn't write anything down.

Then we got him down to a place in the hotel lobby where he could speak to a number of cameras. This was quite difficult, and the setup was quite odd. But Ken delivered an incredibly powerful speech and it was remarkable. Afterwards we got him into the lift to go back up to our room, and he just burst into floods of tears.

Once we were back up, we had to start getting ready to get back to London immediately. There was Ken and Tessa Jowell, me and Seb Coe and a number of others, and we were rushed through Singapore's streets with a police motorcycle escort, to the airport. At first there was a problem with the plane, which led to a frantic scramble to find a flight home. But eventually we made it back and we were rushed through immigration, and then there we were. There was a car waiting to take Ken to meet the Met commissioner, and there was another car waiting to take me home.

And that was that. The celebratory moment had gone. The need to respond to the bombings just took over, quite rightly, and you couldn't really think about the games any more. It was a terrible tragedy. Fifty-two people lost their lives and hundreds of people were injured, Thelma Stober, one of the chief lawyers at the GLA, lost her leg. The high of winning the games vanished entirely. There was a lot to handle, a lot to organise, and a lot to do.

KEN LIVINGSTONE'S SPEECH, SWISSOTEL LOBBY, SINGAPORE, 7 JULY 2005

This was a cowardly attack, which has resulted in injury and loss of life. Our thoughts are with everyone who has been injured, or lost loved ones. I want to thank the emergency services for the way they have responded.

Following the al-Qaeda attacks on September 11th in America we conducted a series of exercises in London in order to be prepared for just such an attack. One of the exercises undertaken by the government, my office and the emergency and security services was based on the possibility of multiple explosions on the transport system during the Friday rush hour. The plan that came out of that exercise is being executed today, with remarkable efficiency and courage, and I praise those staff who are involved.

I'd like to thank Londoners for the calm way in which they have responded to this cowardly attack and echo the advice of the Metropolitan Police Commissioner Sir Ian Blair – do everything possible to assist the police and take the advice of the police about getting home today.

I have no doubt whatsoever that this is a terrorist attack. We did hope in the first few minutes after hearing about the events on the Underground that it might simply be a maintenance tragedy. That was not the case. I have been able to stay in touch through the very excellent communications that were established for the eventuality that I might be out of the city at the time of a terrorist attack and they have worked with remarkable effectiveness. I will be in continual contact until I am back in London.

I want to say one thing specifically to the world today. This was not a terrorist attack against the mighty and the powerful. It was not aimed at Presidents or Prime Ministers. It was aimed at ordinary, working-class Londoners, black and white, Muslim and Christian, Hindu and Jew, young and old. It was an indiscriminate attempt to slaughter, irrespective of any considerations for age, for class, for religion, or whatever.

That isn't an ideology, it isn't even a perverted faith – it is just an indiscriminate attempt at mass murder and we know what the objective is. They seek to divide Londoners. They seek to turn Londoners against each other. I said yesterday to the International Olympic Committee, that the city of London is the greatest in the world, because everybody lives side by side in harmony. Londoners will not be divided by this cowardly attack. They will stand together in solidarity alongside those who have been injured and those who have been bereaved and that is why I'm proud to be the mayor of that city.

Finally, I wish to speak directly to those who came to London today to take life.

I know that you personally do not fear giving up your own life in order to take others – that is why you are so dangerous. But I know you fear that you may fail in your long-term objective to destroy our free society and I can show you why you will fail.

In the days that follow look at our airports, look at our sea ports and look at our railway stations and, even after your cowardly attack, you will see that people from the rest of Britain, people from around the world, will arrive in London to become Londoners and to fulfil their dreams and achieve their potential.

They choose to come to London, as so many have come before, because they come to be free, they come to live the life they choose, they come to be able to be themselves. They flee you because you tell them how they should live. They don't want that and nothing you do, however many of us you kill, will stop that flight to our city where freedom is strong and where people can live in harmony with one another. Whatever you do, however many you kill, you will fail.

CULTURE AND SOFT POWER

PATRICIA BROWN

I did not know that it was possible to actually jump for joy, until I did. It was 6 July 2005, shortly after noon, and after rubbing shoulders with throngs of Olympic delegates, we were sitting holding our breath as IOC president Jacques Rogge drew out his announcement that the thirtieth Olympiad was being 'awarded to … the city of London'.

When London's delegation had walked into Singapore's Raffles hotel ballroom to deliver its presentation, among the 100 delegates were thirty young children who each stood hand-in-hand with a sports ambassador. They were drawn from schools across east London, from twenty-eight different ethnic backgrounds. This was an important element of London's pitch perfect presentation, the combination of a warm welcome to the world with a strong focus on legacy and young people, representing London at its best: showcasing the city's values, diversity and the strength of its cultural and creative heartbeat.

Ken Livingstone had been Mayor of London for just over five years at this time. As such, he not only had to set up his administration, but set the tone for the capital, and we can look back to his legacy as leader of the GLC for aspects that would define his administration, as well as the capital's direction.

LONDON BEFORE THE MAYOR

Livingstone took the helm as Mayor of London in 2000 at a turning point in the capital's story. Neglected by a national government actively planning for its depopulation, buffered by recession and after a period of decline, the city had finally been gathering confidence, intent on determining its own destiny.[1] The post-GLC years had already given rise to a number of initiatives that kept a strategic eye on London. It was one, the London Planning Advisory Committee's *London: World City* report, which in turn spawned the capital's first inward investment body, London First Centre.[2] The centre was chaired by British Airways' Sir Colin Marshall, and was established to leverage the growing interest from business to shape the city's direction.

Staff at LFC knew that quality of life featured highly as a key investment criteria, along with the ability to access and retain talent, so the city's 'unparalleled cultural offer' and depth of creative services featured prominently in LFC's promotional material. London's creative businesses helped lure more design-led business to the city, including the design offices for Samsung, Nissan and Ford; part of the virtuous circle of London's talent pool and creative magnetism.

London's cultural institutions, such as the Imperial War Museum and the V&A, were also helping to refresh the capital, in part as a result of a massive injection of cash from the National Lottery, with awards judiciously distributed to projects that could demonstrate exponential change in terms of audience reach as well as design excellence.[3] This culture-led regeneration and renewal helped to open up parts of London, aimed at generating jobs and opportunities for local people, as well as being part of the early efforts to reinvent our public realm by giving space back to the people. This was the embodiment of the Labour government's 'urban renaissance'.

Livingstone's GLC had played a powerful role in changing the perception of London among its citizens; laying down the tenets of an international, multicultural, multi-everything city, where everyone could find their place, regardless of gender, ethnicity or sexuality. Ten years on, this 'power to be anything you want' featured strongly in LFC's promotional messages.

Similarly, the GLC's focus on culture and creative industries, through its industrial and economic strategies, as well as support for grassroots cultural organisations and festivals – the 'bread and circuses' approach, according to some commentators – had also helped lay the foundation for post-millennium London. Many of the people behind the GLC's strategies and programmes would help set the direction for Livingstone's GLA.

The late 1990s heralded a growing sense of self-determination over London's destiny, with greater confidence and an appetite for doing new things; increasingly championed by the private and cultural sectors.

It was evident that the London of this time could already claim to be – if only it chose to say it – the cultural and creative capital of the world. The strength and depth of the culture sector in London and its cumulative impact outstripped other cities. We led on advertising, design and creative services, and we were strong in fashion and film. Sections of the industry were innovating in technology to build 'Soho-net', which would soon make the Soho area the world leader in special effects for film and advertising.

That the sector could start to be seen and taken seriously as a key economic driver was largely down to a handful of people who first attempted to measure and define it; which led to the 1998 'Creative Industries Mapping Document' that truly cemented the sector within the newly formed Department for Culture, Media and Sport, led by secretary of state Chris Smith. By 2001, when this was updated, it was estimated that the sector generated £112.5 billion in revenue and employed 1.3 million people, 50 per cent of whom were based in London and the south-east.[4]

It was the age of 'Cool Britannia' and glittering receptions hosted by Tony Blair as his government sought to redefine the UK's image away from one of heritage and pinstriped bankers, towards creative entrepreneurs and culture.

LIVINGSTONE: LONDON'S FIRST DIRECTLY ELECTED MAYOR

This was the London that elected Livingstone, giving him leadership over the GLA, the newly formed Transport for London and the London Development Agency, and through them, control and influence over key London promotional agencies, including Think London and Visit London (formerly the London First Centre and the London Tourist Board).

Livingstone had been practising for the role for decades and, having backed cultural and creative industries in his role in the first-incarnation London government, it was easy to persuade him to embrace his cultural brief; especially as a way of asserting London's progressive values and to build London's reputation across the globe.

This was in part why the architects of the Greater London Authority Act 1999 had included culture as a mayoral strategic priority, as they knew that it would play an important part in the mayor's influencing role. The Act required the mayor to establish an independent Cultural Strategy Group, tasked with preparing a draft culture strategy.[5] The final culture strategy was to be published and owned by the mayor, who had the ultimate power to require modifications as well as the duty to ensure that the plan was reviewed periodically.

As an independent mayor, Livingstone chose for his deputy Labour assembly member Nicky Gavron, who'd been at the forefront of London's cultural development for several decades and was as passionate about the arts as about planning and sustainability. He also appointed a number of trusted advisors, including economic advisor John Ross, and Jude Woodward as lead cultural and creative industries advisor.

The confluence of Livingstone's statutory strategic responsibility to produce both cultural and economic development strategies, and his track record for tone-setting through investing in the capital's cultural life, meant that the administration wasted little time in defining its approach to cultural activity. Many were policies drawn from Livingstone's GLC tenure with a twist, updated for a modern era and embracing capitalism; confidently using culture and the creative sector to both define London's global image and leverage its significant wealth creation.

One of Livingstone's first, and symbolic, acts was to commit £25 million to undertake the stuttering reconfiguration of Trafalgar Square. The Greater London Authority Act had transferred responsibility for the square to the mayor and a redesign by Foster and Partners created a better experience and improved connectivity for visitors, providing a stage for many of the events and festivals which were about to be unleashed on the capital. Such events ranged from a St Patrick's Day celebration to the revived free anti-racism music festival, Rise. Livingstone later attributed a 35 per cent decrease in racist attacks between 2001 and 2005 to this and other anti-racist policies in the capital.[6]

While some criticised the approach by saying that it harked back to the 'bread and circuses' policies of the GLC, it formed an important part of the vision and the values the mayor wanted to espouse. Along with the choice of the London Eye for the New Year's Eve fireworks spectacular, Livingstone wanted the world to be in no doubt that London was a modern and ambitious place and the most diverse, inclusive and cosmopolitan city on earth. And he had the LDA's remit and budget and his promotional bodies to help.

Despite London's gathering confidence in the 1990s, it had been lacking a voice on the world stage and it was expected that the London mayor would take on that role. Livingstone was also a 'brand' and while not instantly inclined to travel, he was persuaded of the importance of building international networks. It was especially in the city-to-city role that the new administration started to forge links and began to become a strong player. It was Nicky Gavron who, in

London's rudderless years, was highly influential in the development of the C40 Cities climate change network, ensuring that London had a leadership role in climate and sustainability. Livingstone's endorsement of London's continued role did much to establish the mayoralty as a global leader.

Under Livingstone relationships were built with other city mayors, from New York to Moscow, Paris and Berlin, and partnerships were created with Delhi and Shanghai. It was in London's trade and investment and overseas promotion that these city-to-city relationships came into their own, helping the capital penetrate quickly into business and civic networks.

Meanwhile, the LDA's early work had been boosted by the legacy of the London Development Partnership, a voluntary shadow body, whose work included a major study of London's creative sector. This corresponded surprisingly well with the emerging agenda of the LDA, led by Michael Ward, the former head of Livingstone's Greater London Enterprise Board.

While actively building a platform of bottom-up cultural events, Livingstone and his team took the creative sector into the economic mainstream, to grow London's economy within the 21st-century globalised world. The LDA's significant body of work on the creative industries included the mayor's Commission on the Creative Industries.[7] This was established in 2002 and run by a specialist unit, Creative London. The final report of the commission – 'Creative London' – was intended as a manifesto, guiding the unit's work until it was disbanded in 2006.[8]

The LDA also put major financial backing and resources into some significant initiatives – including Film London, London Fashion Week and London Design Festival – that had already been established by industry leaders to promote and grow different parts of the creative ecosystem. These in turn helped strengthen London's overseas image and its investment proposition.

To provide greater coordination, Livingstone's team formed an umbrella body, London Unlimited, that brought the various promotional bodies and other key organisations together to brand London consistently. It built a network of overseas offices to foster and strengthen local relationships and networks, and to help entice business and investment, visitors and students to London. This coordination was also key in the content and approach to telling London's story; events held overseas would be designed to showcase the diversity of London's cultural offering and its talent, but also frequently promoting the host country or city's culture in London. Again, London was used as a stage, as was seen with the organisation of an international game of chess to mark the Russian Winter Festival in 2007, which was played using giant chess pieces made of ice in both London and Moscow, via satellite.

Even though Livingstone started out as an independent mayor, his ambition for and the way he embraced cultural and creative industries found considerable common cause with the national Labour government. In 2001, Chris Smith was replaced by Tessa Jowell as secretary of state for culture, media and sport and in 2004 the newly re-elected (by then) Labour mayor invited Smith to chair the London Cultural Consortium; a reconfiguration of the Cultural Strategy Group for London, which was tasked with the role of taking forward the implementation of the 'Culture Strategy for London'. This ten-year framework, published in April 2004, aimed to develop London as a centre of cultural excellence and creativity and was thought to be the world's first-ever integrated cultural plan: not only a strategic and coordinated approach to arts, sport, heritage and creative industries in the capital, but strategically linked to wider issues – such as transport, spatial development, the economy and the environment.[9]

During the first two mayoral terms, both government and private sector money was poured into London's renewal. Commercial investment in large-scale development was opening up swathes of London, and the business community was becoming a major influencer and investor in shaping London's streets and spaces to create a walkable, liveable London. Probably the most high-profile example was the establishment of business improvement districts, based on the North American model, and first introduced by Central London Partnership, with LDA financial backing.[10]

During this time funds from the Lottery, LDA and TfL were rebuilding or creating cultural venues and London's public realm infrastructure. The architect of the UK government's 'urban renaissance' policy, Richard Rogers, was also advising the mayor in his approach to design, especially on housing and public space. There was an increased sense of 'public-ness', and stages large and small were emerging – spaces for events and gatherings and for simply enjoying being in the city, frequently led by cultural institutions.

Across the city high-quality public art was taking a greater priority, exemplified by the commissioning of art for the fourth plinth in Trafalgar Square, which first occurred in 1999. Initially conceived by Royal Society of Arts chair Prue Leith, this led to the GLA's Fourth Plinth Commission, that has since become one of the most high-profile public art commissions in the world.

This was the background to London winning the 2012 Olympics, largely thanks to culture secretary Tessa Jowell, who had challenged the opposition to a bid among Blair and his Cabinet. The mayoral family set to work on its plans to make the city Olympics-ready and lay the foundation for legacy, unlocking investment in a range of transport projects. Most are mentioned elsewhere in this book and include the stalled upgrade of King's Cross Station, helping to cement the future of Argent's long-evolved King's Cross project, and the upgrade and extension of the east London line into London Overground.

Livingstone's agencies used the games to win business and tourism for London and the UK, and worked alongside the Department for

Culture, Media and Sport leadership of the Cultural Olympiad, to embed a wider cultural offer into the Olympic visitor experience.

JOHNSON'S TENURE

It was a new mayor, Boris Johnson, who would eventually lead London in 2012, and he had inherited a confident global city. Johnson was another 'personality mayor' who, recognising a good opportunity, was happy to rely on London's global creative pre-eminence to provide stories and memorable moments to drive home his message that London was the 'greatest city on earth'. In fact, he was content with continuity in this area; Livingstone's appointee Jude Woodward stayed for a short time, while another Livingstone aide, Neale Coleman, remained his Olympic advisor right through to the 2012 games.

It was Justine Simons who would provide the most significant consistency. Having started during Lola Young's tenure as head of culture, Simons worked alongside Munira Mirza when Mirza joined City Hall in 2008, initially as Johnson's cultural advisor, and eventually became deputy mayor for education and culture in 2012. Johnson's Cultural Strategy Group was chaired from 2008 to 2012 by Whitechapel Gallery director Iwona Blazwick. The former editor of the *Evening Standard*, Veronica Wadley, became a senior advisor to the Mayor of London in 2012, and subsequently as chair of the Arts Council London, an appointment that attracted a fair amount of controversy.[11]

It was often observed that Johnson had little interest in policy details, and was happy to largely delegate this to his deputies and trusted advisors. Culture was no exception, and Mirza steered the mayor's cultural policy throughout his tenure, drawing on Simons and a strong team, both of whom were seen as helpful fixers by some creative sector leaders.

While the mayor largely maintained the architecture of the GLA's events programme, such as the Fourth Plinth Commission and the Big Dance, Johnson's City Hall still put its stamp on the capital's cultural life. With the publication in late 2008 of its cultural strategy, 'Cultural Metropolis', chunks of Livingstone's 'bread and circuses' policy were abandoned, including paring back events in Trafalgar Square.[12]

The strategy reflected the administration's belief in the arts being challenging rather than simply accessible, with a pitch for excellence (or, according to some, elitism). Mirza challenged the assumption that young people only liked art that they could immediately relate to, restricted to hip-hop and movies, and instead wanted to offer access to high culture. Music education was a feature: No Strings Attached, backed by Julian Lloyd Webber, encouraged people to donate unused musical instruments to be used by children; an annual schools music festival was launched, while the mayor's Fund for Young Musicians raised money for music scholarships. The strategy looked forward to the Olympics, and included plans for a pan-London festival entitled 'The Story of London', as a celebration of London's people and history, which was somewhat scaled back in its actual delivery.

The mayor looked to Daniel Moylan, then deputy chair of TfL and deputy leader of Kensington and Chelsea Council, to champion the approach to London's public realm ahead of the Olympics. Moylan was behind the radical re-modelling of Exhibition Road, financially supported by the mayor, and intended to provide an improved public realm and visitor experience to one of London's core cultural quarters.

The global financial downturn started just after Johnson's first term in office began and hit London's financial services sector hard. Two years later, the 2010 general election ushered in a government that was committed to deep cuts to public spending and a 'bonfire of the quangos' that would formally disband the LDA in 2012.

Ahead of this, Johnson began his own cuts as part of the regime change. While sparing the Party in the Mall in London, he cut back heavily on the high-profile events programme planned to take place throughout Beijing for the Beijing Olympic handover. London Unlimited was axed, as was Think London's budget, eventually merging the city's promotional bodies into one institution, London & Partners. This reform resulted from a desire to hone a coordinated set of messaging and marketing and to offer a single portal in the run-up to the Olympics, all with a reduced budget. Overseas offices remained, although GLA staff were removed, and the strategy that had begun in 2006 was continued, forging links with international business ahead of the games, culminating in the Mayor of London's 2012 Business Programme; engaging over 200 business leaders from twenty-eight countries in tailored seminars, networking events and tours of London's cultural highlights, as well as attending the games themselves.[13]

This linked to the government-supported Tech City UK, capitalising on the growth of digital economy businesses. Many of these were clustered around Shoreditch, giving rise to Prime Minister Cameron's branding of the area as 'Silicon Roundabout'. Regardless of the hype around this it became a huge growth sector, with a 92 per cent increase in new digital companies incorporated in inner London between 2010 and 2013, which provided 251,590 jobs by 2015.[14]

In fact, the growth of this creative cluster also started having a profound impact on the look and feel of London. The property industry started to respond to the growing desire for flexible, well-designed, interesting spaces; a trend set particularly by Derwent London, illustrated by the success of its Tea Building and White Collar Factory in Shoreditch.

In a cruel twist of timing, the LDA closed its doors just ahead of London's 2012 spectacular that it helped to engineer. Along with the LDA's demise went the funding for London's creative infrastructure. While the culture team fought successfully to have some budgets moved into City Hall, London's economic development knowledge and approach was weakened and, arguably, it has never fully recovered.

Undoubtedly, London scrubbed up well in 2012 and delivered thousands of events in the public realm that were programmed to complement – rather than compete with – the sporting calendar, to provide additional colour when the media was in town. As stories and images of London's civic triumph spread around the globe – and even as austerity was taking chunks out of London's civic life – London was changing and growing. Globalisation, and the sheer amount of mobile foreign investment into London's real estate, actively wooed by Johnson's administration, meant that London's character shape-shifted; parts of the city flipped from being part of an 'urban renaissance' into, arguably, a form of over-gentrification.

Mark Twain's exhortation to buy land, since 'they're not making it any more' rang particularly true. By the end of Johnson's final term, London had reached a tipping point. Its population, housing growth and land use changes – accelerated by permitted development rights, which allow for a change of use without applying for planning permission – had started to undermine the city's cultural ecosystem.

This had an impact across the board: over the decade to 2019 London lost 35 per cent of its grassroots music venues and 61 per cent of its LGBT+ venues. There were approximately 14,000 artists on waiting lists for studios.[15]

London's film industry also illustrates the tensions in demand, and the significant brake on investment into the capital that results from this tension. In 2019 film brought in £1.3 billion of inward investment to London and 4,000 production companies had a combined turnover of £2 billion.[16] Since 2010, feature and TV drama filming in the capital has increased by 121 per cent.[17] Yet while the demand for the UK's film facilities and infrastructure is constant and increasing, valuable studio space has been lost over this period, such as Teddington Studios and part of the BBC Television Centre at White City – largely to property development – and new investment has struggled to find space in or close to London. There will be a welcome expansion in Barking and Dagenham, where the borough is investing £110 million to create a studio and entertainment complex covering twenty-two acres which is expected to create around 1,200 jobs; jobs that are, given their technical and creative nature, largely 'AI-proof' according to Adrian Wootton of the British Film Commission.[18]

KHAN'S MAYORALTY

Concerns about creative space in the capital have also worried the Cultural Strategy Group. Encouraged by Munira Mirza, the group set out a series of potential solutions in a briefing offered to 2016 mayoral candidates. Sadiq Khan alone responded directly to this briefing, and placed culture among his top priorities from the start of his mayoralty, appointing Justine Simons as deputy mayor for culture and creative industries. Indeed, an important thread in London's cultural story is of continuity, of policy and key officers, offering sustained relationships and institutional memory.

Within weeks of taking office, Khan found himself leading a Remain-voting capital city, out of step with many parts of the UK which had voted Leave. The administration lost no time in mobilising the city's cultural community in support of his response: the London Is Open campaign, established to celebrate the values that had made London the city that it is.

To strengthen its direct foreign investment programme in the face of Brexit the mayor increased London & Partners' budget – by £1.355 million in 2018/19, and by £1.236 million in subsequent years.[19] This increase was provided specifically to help grow its European net-work, ensuring that London remains strongly connected to business opportunities.

Alongside Brexit, London's tragic escalation of knife crime and terrorist attacks mean that Khan has had his work cut out. His administration has also had to grapple with other challenges, in part born from the unintended consequences of success: expansion and growth; competing demands for diminishing space and financial resources. Yet he remained steadfast to culture as a priority and his team was sure-footed on what was needed. They knew the scale of the problem and how to both 'hard wire' culture into London and future-proof it.

The mayor's 2018 strategy, 'Culture for all Londoners', set out a vision and plan to sustain London's position as a global capital of culture, while a reconfigured 'cultural leadership board' brings together people who help guide specific leadership areas. This is chaired by Ben Evans, who as co-founder and director of London Design Festival is a key figure in the promotion of London's creativity.[20]

The strategy seeks to simultaneously maintain London's 'world city' status while also helping more Londoners experience and create culture on their doorstep. What sets the current approach apart is how it meshes with the mayor's wider strategies, especially in strengthening the relationship between culture and planning policy, with a dedicated chapter on heritage and culture in Khan's draft London Plan. London will probably be the first city to protect artists' studios in its strategic planning strategy, which fits in well with Khan's emphasis on 'good growth'.

The fact that large parts of London are now unaffordable to the artists and creatives that helped give London its vibrancy means the city must work on various fronts to stave off further damage. It is for that reason many of the mayor's initiatives focus on ways of supporting the cultural infrastructure, guided by a 'Cultural Infrastructure Plan', setting out how London can support and grow cultural spaces for generations to come.

A 'Culture at Risk Office' was established as a dedicated frontline emergency service – a 'bat phone' – offering help and advice. Six creative enterprise zones – delivered in partnership with London boroughs – are set to deliver 40,000 square-feet of permanent studio space, while the Creative Land Trust has been established to further support affordable creative workspace.

The capital's 24-hour economy is championed by Amy Lamé, who was made the Night Czar in 2016 and is supported by a Night Time

Commission. A 'Sounds Like London' programme was also created to celebrate London's music scene. Waltham Forest was the first borough to become the London Borough of Culture, inspired by the UK City of Culture and the European Capital of Culture programmes, with the ambition of putting culture at the heart of local communities. Brent followed in 2020.

This chapter began with the Olympics and the plans to build a legacy through the regeneration of east London, so it is fitting that one of the most ambitious programmes for the capital is East Bank, a new culture and education district at the Queen Elizabeth Olympic Park. Meanwhile, heading further east, the Thames Estuary Production Corridor is a collaboration between authorities in Essex, Kent and London to – among other things – utilise the land the area offers in support of the creative sector.

This is an example of the collaboration that London increasingly needs, since the city is not an island. Nonetheless, some say that there has been a rise in 'London envy', even though its mayors have, mostly, seen London as a trojan horse for investment and tourism into the UK more generally. The creation of city mayors is a policy that has strengthened the economic performance of English city-regions and Sadiq Khan participates regularly in a forum that shares best practice and dialogue.

Khan is now vice-chair of the C40 Cities Climate Leadership Group steering committee and, in the face of Brexit, these global networks are even more critical to London's sustained 'soft power' role. Maintaining a global profile has not been easy for London's mayors, given that international travel can leave them open to media criticism. Over time critics have become noisier and the politics of London meaner, which has reduced City Hall's appetite for international travel further. This factor, in turn, has led to increasing criticism of Khan as lacking in a new big picture and vision for London.

At the start of this story was the recognition that London's economic destiny was dependent on talent, and it is the talent, creativity and energy of the city's people and business community that were and remain part of its success story. Maybe what is missing is the hunger that London felt in the late 1990s, when the capital's businesses were ready to lend their voice and money to be part of a new solution.

While all three mayors have come to the cultural brief from a different point of view and intent, it's arguable if any of them have had a true personal passion for culture. Though in different ways, each mayor has grasped the importance and potential of the portfolio to help fulfil their ambition for the city. Throughout, culture has been at the table; reflecting its importance in City Hall policies and approach.

What is certain is that London has plotted a positive path over the past twenty years. Its creative economy has been an important part of this, responsible for one in six of the capital's jobs. The number of jobs in the sector has grown by 31.8 per cent between 2011 and 2017, against 20.8 per cent for the economy as a whole.[21] Yet changes affecting the city outlined elsewhere mean that the mayor has to work hard to sustain the fabric that has helped lead to that success and is so key to both quality of life and the success of the city's economy. London's cultural roots have to be nurtured to sustain a healthy ecology where talent can continue to flourish, contributing to an industry that now generates £52 billion for the city every year, with a further £40 billion spent through the supply chain.[22] As such, culture is vital to London's economy. But more than that, it is intrinsically bound up with the UK's soft power as well as being vital to the wellbeing of Londoners, the values of the city and its civic life.

21

CYCLING IN LONDON

ISABEL DEDRING

Over the first two decades of London's mayoralty, cycling in the city has been transformed. There have been a number of big inflection points in this story, but none bigger than 2011.

In the early years of the mayoralty, cycling was not a top priority for London government. Ken supported cycling as part of his commitment to action on climate change. But it was just one of the many priorities for his administration, and it had a small political profile. What miniscule cycling budget there was was partly thanks to the Green Party who held the balance of power in the assembly, which had to approve the mayoral budget.

Boris Johnson arrived at City Hall in 2008 with a personal passion for cycling and a stated commitment to get more people cycling in London. In the run-up to the election at TfL we worked through how we might deliver the manifesto commitments made by the individual candidates. Xavier Brice (now running Sustrans, which strives to make it easier for people to cycle and walk) and others developed some early work that we had done for Ken further – ideas for a cycle-hire scheme, a network of fast commuter-friendly cycling routes and neighbourhood-based, high-quality cycling zones. In the weeks after the election, we presented our ideas to Boris. A few 'recce' cycle trips with TfL later – including one in which he was nearly knocked off his bike – and the plan was largely agreed.

The first cycle 'superhighways' and the cycle-hire scheme formed the bones of the initial approach that was adopted, but the resourcing was not in place to deliver a truly ambitious and high-quality plan. It was still a relatively niche area, and it was in competition with many other transport priorities. However, there were a number of things that came together in 2011 that accelerated the pace of change.

Boris had been a strong personal advocate for cycling, which made it a target but also raised its profile. The first superhighways were less than super in many places – they were not entirely segregated from other traffic, and they were criticised for not being built to a sufficiently high standard. As the 2012 mayoral election loomed on the horizon, all the mayoral candidates were pressed to sign up to the 'Love London, Go Dutch' commitment launched by the London Cycling Campaign, which argued that people should be able to cycle safely 'from ages eight to eighty'. The political opposition in the assembly helped pile on the pressure – Val Shawcross, transport lead for Labour, and Caroline Pidgeon for the Lib Dems were both brilliant, peppering us with a barrage of uncomfortable, but effective queries each month at Mayor's Question Time: 'What are the top-fifty most dangerous junctions in London?' 'How many people have died and where?' 'What are you doing about it?'

At the same time, outside lobby groups were changing. People like Danny Williams, who runs the blog 'Cyclist in the City', were raising the profile of cycling in London and influencing policy very effectively through social media. The third sector had become suddenly more agile, with new 'tools' and constituents, and far more effective and hence politically 'scarier'.

Then, tragically, there were a number of high-profile cyclist deaths in 2011. Brian Dorling, a 58-year-old man with young children, was killed by a lorry at Bow roundabout in October. Just over two weeks later, a 34-year-old woman named Svitlana Tereschenko was killed on the other side of the same roundabout. The atmosphere became febrile. There were a series of candlelight vigils held in Bow, which had been long recognised as a notorious blackspot for cycling in London. There were cyclist 'die-ins', including outside TfL headquarters, with hundreds of people lying down in the middle of the road.

A number of key journalists took particular interest in the issue, including Tom Edwards, transport correspondent for BBC London, and Ross Lydall at the *Evening Standard*. At *The Times*, Kaya Burgess and then editor James Harding ran a campaign on cycle safety after one of their journalists had a serious accident. I remember an intense meeting with Boris in *The Times* offices in St Katherine's Dock where James raked us over the coals.

For me personally, a turning point came with the development of the Blackfriars Bridge northern junction. I knew that what we were doing needed to be better, but I wasn't sure exactly what this looked like. We didn't have the right people in the GLA, with the right experience, to design what was needed. We had put forward a proposal to improve cycling provision that wasn't adequate, and it became a focal point for criticism of the mayor. I decided to reach out to some of the cycling bloggers personally – I'd never met them before, and I didn't know what to expect. So we had a sort of cloak-and-dagger meeting on Blackfriars Bridge ('I'll be wearing a green raincoat' type of thing), we looked at the junction together and then went and had a coffee. They more or less drew a picture on a napkin of what a good design would be for the junction – and this basically became what was built.

This signalled the beginning of an exciting period where I worked behind the scenes with those 'outside the tent' to work in detail on better interventions – which in parallel built political consensus.

However, we still had loads of difficult moments. The 'mini-Holland' proposals to improve cycling conditions in Waltham Forest led to protests, with a coffin being carried through the area to proclaim the death of the high street. The proposed east–west cycle superhighway running along the Thames became an epic political battleground, and led to months of meetings between Andrew Gilligan, the new cycling commissioner, TfL and players from key institutions ranging from Buckingham Palace to the Tower of London about individual metres of road, timings of specific traffic lights and numerous iterations of bollard designs. We had to get our proposed budget – £1 billion over ten years – through the TfL board: the board members were split, and we needed the support from all of our 'fifth column' of co-conspirators – officials, journalists, political opponents and bloggers. We were texting each other during the real-time broadcast of the meeting and we were elated when we got it through.

Today, cycling continues to evolve at pace in London thanks in part to the key development in 2011. It shows how the non-linear pace of politics (which can sometimes be glacial) can be a force for good – once things get going, they can move fast. It is an example of the positive power of social media in politics – connecting people who aren't 'the usual suspects' and creating porosity in government. It shows how having a small number of individuals, who are formally on opposing sides of a debate, but who share a common aim, can work together to deliver a step-change for our city.

22

ARCHITECTURE AND DESIGN
DEYAN SUDJIC

INTRODUCTION

Being the Mayor of London is a highly personalised position, perhaps inevitably focused on one individual and their 'vision' for the capital. In her analysis of Ken Livingstone's 2004 London Plan and Boris Johnson's 2009 equivalent, LSE's Nancy Holman makes the essential point that both mayors produced highly personal visions rather than abstract systems for London's future growth.[1] This stood in stark contrast to the Abercrombie Plan of 1944 and the Greater London Development Plan of 1969, which were the most significant previous attempts to plan the UK's capital city in modern times. Livingstone's plan even went as far as to use the phrase 'my vision for London'.[2] But have these individualised mayoral visions for the capital been realised?

AN UN-BRITISH APPROACH?

Both Livingstone and Johnson's approach to setting out their visions for London had more in common with the practices of mainland Europe, and the United States, where mayors and presidents alike have delighted in letting loose bulldozers and cranes to build cities in their own image. From Barcelona to Shanghai, city mayors have taken to collecting trophy buildings designed by what have been described as a 'flying circus' of a group of perpetually jet-lagged architects.

The role of the Mayor of Paris is one that the French government has abolished more than once in the past, when its incumbents challenged governmental authority or risked becoming too politically powerful. On stepping into the role, Jacques Chirac declared: '*L'architecte en chef, c'est moi*' ('The chief architect is me'), before killing off the Les Halles markets redevelopment plan that had been initiated by the President, Valery Giscard d'Estaing, in favour of his own choice.[3]

Until the introduction of directly elected mayors, this was simply not the kind of thing that a British politician would have dared to say, or still less try to do. Ever since the disgraced former Newcastle council boss, T. Dan Smith, tried to bring the design of Brasília and Arne Jacobsen to Tyneside, the whole idea of combining politics with architecture has felt toxic. It is inconceivable that a traditional Labour council leader would ever have claimed, as Livingstone did, that it was his duty as mayor to lead, rather than to listen; a destiny manifest in his decisions on everything from questions of aesthetics, to the westwards extension of the Congestion Charge Zone. Nor would such a figure earmark £100,000 from the Greater London Authority's budget, as Livingstone did, to defend his personal choice of location for a singularly lifeless tribute to Nelson Mandela in court.[4]

AN UNPLANNABLE CITY?

Both Livingstone and Johnson have relished the chance to demonstrate that they are indeed London's architect in chief. But this hubris has had less of an impact than they might have hoped. London has tended to shrug off attempts to tame or direct its growth, ever since its citizens ignored the attempts of Tudor monarchs to prevent the growth of the suburbs outside its city walls, or later refused to accept Christopher Wren's masterplan for the city's reconstruction after the Great Fire in 1666.

London is a city of unintended consequences as much as it is one of personal visions. Its long rush westwards, for example, was given a massive and entirely unintended boost by the wartime creation of a heavy bomber aerodrome at Heathrow that later became Europe's busiest airport. The great lurch east of the 1990s, driven by the eruption of the Canary Wharf development, was an equally unintended consequence of the area's enterprise zone status and the establishment of the Urban Development Corporation, which was intended to support industrial employment rather than the building of skyscrapers.

Certainly London has had large-scale urban visions in the past. Regency London saw John Nash build the Mall, Haymarket, Piccadilly Circus and Regent Street on a scale heroic enough to inspire Napoleon III to remodel Paris. Later, the London Underground would set the pace for the Paris metro. The Barbican, London Wall and Paternoster Square were all the product of carefully considered planning strategies, not all of which proved successful in the long term. But in most of its history London has changed and grown almost of its own accord, through pragmatism rather than by design.

All three mayors have pursued projects based on their own personal preferences. They have been at their most effective when they have kept their egos in check, and used their interventions to nudge the city rather than attempt to force it into patterns with which it is uncomfortable. Sometimes they might have done better not to push it even faster down a path on which it was already rushing. The results have been mixed, but we can see something of each of Livingstone, Johnson and Khan in the ever-changing London of 2020.

LIVINGSTONE'S LONDON

It could be said that a key positive development under Livingstone was the introduction of the Oyster card, a tiny object that eventually led to the contactless payment system that replaced it in 2014. The system has become a distillation of all the achievements of Transport for London, the integrated transport system which must be seen as one of the most transformational and enduring aspects of his time in office.

But perhaps a more conspicuous and quintessentially Livingstonian artefact is the Shard, Renzo Piano's 310-metre-high skyscraper, which sits next to London Bridge Station. The building sums up so many aspects of Livingstone's ideas about London. Livingstone's London Plan of 2004 refers to London as a 'world city' no fewer than forty-four times.[5] His essential vision was to work with the City of London Corporation to make London the world's financial capital. This was the key to persuading central government to fund investment in the capital, from transport to the Olympics. In Livingstone's mind, a world city demanded a visible expression of its status. It would have to look the part, which meant a slightly needy, attention-seeking skyscraper-decked skyline to match that of Shanghai.

Since construction finished in 2012, it is hard to remember just how much of a reversal of the conventional wisdom about London it represents. In 1984, it took nothing more challenging than an insignificant extension to the National Gallery, less than 100ft tall, to goad the Prince of Wales and his supporters to such a fever pitch of fury that it took twenty years for the architectural profession to fully recover. The Mies van der Rohe development opposite the Mansion House involved a tower that was just eighteen floors high, which the Prince of Wales vetoed for fear of the damage it would do to London's skyline.[6]

In 2001, shortly after the Taliban's destruction of the two ancient Buddhas of Bamiyan in the Hazarajat region of Afghanistan, Ken Livingstone was shameless enough to call English Heritage 'the Heritage Taliban' for trying to stop business tycoon Gerald Ronson from building a tower at 110 Bishopsgate, immediately east of Liverpool Street Station.[7] Livingstone suggested that it was an investment in the future of London. But Heron Tower turned out to be a 46-storey-high battering ram, tipped by a decorative steel needle, that tore its way through the previously accepted view of what central London should look like. It set a precedent for countless other towers.

It was deputy Prime Minister and secretary of state for environment, transport and the regions John Prescott who took the final decisions on both the Ronson tower at 110 Bishopsgate, designed by Kohn Pederson Fox, and on the still more damaging Vauxhall Cross residential tower. Neither were of a size to match the Shard, yet another short-lived attempt at Europe's tallest tower – the building that Livingstone personally made possible by directing TfL to sign a lease for ten floors of its office space off-plan, transforming the fragile finances for the project. In the event, office rents rose fast enough for TfL to make a profit when they were bought out of their lease before the project was completed. Their signature on a lease had done its job. It made the development look credible to the banks to finance the project.

The Commission for Architecture and the Built Environment (CABE), established in Tony Blair's first term in office and charged with safeguarding architectural quality, played its part in the development of London too. Rather than object to the scale of the new buildings, it concentrated on ensuring that approved architects got to build them. 'The city certainly won't draw a line that says "people can go this high, and no higher"', CABE's deputy chair Paul Finch said at the time.[8] 'Developers believe that they stand a better chance of getting planning permission if they use a good architect, and that is leading to the kind of architecture we are seeing now'. It's the reason that Sellars talked to Renzo Piano about the Shard project and sidelined its original architects, Broadway Malyan.

Livingstone had planned on giving London skyscrapers, and also 100 new urban public spaces. In the end, the city got several hundred towers, but only a fraction of the 100 public spaces.

BORIS JOHNSON

When CABE was set up in 1999, London still looked like the same city that Canaletto had painted in the mid-1700s. It had the dome of

St Paul's at its centre. The tallest new structure, known as the NatWest Tower when it was completed – and now called Tower 42 – was an isolated one-off. But London has since sprouted Europe's most conspicuous high-rise developments: one at Canary Wharf; another around Bishopsgate in the City of London; and a third concentration of residential towers around Vauxhall. Despite being elected with a promise to stop the march of the 'phallocrats' and to prevent London from turning into 'Dubai-on-Thames', Johnson did nothing to stem the ever-increasing number of towers.[9]

The Johnson years had more than their share of fiascos: the Garden Bridge that was supposed to cost the taxpayer nothing; the ill-judged Orbit project in the Olympic Park; and the little-used Emirates Air Line cable car across the Thames between the Royal Docks and Greenwich. All three were advertised as free gifts to the London electorate, but each turned out to come with expensive strings inextricably attached.

A more positive initiative, the Mayor of London's 'Housing Design Guide' of 2010, insisted on higher standards for housing, including a minimum ceiling height of 2.5 metres and space standards that resurrected the Parker Morris approach of the welfare state.[10] Its impact is visible throughout the capital, bringing a sobriety that is a deliberate contrast to the increasingly wilful shape-making of the more conspicuous of the new office towers on either bank of the Thames.

But there are some who have taken a sceptical view of this too. An architectural think tank associated with Haworth Tompkins produced a paper entitled 'The Emperor's New Housing', describing Johnson's design guide as a response to the unintended consequences of Livingstone's densification policies.[11] The report endorsed the minimum room sizes it demands, but mocked Johnson's bid to create a new London housing vernacular, characterised by brick and more brick, punctuated by portrait format full-height windows with deep reveals. The report stated that better results come from allowing architects to experiment, rather than insisting on every developer building the same thing. A more damning charge for Johnson was that he was focusing on quality housing rather than quantity at a time of an acute shortage of affordable housing across the capital.

SADIQ KHAN

Summing up Boris Johnson's time in City Hall, ahead of the 2016 election, the *Observer*'s Rowan Moore pitied any successor who would have to deal with a legacy that mixed unbridled development with occasional, sizeable vanity projects.[12] Sadiq Khan has found himself having to cancel at least one of these in the Garden Bridge, and having to acknowledge that affordable housing is 'a marathon and not a sprint'.[13]

Sadiq Khan's draft London Plan, submitted to his predecessor's Conservative government at the end of 2019, was never going to have it easy. Johnson and Khan appear to have a relationship that reverses the dynamic of that between US Presidents Donald Trump and Barack Obama, with Johnson finding any success on Khan's part unbearable. Khan's plan, submitted to the government at the end of 2019, was thrown back in his face by Johnson's secretary of state for housing, communities and local government Robert Jenrick.

But it too was based on an idea of what London should become. Khan's plan suggested a continued rate of growth of an additional 70,000 people every year, which he described as 'a once in a lifetime opportunity'.[14] Khan's London, if he gets his way, will see outer suburbs such as Kingston take on a more urban quality to accommodate that growth. New housing will go on land owned by TfL, all around the city, a policy that the mayor's opponents characterised as 'war on the suburbs'.[15] Livingstone, by way of contrast, wanted to build tall and increase densities in the inner boroughs.

Khan has also had to face the impact of the coronavirus pandemic on TfL, which forced him to accept a bailout by Westminster on humiliating terms. As a result, he has raised the possibility of abandoning City Hall, the home of the Mayor of London since 2000. Taking advantage of a break clause in the lease in 2021 would save £55 million in rent over five years.[16] It is proposed that the GLA could move into the Crystal, an exhibition space in the Royal Docks designed by Wilkinson Eyre. The Crystal was acquired by the GLA in 2019 from Siemens, who built it as a showcase for environmental technologies after it became clear that it was failing to attract the anticipated audience. At the time of writing, the future home of the mayoralty remains uncertain.

CITY HALL

Buildings carry symbolic messages. They can be messages that are intended from the outset, and others that they acquire over time. When the Greater London Authority was set up twenty years ago, restoring local government to the capital after Margaret Thatcher abolished the GLC in 1986, the Blair government felt that there could be no going back to the majestic Edwardian County Hall building, even if it had been possible to. It belonged to another era of civic government, when the mayor was a ceremonial figure, weighed down with gold chains that showed that real power was held elsewhere. County Hall sat facing the Houses of Parliament and Westminster across the river. It had allowed Livingstone to embarrass Margaret Thatcher in the 1980s by using its façade to post constantly rising unemployment figures. She made sure that she and her successors would never be embarrassed again by shutting the GLC down, and selling the building.

The new GLA was the product of the private finance era. Developers were asked to bid for the chance to design, construct and operate an assembly. Norman Foster, in those days working with Ken Shuttleworth, beat Will Alsop and a plan to convert a neo-classical insurance headquarters in Holborn. For the owners of the City Hall site, it marked the end of a three-decade-long struggle to create a development that

would be both fundable, and could navigate its way through a fluctu-
ating planning system. Owned for many years by the government of
Kuwait, every architectural approach had been attempted, including
commissioning Philip Johnson, the chameleon-like post-modernist,
to design a larger-than-life replica of the Houses of Parliament. The
Kuwaitis proposed building it in stages, and wanted to name every
building for a Conservative Prime Minister, starting with Lord North
and finishing with Margaret Thatcher. Eventually they sold the land
to a group who named the area 'More London', and used City Hall as
the catalyst for a wider scheme that is now fully occupied – and once
more owned by Kuwait.

Politics can sometimes be about as interesting as reading from
a telephone directory. However, City Hall tries valiantly to make
it appear more interesting. The 500 staff and twenty-five assembly
members could have vanished into an anonymous office block, which
perhaps would have been the financially responsible option. But an
invisible government is a government without democratic legitimacy,
and City Hall's symbolic message is as significant as its practical
purpose. Livingstone was dismissive initially. A 'glass testicle', he
called it. But then with his skill for meaningless gestures, he insisted
on downsizing the office that was allocated to him, to give his support
staff better views.

Back in 2002, City Hall caused a stir. Before the invasion of high
rises, the building stood out as one of the most conspicuous and distinctive buildings of its time. London had given Britain its first taste
of what the architecture of modern democracy looked like well before
Edinburgh opened its Enric Miralles-designed parliament and Cardiff
completed the Welsh Assembly, designed by Richard Rogers. Inside,
the building gave municipal politics the same treatment that Australia gives to cricket. No more fuddy-duddy cricket whites, and V-neck
sweaters, but floodlit matches played in lime-green pyjamas. Or, in the
case of City Hall, purple carpets and yellow walls that look good on
television.

The centre of City Hall has been scooped out to make room for the debating chamber, which sits at the bottom of a spiralling ramp of baroque complexity. It is meant to celebrate the symbolic democratic heart of the building. But it is almost comically overblown. The London Assembly and its committees use it just a few times a month, in front of sparse audiences. The rest of the year it is an empty gesture – in the most literal sense. It reveals an all-powerful mayor, and twenty-five elected members, who essentially form the studio audience for a day-long mayoral TV quiz show, played out ten times a year. Perhaps the realisation that City Hall was built for a different form of civic government to the one that we actually have is partly behind Khan's plans to abandon it. But it remains a highly visible landmark, in a part of London typically crowded with people, sharing the skyline with the Tower of London. To move to the Royal Docks, to a building that speaks the architectural language of a stealth bomber, would send out a far from confident message about the future of London's mayoral system. Regardless of Khan's decision, the future of City Hall, like the mayoralty itself, remains uncertain.

23

BREXIT

LEAH KREITZMAN

I am writing this chapter four years to the day since the EU referendum of 23 June 2016, but I still remember it vividly.

Sadiq had only been elected six weeks before, after what was, by common agreement, a very bitter mayoral election, with very personal attacks on Sadiq from Zac Goldsmith, the Tory candidate, unleashing Islamophobic abuse and vitriol into a political campaign in a way not seen in this country before. But, just a few weeks later, Sadiq was sharing a stage with the then Tory Prime Minister, David Cameron, at Remain rallies – because he realised that he had to do all he could to win the referendum. We had a lot on our plate, as we were still setting up a new City Hall administration, but Sadiq threw himself into the campaign regardless.

As polling day drew nearer, we knew that the result was going to be closer than it should have been. But we were optimistic. Trump had not yet been elected and Sadiq, who had won the mayoral election very convincingly on an unapologetically progressive platform, had campaigned hard for Remain. So, I went to bed relatively early thinking that we would win – Nigel Farage had already conceded defeat. It was to be a rude awakening.

The next day in the office was hard. I remember that the younger members of the team, for whom being European was central to their identity, were particularly upset. Many had European partners and relatives. The blow from this referendum defeat was a counterweight to the high of the mayoral election victory the month before.

With the referendum lost, we knew we needed both to reassure Londoners and project confidence in the future of the city. We launched the London is Open campaign immediately and the hashtag #LondonIsOpen was tweeted by the official Mayor of London account that afternoon.

London is Open had dual objectives of restoring the confidence of London businesses and reassuring Londoners that our city's values hadn't changed. The business community was anxious, but so were many ordinary Londoners. There was a big spike in xenophobic and racist hate crime in the weeks and months after the referendum and many European Londoners were worried about what Brexit would mean for them. Sadiq knew that he had to send a message to the world that London was open for business, to investment, trade, talent, tourists, as well as a message to Londoners – especially those from minority and migrant communities – that the city was still open and inclusive to people of different backgrounds and that all were welcome here.

From that moment on Brexit loomed large and responding to the risk that it posed to London and our position in the world took up a huge amount of City Hall's time and resources. Sadiq's diary filled up with business events, including dinners for the Confederation of British Industry and other business groups, and lots of one-to-one meetings with London's business leaders. We also travelled to Davos to meet with global CEOs and took trade missions to New York and Chicago to bang the drum for inward investment. We convened all the twenty-seven EU ambassadors in City Hall to talk about how we could best serve their citizens in London. We also commissioned a study early on, with London & Partners and the City of London Corporation, on how to communicate London to business and leisure tourism audiences, given Brexit – and where it was most crucial we targeted those communications. Germany and France came out as particularly important so we opened, for the first time, offices in Berlin and Paris.

Internally the mayor established the EU Exit Working Group, which brought together most of his deputy mayors, mayoral and executive directors, as it became apparent that Brexit was going to affect all aspects of City Hall's remit. Sadiq also set up the Brexit Expert Advisory Panel to give a sectoral perspective from London's leading industries to inform our lobbying of government.

It was gruelling, and obviously it was additional to lots of things we had planned. But we were overwhelmed by offers of support from businesses, creatives and the civil society of London. While the London is Open campaign budget is small, particularly compared to Whitehall-run Brexit campaigns, the in-kind support it has received and its impact has been huge. I think we worked out that we secured over £5 million in value in kind for the campaign to date. For example, the New West End Company dressed their district in London is Open banners, our campaign films were shown on the big screens everywhere from Piccadilly Circus to Wembley Stadium to Heathrow, Turner Prize winning artists created new work for the campaign and brands from Formula 1, the National Football League and Major League Baseball to MTV and Westfield carried our message. Everyone wanted to get behind it. I think the whole campaign is a great illustration of the way that the mayor can bring London together and amplify the city's voice.

The impact of the referendum result defined Sadiq's first term and it will be felt for years to come, but it also meant that London and Londoners could restate their values – of inclusivity and openness – and send a message to an increasingly insular and nativist world that our city would continue to look outwards.

PART FOUR

EVALUATION

CONCLUSION: THE GLA AT TWENTY AND THE FUTURE OF LONDON GOVERNMENT

BEN ROGERS AND TONY TRAVERS

London is London. The city's very familiarity to people makes it easy to overlook its extraordinary nature. As one of the world's two or three leading global cities, it plays a major role – some argue too much so – in the UK's economy, cultural and political life and its standing in the world. Yet, as we have outlined in our introduction, the metropolis has never had a settled form of government. Any Londoner over sixty will have lived under four distinct municipal regimes.

SUCCESSES

So how has the latest attempt to come up with a way of governing 'the ungovernable' city fared? What should we make of the UK's first big-city experiment with a directly elected mayor?

Overall, the verdict is positive. Giving London a directly elected mayor has worked. Perhaps the greatest tribute to its success is that it has been, for twenty years, overwhelmingly viewed – at least until very recently – as a settled fact of British institutional life. Few have seriously called for its abolition and most polls have suggested Londoners support the office. Indeed, subsequent governments have sought to roll out a variant of the model, introducing directly elected 'metro mayors' in most larger city regions and possibly across all areas of England.[1] Given that a Mayor of London was, by UK standards, a radical and ambitious policy innovation, produced quickly in a country that prides itself on institutional conservatism, the achievement is impressive.

The Greater London Authority has developed much as its creators wanted and expected. In areas such as planning, housing, transport, skills, economic development and environmental management, it has provided strategic leadership, and has operated as a purposeful counter-balance to the interests of the boroughs but not pointlessly competing with them, as the GLC was seen to do. The mayor has provided a voice for the capital, with a vast electoral mandate, a high-profile but accountable leader, strong direct relations to the people of London and (again, until recently) influence over national government. Mayors have used their mandate and powers to introduce the congestion charge, progress with Crossrail and help secure and deliver the Olympics. Much as its creators hoped, the GLA has also gained new powers as the new institution has won the confidence of ministers.

THE UNEXPECTED

Yet, some of the ways the role of mayor has developed would surely surprise those who set it up. First, few people in the run-up to 2000 could have foreseen the speed with which London would, over the next couple of decades, establish itself as one of the world's most admired and dynamic megacities. Much like the skyscrapers that suddenly reached into its skyline, the metropolis has grown and expanded. This success, in turn, gave the mayor an unexpectedly prominent global profile. The Mayor of London became a player on the global stage, presiding over the Olympics and Paralympics, welcoming investors, hosting international conventions, leading global trade missions, convening urban summits. By the end of Boris Johnson's time as mayor, he was, arguably, at least as well known internationally as the

Prime Minister, David Cameron. President Trump's attacks on Sadiq Khan have paradoxically raised the latter's international profile.

Those who set up the mayoralty always envisaged that it would provide a 'voice for the capital'. But this was approached as a way of corralling the boroughs, championing London in its dealings with national government and selling it overseas. Livingstone, Johnson and Khan have certainly done all of those things, but the Mayor of London has also ended up speaking for the city in ways that were not foreseen, particularly at times of triumph and tragedy. Whether celebrating the Olympics, making rallying speeches in the face of terrorist attacks, or mourning those lost in the Grenfell fire and the coronavirus pandemic, all three mayors have provided leadership and unity through good times and bad.

Again, the mayoralty's founding fathers – or more properly its founding parents, as women like Nicky Gavron, Liz Meek and Genie Turton played major roles – always hoped that it would inject new life into British politics, in part by attracting a different and more independent sort of person, and in part by serving as a proving ground for national leaders. Before the creation of the devolved authorities in Scotland, Wales, London and, latterly, city regional mayors, the only way of gaining the experience of powerful office in the UK was through becoming a Cabinet minister. All power resided in SW1. This hegemony has been weakened.

The mayoralty helped to do that. But its creators might have been surprised by the back stories of all three mayors. One of the hopes of Tony Blair and other champions of the mayoral model was that it would attract new talent into politics. But Livingstone, Johnson and Khan entered the race as party politicians. In fact all were sitting MPs. And while several independents have run for mayor and the names of many non-politicians have been touted as possible candidates (e.g. Greg Dyke, Nick Ferrari, Peter Bazalgette, Lord Alan Sugar and Richard Branson), no one from outside the party system has come close to winning and no well-known non-politicians have made a serious run for the office. London has yet to have a figure such as Arnold Schwarzenegger or Mike Bloomberg propelled into City Hall.

But the first two mayors certainly injected new energy into the political system. Ken Livingstone, running as an independent, had taken on and beaten the New Labour machine in the first mayoral election, while Boris Johnson used the mayoralty to transform his image from a journalistic 'court jester' to a Conservative heavyweight, leading Brexiter and landside-winning Prime Minister. Sadiq Khan is, so far, the most conventional of the three, though even he stands out as the first Muslim to run a major Western city – a fact much commented on abroad, even if most Londoners seem to have taken it in their stride. It says much about the individuality of the characters who have become mayors and their relation to the Londoners who elected them that each has been called by their first name. In the time that national government has been led by Blair, Brown, Cameron and May, London has had Ken, Boris and Sadiq in City Hall.

UNFINISHED BUSINESS

While there have been surprises, there have also been disappointments. First, devolution. While the devolved authorities in Scotland, Wales and London reduced Westminster's monopoly of power, and though the mayoralty has gained new powers over time (see Chapters 4 and 7), London government remains weak by international standards. England within the UK had an exceptionally centralised system of government twenty years ago and that remains the case today. In contrast to mayors in cities such as New York, Tokyo and even Paris, the Mayor of London has very limited powers to design and redesign or to raise and lower taxes. In fact, the last ten years have been ones of fiscal centralisation in England, as a decade of government cuts have led to a substantial decline in sub-national public spending relative to Westminster and Whitehall. London political, business and civil society leaders, business groups and think tanks have called for the mayor to be given more power – especially fiscal power – almost since before the mayoralty was established and winning more power remains the priority for London government going forward. Having appointed the London Finance Commission in 2013, Boris Johnson campaigned energetically and loudly for fiscal devolution while he was mayor, but he has shown little interest in delivering it since becoming Prime Minister.

Second, the London Assembly. The assembly was, as described in Chapter 2, designed deliberately as a relatively weak, 'scrutiny' body. It was given no power to approve or disapprove of a mayor's decisions (except by using a hard-to-achieve budget veto) or to pass legislation. Moreover, while the mayor's role has evolved considerably over twenty years, the assembly's has barely changed. Some scrutiny has been effective, but much has been tactical rather than strategic. The additional member voting system has ensured a relatively widely representative array of member, with minority party Green and UKIP members taking their place alongside Labour, Conservative and Liberal Democrat ones. Ken Livingstone worked particularly closely with the Greens, notably assembly member (now Baroness) Jenny Jones. Other assembly members such as Nicky Gavron also proved influential in delivering environmental outcomes. Fifteen assembly members have gone on to become MPs, including David Lammy, currently shadow secretary of state for justice, and James Cleverly, until recently chair of the Conservative Party and currently minister in the Foreign Office.

But it is hard to avoid the feeling that there is 'unfinished business' where the assembly is concerned. Does it make sense to go to the bother of electing and resourcing an institution with so little power? There could be an argument for giving the existing assembly more power, especially if the mayor were to accrue more power. Alternatively, other ways to hold the mayor to account have been suggested, such as by transferring scrutiny powers to the boroughs. The case for the latter possibility has been given impetus by the rise of metro mayors in other parts of the country. In cities such as Liverpool and

Manchester, mayors are answerable not to an independent assembly but effectively sit alongside local council leaders as 'first among equals'. It is telling that while few politicians or commentators have called for the abolition of the mayoralty, rather more have made the case for a radical rethink of the assembly.

LONDON WITHIN THE UK

As discussed in Chapter 12, in the twenty years since the GLA was created, London's economy grew relative to that of the rest of the UK. London's growing economic dominance, along with the concentration of political power, cultural institutions and transport investment in the city, has understandably provoked something of a backlash across the country at large, and this has become particularly pronounced in the years following the global financial crisis. Dozens of newspaper articles have appeared attacking the capital for enjoying too much investment, too much success and too much power.[2] More recently, think tanks, notably the IPPR North, have published a series of papers arguing London was privileged and that regional inequality in the UK was significantly worse than elsewhere.[3] Economic and other differences between London and the rest of England were mobilised during the 2019 general election.[4]

In reality, despite its relatively high gross value added per head, London remains the UK's largest concentration of deprived households and faces enormous pressure on its housing and other infrastructure.[5] Accusations that London controls the rest of the country in an over-centralised way, imposing 'metropolitan elite views' on the rest, generally conflate London as the seat of government and London as a home of 9 million people. Moreover, despite perceptions of London being 'removed' from the rest of the country, the city remains (by some distance) the largest concentration of UK-born people anywhere in the country.[6]

Nevertheless, the Johnson government elected in December 2019 was committed to 'levelling-up' income and wealth between

London and other regions. Covid-19 and Brexit will surely affect the levelling-up agenda. The government might well come to see investment in London as essential to economic recovery and a more 'global Britain'. Or it is possible that the twin shocks of the virus and leaving the EU will, accidentally, 'level down' the country. Only time will tell.

2020: A THREAT TO THE 2000 LONDON SETTLEMENT?

2020 proved to be a unique year. It started normally enough, but by March it became clear that the global pandemic would require a major public health response. This response turned out to be a government-imposed 'lockdown' in late March, with the population required to stay at home and work from there if possible. Millions of employees were 'furloughed' and the UK economy shrank by over a fifth in the first half of the year.[7] Efforts were made to re-kindle economic activity, carefully, from late June. But the 'stay at home' messaging by the UK proved so effective that the return to places of work was slower in Britain than other comparable countries.[8] City centres were particularly badly hit because of their reliance on high-capacity public transport. In the depth of lockdown, London Underground journeys fell by 96 per cent and bus travel by 86 per cent.[9] During the Second World War, public transport and the London economy had continued to function despite bombing and war damage. Nothing since cholera and, before that, bubonic plague had affected London's, and particularly the city centre's, economy so profoundly.[10]

In the weeks when the Covid-19 challenge was emerging, the UK government's secretary of state for housing, communities and local government, Robert Jenrick, published his response to mayor Sadiq Khan's proposed revision of the London Plan.[11] The letter was unapologetically critical of Khan's proposals. The tone of the letter was so dismissive of the mayor and his use of his powers that it is worth quoting at length:

Housing delivery in London under your mayoralty has been deeply disappointing, over the last three years housing delivery has averaged just 37,000 a year; falling short of the existing Plan target and well below your assessment of housing need. Over the same period, other Mayors such as in the West Midlands have gripped their local need for housing and recognised the opportunities this brings, leading significant increases in the delivery of homes ... Clearly, the housing delivery shortfall you have overseen has led to worsening affordability for Londoners ... Critical strategic sites have stalled, epitomised by your Development Corporation in Old Oak and Park Royal being forced to turn away £250 million of Government funding because of your inability to work successfully with the main landowner. You also turned away £1 billion of investment we offered to deliver Affordable Homes, because of the support and oversight that would accompany this. You have put a series of onerous conditions on estate regeneration schemes for them to be eligible for grant-funding, such as the requirement for residents' ballots. In attaching such conditions, you are jeopardising housing delivery and this approach will make it significantly more difficult to deliver the Plan's targets and homes needed.

For these reasons I am left with no choice but to exercise my powers to direct changes. Your Plan must be brought to the minimum level I would expect to deliver the homes to start serving Londoners in the way they deserve. However, this must be the baseline and given this, I ask that you start considering the next London Plan immediately and how this will meet the higher level and broader housing needs of London.

Jenrick had, in effect, taken control of the London Plan and, thus, of the number of homes to be built by the boroughs in future years, which his letter suggests must be revised upwards significantly, from 52,000 to 66,000.[12] Few commentators believe that a significantly higher target would ever be achieved, particularly given the unwillingness among some Conservative boroughs to increase their housing delivery at the scale suggested. An intervention of this kind would have been inconceivable in Scotland or Wales and had the effect of showing the government's understanding of devolution in England: devolved power could be tolerated, but only if it delivered to national policy objectives.

Covid-19 provided an opportunity for another Whitehall intervention in the mayor's powers. When the government mandated people to stay at home, Transport for London's fare revenues declined by about 90 per cent.[13] Because public transport in Britain has been required to set fares to cover more of its operating costs than in most comparable countries, this loss of revenue pushed TfL towards bankruptcy very fast. After a period of public debate, the Department of Transport agreed a £1.6 billion bailout, of which £1.1 billion would be in the form of a government grant and £500 million would be borrowed by TfL.

As with Robert Jenrick's intervention in relation to the London Plan, transport secretary Grant Shapps used the funding settlement to impose new conditions on the Mayor of London:

> To put TfL on a sustainable footing for the longer term and help safeguard its future, the mayor has agreed that the government will carry out an immediate and broad-ranging review of the organisation's future financial position and structure, including the potential for efficiencies. Two special representatives will represent the government on TfL's board, its finance committee and its programmes and investment committee, in order to ensure best value for money for the taxpayer.[14]

Other conditions were imposed on Khan, such as the suspension of concessionary fares and an increase in the period of operation and level of congestion charging. Consultants KPMG were appointed to review TfL's finances.

With the 2020 mayoral election suspended, TfL's need for support provided an excellent opportunity for Conservative politicians to attack the Labour mayor. A way of putting the political background into context is to compare the TfL funding package with the significantly bigger one given to the private companies running the national railways, including most of London's commuter lines. Total grants of £3.5 billion were given to these companies (including some with recent performance data far worse than TfL's) to cover the first few months of the effects of Covid-19, although there were no strings attached.[15] Similarly, bailouts were given to bus and tram operators outside London with no conditions attached.[16] In fairness, Khan's approach to the government and TfL's funding has had independent critics outside the Conservative Party and government.[17] But the politics of supporting London's transport system during Covid-19 and its aftermath will be an important test in judging how the city's devolved government evolves.

In August 2020 the UK government published a planning white paper with proposals to move towards a more 'zoning' based system in England.[18] Given the importance of the London Plan to the mayor's capacity to influence the development of the city, it was surprising that the document did not mention either the plan or the mayor at any point. There was a reference to a mayoral 'Community Infrastructure Levy', but not of a kind that revealed any ongoing role for the mayor in strategic planning. Against the backdrop of the government's over-ruling of Sadiq Khan's London Plan and, separately, the intervention with TfL, this omission may prove suggestive of a down-grading of the GLA's future planning powers.

THE FUTURE

Despite the twenty years of gradual, politically moderate, evolution of the office of Mayor of London, there are now clear signals that the present government, led by a Prime Minister who clearly relished his previous job as mayor and seemed to genuinely love the city he ran, may well start to reverse the reforms of 2000. For the first time since the GLA was created, articles have appeared in the press suggesting the need for a review of the governance of London or even that aboli-tion should be considered.[19] The delayed 2020 mayoral and assembly elections are planned to take place on 6 May 2021. By chance, this will be the day that the GLA's lifespan will exceed that of the GLC's. There are three possible ways forward from here.

First, it is possible that the GLA will be given additional powers as part of the government's wider commitment to extend devolution within England. A white paper on the subject was expected during the summer of 2020 and it is conceivable, notwithstanding the issues considered above, that such a document could offer London and other cities more power over provision, such as post-school education, skills, public health, housing and transport.[20] Greater fiscal freedom would be an element of genuine devolution.

Second, it is possible that the government will decide that the Mayor of London and the London Assembly should be abolished. Given the particular history of London's city-wide government since the 1830s, notably the abolition of the Metropolitan Board of Works, the LCC and GLC, it would be naïve to rule out such a development. Leading Conservatives from Lord Salisbury to Margaret Thatcher have been discomforted by the scale, expenditure and progressive policies of the capital's government. The fact that the Conservatives as a party find it increasingly hard to win in London creates, arguably, an additional incentive to downgrade its government.

Third, and the most likely option, is that there will be a period until the mid-2020s when the mayor and assembly are subject to minor re-forms which reduce their authority but which leave the GLA in place.[21] The key question then will be: what does the Labour opposition intend to do if and when it gets into government? Labour has done well in winning city-regional mayoralties in London, Greater Manchester and Liverpool and might be expected to produce future manifesto commitments to enhance the powers of such public officials. But there were no such detailed promises during the 2019 election. A period of politically bleak stasis may lie ahead.

Covid-19 will affect the UK and the rest of the world for years to come. The government has had to provide the mayor, the boroughs and local authorities across the country with substantial additional resources. The Covid-19 lockdown further delayed the opening of Crossrail and has led to a continuing reduction in the use of public transport. Central London, in common with Manhattan and other global city downtowns, has been hit far harder than other parts of the city and country. It is possible that the short-term effects of Covid-19 and the lockdown will translate into longer-term change in the structure of the city's economy, potentially making it more polycentric. If such a change happens it is conceivable London will expand outwards once again. Planning policy will be important in determining the longer-term future both of London's international core, but also of its suburbs and semi-rural edge.

Central government, City Hall and the boroughs will make decisions during 2020 and 2021 that affect London's long-term future. Because of the importance of central London to the British rail system, any permanent change affecting the city centre's economy will also impinge on the national railways' future. A shift away from public transport would mean more road building and worse traffic congestion. Britain's theatre, opera, ballet and other performing arts also rely on central London's agglomerated market. Structural changes in the London economy could affect economic sectors across the whole of the UK, and not in a good way.

The Mayor of London will need to be a key player in articulating the policy options facing the city post-Covid. Beyond platitudes about 'building back better', decisions will need to be taken about how to recover confidence in public transport, crowded places and moving around during rush hour. Significantly more housing may need to be built in inner and central London (closer to the residential densities of New York and Paris) to allow different working patterns to sustain the central area. Social distancing is the enemy of agglomeration and thus of city centres. London may have recovered from plague, cholera, the Great Fire and the Blitz in recent centuries, but changing work patterns and contemporary opportunities for remote, internet-based employment will change city centres for ever. Public policy will influence what change occurs and how fast.

London's mayor at twenty had (gradually, and over time) been given a number of new powers and, at the end of 2020, survives, albeit with a question mark hanging over the office and also over its future scope and powers. Given the turbulent, culture-war-ridden nature of UK and international politics in recent years, it is perhaps a tribute to Ken Livingstone, Boris Johnson and Sadiq Khan that the position has evolved in a way robust enough to survive in a political system as prone to knee-jerk reform as Britain. In late 2020, survival as the precursor to a potentially better future may be the least-worst way ahead, not only for the Mayor of London but for the UK's political system more generally.

Outcomes include Crossrail, the London Overground, Tube upgrades, the Oyster card/ticketing systems, congestion charging, the bike-hire scheme, cycle superhighways and extensions to the DLR. Police numbers were probably protected by successive mayors, particularly since 2010. The Olympics would almost certainly not have been won or so effectively delivered without mayoral involvement. Latterly, the mayor has made major steps towards air quality improvement of a kind Whitehall would never have attempted. Politically and culturally, the Mayor of London has become a symbol of the city.

COUNTERFACTUAL: LONDON
WITHOUT THE MAYORALTY

This book has been dedicated to chronicling the creation and development of London's mayoralty and analysing its influence. But what if the GLA had not been established and London had continued to muddle on with the arrangements put in place after the abolition of the GLC? Thinking along these counterfactual lines presents another, in our case final, way of exploring the difference that the Mayor of London has made.

There would have been no congestion charge and almost certainly no Olympics. Quite possibly Crossrail would not have been given final approval and it is likely that there would have been less public transport investment. There would be no London Overground. There would probably be fewer skyscrapers and (even) less new housing. Neither bendy buses nor their new Routemaster successors would have hit the streets. There would be no cable car from the Royal Docks to North Greenwich and possibly no city-owned cycle-hire scheme or cycle superhighways. There might have been fewer police and a less conscious policy of celebrating London's remarkable ethnic and religious diversity. Air quality and pollution would almost certainly have been worse.

The economy was growing relatively fast before 2000, with a resurgence that began as far back as the mid-1980s. Population was also beginning to rise quickly. With less investment, it is possible that overall economic and population growth would have been lower if there had been no mayor, but not significantly so.

It is likely that there would have been pressures to reform the boroughs. Many commentators believe that the current number of boroughs is too large and that there should be amalgamations. By 2020, London would have had no city-wide government for thirty-four years and the pressure for some kind of 'senate' of powerful borough leaders might have been hard to resist. Would the ancient City of London have survived such a change?

Consideration of a coordination mechanism for the wider south-east (i.e. London, the south-east and the east of England) might have loomed larger. With no mayor or other city-wide governance institution, it might have been easier to develop a 'greater London' entity to deal with transport, roads, housing and other regional issues. It is possible that central government might have instituted such a mechanism as it did with the Northern Powerhouse.

Outside London, it is likely that there would have been no impetus from Prime Ministers Blair and Cameron to require directly elected mayors in Greater Manchester, Liverpool, West Midlands and elsewhere. Combined authorities would doubtless have emerged, but not mayors.

It's unlikely Boris Johnson would have become Prime Minister if he had not had the opportunity to be a popular and reasonably successful Mayor of London. It is conceivable that without the existence of the office of Mayor of London, Boris Johnson would never have become so powerful within British politics that he could, personally, have got Brexit over the line. In this sense, the creation of a mayor to lead London, that most cosmopolitan of cities, may, ironically, have accidentally facilitated the UK's departure from the European Union.

ACKNOWLEDGEMENTS

The editors are hugely indebted to the many people who have given their expert advice, comments and time, both in the researching and writing of this book and throughout the years. We are, of course, extremely grateful to our external authors, who have contributed a diverse and fascinating set of perspectives to Part Three of this book. We would also like to thank all of the project's interviewees, anonymous and named, for their time and insights.

The idea for this book had its origins in a conversation between Jeremy Skinner (of the GLA) and Tony Travers in a café on Shad Thames in 2017. Huge thanks are also due to our colleagues at Centre for London, and particularly to Ben Rogers. We are also especially grateful to Robert Gordon Clark of London Communications Agency for his assistance, advice and support throughout. We would also like to thank James Lilford and his colleagues at Biteback for their extensive assistance throughout.

NOTES

1: THE ROAD TO REFORM

1   Tony Travers, *The Politics of London: Governing an Ungovernable City* (Basingstoke: Palgrave Macmillan, 2003), pp. 21–42.

2   Ben Pimlott and Nirmala Rao, *Governing London* (Oxford: Oxford University Press, 2002), pp. 31–43.

3   'Population Growth in London, 1939–2015', Greater London Authority, January 2015, https://data.london.gov.uk/dataset/population-change-1939-2015 (accessed September 2020).

4   Ibid., p. 104.

5   Michael Hebbert and Ann Dickins Edge, *Dismantlers: The London Residuary Body* (London: Suntory-Toyota International Centre for Economics and Related Disciplines, LSE, 1994), pp. 31–2.

6   Michael Hebbert and Tony Travers (eds), *The London Government Handbook* (London: Cassell, 1988), pp. 3–4.

7   See, for example: David Owen, *The Government of Victorian London 1855–1889: The Metropolitan Board of Works, the Vestries and the City Corporation* (London: Belknap Press of Harvard University Press, 1982); Ken Young and Patricia L. Garside, *Metropolitan London: Politics and Urban Change 1837–1981* (London: Edward Arnold, 1982); and John Davis, *Reforming London: The London Government Problem, 1855–1900* (Oxford: Clarendon Press, 1988).

8   Michael Hebbert and Ann Dickins Edge, *Dismantlers: The London Residuary Body*.

9   Michael Hebbert and Tony Travers (eds), *The London Government Handbook*, pp. 136–9.

10 '1987 Labour Party Manifesto: Britain will win with Labour', Labour Party, 1987, http://www.labour-party.org.uk/manifestos/1987/1987-labour-manifesto.shtml (accessed August 2020).

11 Michael Hebbert and Tony Travers (eds), *The London Government Handbook*, pp. 79–81.

12 Tony Travers, *The Politics of London: Governing an Ungovernable City*, p. 34.

13 John Hall, 'The Role of Business in London Local and Regional Government: How it Became Recognised as a Significant Player', *Local Government Studies* (June 2006), vol. 32, no. 3, pp. 311–40.

14 Tony Travers, *The Politics of London: Governing an Ungovernable City*, p. 33.

15 Andrew Hosken, *Ken: The Ups and Downs of Ken Livingstone* (London: Arcadia, 2008), p. 28.

16 See: 'London Borough Council Elections 3 May 2018', Greater London Authority, 2018, borough results tables, p. xi.

17 'Central London Rail Study', Department of Transport, January 1989, https://www.railwaysarchive.co.uk/documents/DoT_CentralLondonRailStudy1989.pdf (accessed August 2020).

18 Christian Wolmar, *The Subterranean Railway: How the London Underground was Built and How it Changed the City Forever*, (London: Atlantic Books, 2004), p. 308.

19 Scott L. Greer and Mark Sandford, 'The GLA and Whitehall', *Local Government Studies* (June 2006), vol. 32, no. 3, pp. 239–53, p. 244.

20 Tony Travers, *London's Boroughs at 50* (London: Biteback Publishing, 2015), p. 219.

21 See: 'Local Government' by Tony Travers, in Anthony Seldon (ed.), *The Blair Effect* (London: Little, Brown, 2001), p. 123.

22 'London in the 21st Century: London's Future', Architecture Foundation, 17 April 1996, https://www.architecturefoundation.org.uk/programme/1996/london-in-the-21st-century/preparing-for-the-21st-century-londons-future (accessed September 2020).

23 Ben Pimlott and Nirmala Rao, *Governing London*, pp. 62–78.

24 Philip Johnston, 'Black Wednesday: The day that Britain went over the edge', *Daily Telegraph*, 10 September 2012.

25 Tony Travers, George Jones, Michael Hebbert and June Burnham, *The Government of London*, (York: Joseph Rowntree Foundation, 1991), p. 66.

26 Tony Travers, *The Politics of London: Governing an Ungovernable City*, pp. 43–5.

27 Richard Wachman, 'Is now the time for another prawn cocktail offensive?', *The Guardian*, 10 March 2002.

28 '1997 Conservative Party General Election Manifesto: You can only be sure with the Conservatives', Conservative Party, 1997 http://www.conservativemanifesto.com/1997/1997-conservative-manifesto.shtml (accessed August 2020).

29 The Conservative Party's 1999 proposals for the assembly can be found in Hansard, House of Commons Debate, 19 January 1999, vol. 323, cc. 728–84.

30 Mark Sandford, 'The Greater London Authority', 05817, House of Commons Library, 7 June 2018, pp. 16–17.

2: CREATING THE GLA

1 Tony Blair, *A Journey*, (London: Hutchinson, 2010), p. 24.

2 'New Leadership for London: The Government's Proposals for a Greater London Authority', Department of the Environment, Transport and the Regions, 1997.

3 Interview with Len Duvall, 23 April 2020.

4 Hansard, House of Commons Debate, 5 June 1991, vol. 192, cc. 285–338.

5 Quoted in Michael Hebbert, 'Governing the Capital' in Andy Thornley (ed.), *The Crisis of London* (London: Routledge, 1992), p. 134.

6 '1992 Labour Party Manifesto: It's time to get Britain working again', Labour Party, 1992, http://www.labour-party.org.uk/manifestos/1992/1992-labour-manifesto.shtml (accessed August 2020).

7 Hansard, House of Commons Debate, 5 June 1991, vol. 192, cc. 285–338.

8 '1992 Conservative Party General Election Manifesto: The Best Future for Britain', Conservative Party, 1992, http://www.conservativemanifesto.com/1992/1992-conservative-manifesto.shtml (accessed August 2020).

9 'Labour Party Manifesto: new Labour because Britain deserves better', Labour Party, 1997, http://www.labour-party.org.uk/manifestos/1997/1997-labour-manifesto.shtml (accessed August 2020).

10 Interview with Simon Jenkins, 19 April 2020.

11 Robert Gordon Clark, 'London 1990 to 2020. And what must happen next', OnLondon, 3 March 2020, https://www.onlondon.co.uk/robert-gordon-clark-london-1990-to-2020-and-what-must-happen-next/ (accessed September 2020).

12 Nick Raynsford, Centre for London seminar, 9 March 2020.

13 Quoted in John Carvel, *Turn Again Livingstone* (London: Profile, 1999), p. 255.

14 Nick Raynsford, Centre for London seminar.

15 Interview with Liz Meek, 27 April 2020.

16 Genie Turton, Centre for London seminar, 24 February 2020.

17 Tony Travers, *The Politics of London: Governing an Ungovernable City*.

18 New Leadership for London: The Government's Proposals for a Greater London Authority', Department of the Environment, Transport and the Regions.

19 'A Mayor and Assembly for London', Department of the Environment, Transport and the Regions, 1998.

20 Matt Qvortrup, 'Democracy by delegation: the decision to hold referendums in the United Kingdom', *Representation* (August 2006), vol. 42, issue 1, pp. 59–72.

21 'Greater London Authority Bill: A Mayor and Assembly for London', House of Commons Library, Research Paper 98/115, 11 December 1998.

22 Tony Travers, *The Politics of London*, p. 62.

23 Hansard, House of Commons Debate, 14 December 1998, vol. 322.

24 Ibid.

25 'Who's in the running for Mayor', BBC News, 10 April 1998.

26 'Poll of Londoners', MORI, 1 March 1998, https://www.ipsos.com/ipsos-mori/en-uk/poll-londoners (accessed August 2020).

27 Simon Jeffrey, 'The rise and fall of Jeffrey Archer', *The Guardian*, 19 July 2001.

28 Tony Travers, *The Politics of London*, p. 70.

29 John Carvel, *Turn Again Livingstone*, p. 3.

30 Hansard, House of Commons Debate, 6 June 1997, vol. 295.

31 Tony Blair, *A Journey*, p. 267.

32 Ken Livingstone, *You Can't Say That: Memoirs* (London: Faber and Faber, 2011).

33 Tony Travers, *The Politics of London*, p. 72.

34 Ken Livingstone, *You Can't Say That: Memoirs*.

35 Bob Chilton, Centre for London seminar, 9 March 2020.

3: MAKING THE MAYORALTY: 2000–2001

1 Julia Hartley-Brewer, 'Bunged-up machines cause chaos at count', *The Guardian*, 6 May 2000.

2 Tony Blair, *A Journey*, p. 267.

3 Interview with Len Duvall, 23 April 2020.

4 Mayor's Question Time, Greater London Authority, 24 May 2000, https://www.london.gov.uk/about-us/londonassembly/meetings/CeListDocuments.aspx?CommitteeId=0&MeetingId=3528&DF=24%2F05%2F2000&Ver=2 (accessed August 2020).

5 Mayor's report to the London Assembly, 24 May 2000.

6 Ken Livingstone, *You Can't Say That*, p. 425, and Seumas Milne, 'Livingstone in car plant talks', *The Guardian*, 9 May 2000.

7 Mayor's report to the London Assembly, 29 June 2000.

8 Ibid.

9 Ken Livingstone, *You Can't Say That*, p. 427.

10 'Fourth report of the Mayor of London to the London Assembly' 13 September 2000, https://www.london.gov.uk/about-us/londonassembly/meetings/Data/London%20Assembly%20(Mayor's%20Question%20Time)/20000913/Agenda/Mayor's%20report%20PDF.pdf (accessed August 2020).

11 David Bond, 'Government "no" to Picketts Lock', *Evening Standard*, 4 October 2001.

12 'Minutes of the meeting of the Assembly – 15 November 2000', Greater London Authority, https://www.london.gov.uk/about-us/londonassembly/meetings/Data/London%20Assembly%20(Mayor's%20Question%20Time)/20001115/Minutes/Appendix%20A%20PDF.pdf (accessed August 2020).

13 Ken Livingstone, *You Can't Say That*, p. 437.

14 Mayor's Question Time, Greater London Authority, 24 May 2000.

15 Martin G. Richards, *Congestion Charging in London: The Policy and the Politics* (Basingstoke: Palgrave Macmillan, 2006), p. 99.

16 Ken Livingstone, *You Can't Say That*, p. 397.

17 'Mayor's report to the London Assembly', Greater London Authority, 18 October 2000, https://www.london.gov.uk/moderngov/Data/London%20Assembly%20(Mayor's%20Question%20Time)/20001018/Agenda/Report%20PDF.pdf (accessed August 2020).

18 Louise Butcher, 'London Underground PPP: background', SN1307, House of Commons Library, 16 January 2012.

19 Liz Meek, Centre for London seminar, 24 February 2020.

20 'Mayor's report to the London Assembly', Greater London Authority, 27 July 2000, https://www.london.gov.uk/about-us/londonassembly/meetings/Data/London%20Assembly%20(Mayor's%20Question%20Time)/20000727/Agenda/MQT%20report%20PDF.pdf (accessed August 2020).

21 'Towards the London Plan: Initial proposals for the Mayor's Spatial Development Strategy', Greater London Authority, May 2001, https://www.london.gov.uk/about-us/londonassembly/meetings/Data/Spatial%20Development%20Strategy%20Investigative%20Committte/20010516/Agenda/5%20Appendix%20PDF.pdf (accessed August 2020).

22 Tony Travers, *The Politics of London*, p. 190.

23 Ken Livingstone, *You Can't Say That*.

4: 'HAVING A MAYOR': TWENTY YEARS OF THE MAYORALTY

1 'The London Plan', Greater London Authority, February 2004, https://www.london.gov.uk/what-we-do/planning/london-plan/past-versions-and-alterations-london-plan/london-plan-2004 (accessed August 2020).

2 'GLA: Two Years On', November 2002, London Communications Agency archive.

3 'Shard is Londoners' second-favourite skyscraper', LondonSE1, 27 March 2014, https://www.london-se1.co.uk/news/view/7491 (accessed August 2020).

4 Interview with Ken Livingstone, 13 April 2020.

5 'July 2003 briefing', London Communications Agency archive.

6 Patrick Wintour, 'NEC rejects Livingstone bid to rejoin Labour', *The Guardian*, 24 July 2002.

7 Louise Butcher, 'London Underground PPP: background'.

8 'Congestion charging: Impacts Monitoring, Second Annual Report', Transport for London, April 2014 http://content.tfl.gov.uk/impacts-monitoring-report-2.pdf (accessed August 2020), pp. 2–5.

9 Ken Livingstone, *You Can't Say That*.

10 James Kirkup, 'Boris Johnson scraps congestion charge for 4x4 vehicles', *Daily Telegraph*, 8 July 2008.

11 'GLA: Three Years On', August 2003, London Communications Agency archive.

12 'Has Boris Johnson saved every Londoner £445?', Full Fact, 7 March 2012, https://fullfact.org/news/has-boris-johnson-saved-every-londoner-445/ (accessed August 2020).

13 Ken Livingstone, *You Can't Say That*, p. 18.

14 Matthew Beard, 'Livingstone suspended for four weeks over Nazi gibe', *The Independent*, 25 February 2006.

15 'Livingstone invites cleric back', BBC News, 12 July 2004 and Peter Tatchell, 'An embrace that shames London', *New Statesman*, 24 January 2005.

16 David Hirsh, 'Livingstone and the ayatollahs', *The Guardian*, 22 March 2006, and Ken Livingstone, *You Can't Say That*.

17 Simon Jenkins, 'Livingstone should guard his tongue but not spare his language', *The Guardian*, 31 March 2006.

18 'GLA Office – Brussels', Greater London Authority, 16 July 2003, https://www.london.gov.uk/questions/2003/1297 (accessed August 2020).

19 'Newsletter', August 2007, London Communications Agency archive.

20 Anonymous interview.

21 Sara Hughes, *Repowering Cities: Governing Climate Change Mitigation in New York City, Los Angeles, and Toronto* (London: Cornell University Press, 2019), p. 28.

22 'Action Today to Protect Tomorrow: The Mayor's Climate Change Action Plan', Greater London Authority, February 2007, http://www.energyforlondon.org/wp-content/uploads/2016/07/CCAP-2007.pdf (accessed August 2020).

23 'Livingstone and companies tie up on emissions', *Financial Times*, 10 December 2007.

24 Simione Talanoa, 'Mayor announces start of a groundbreaking programme to green London's public buildings', Climate Action, 3 March 2008, http://www.climateaction.org/news/mayor_announces_start_of_a_groundbreaking_programme_to_green_londons_public (accessed August 2020).
25 London Communications Agency archive.
26 Ibid.
27 Katherine Barney, 'Scandal of LDA's missing millions', *Evening Standard*, 16 July 2008.
28 Andrew Gimson, *Boris: The Making of the Prime Minister* (London: Simon & Schuster, 2016).
29 'Johnson is a Tory mayor candidate', BBC News, 27 September 2007, the other candidates were Victoria Borwick, Warwick Lightfoot and Andrew Boff.
30 'Ferrari will not be Tories' mayor', BBC News, 2 August 2006.
31 'Mayoral debate transcript', BBC News, 20 April 2008.
32 Sonia Purnell, *Just Boris: A Tale of Blond Ambition* (London: Aurum, 2012), p. 350.
33 'Mayor of London and London Assembly Elections: Results 2008', London Elects, https://www.londonelects.org.uk/im-voter/election-results (accessed August 2020).
34 In 2008 turnout was 45 per cent, which was up 8 per cent on the previous election in 2004.
35 Sonia Purnell, *Just Boris*, p. 314.
36 Sonia Purnell, *Just Boris*, p. 353–4.
37 Interview with former City Hall official, 27 May 2020.
38 Esther Addley and Rupert Neate, 'Boris Johnson's early days as mayor: "It was total, total chaos"', *The Guardian*, 16 July 2009.
39 Andrew Gimson, *Boris: The Making of the Prime Minister*.
40 Sonia Purnell, *Just Boris*, p. 372.
41 'Has Boris Johnson saved every Londoner £445?', Full Fact and 'Newsletter', September 2011, London Communications Agency archive.
42 Sonia Purnell, *Just Boris*, p. 390.
43 Esther Addley and Rupert Neate, 'Boris Johnson's early days as mayor: "It was total, total chaos"'.
44 Andrew Gimson, *Boris: The Making of the Prime Minister*.
45 'Knife "arches" urged for schools', BBC News, 5 June 2008.
46 'Boris Johnson: What's his track record?', BBC News, 23 July 2019.
47 'London Mayor Boris Johnson carries riot clean-up brush', BBC News, 9 August 2011.
48 Andrew Gimson, *Boris: The Making of the Prime Minister*, and Sonia Purnell, *Just Boris* p. 431.
49 Andrew Gimson, *Boris: The Making of the Prime Minister*.
50 'Boris Johnson criticised for "Kosovo" benefits remark, BBC News, 28 October 2010.
51 'Raising the capital: The report of the London Finance Commission', London Finance Commission, May 2013, https://www.london.gov.uk/sites/default/files/gla_migrate_files_destination/Raising%20the%20capital_0.pdf (accessed August 2020).
52 'Met getting £90m to keep police numbers up on capital's streets', *Evening Standard*, 30 January 2012, and 'Boris Johnson: What's his track record', BBC News.
53 'Newsletter', May 2009, London Communications Agency archive.
54 'Newsletter', August 2010, London Communications Agency archive.
55 Sonia Purnell, *Just Boris*, p. 411.
56 'Newsletter', August 2010, London Communications Agency archive.
57 'Boris says "no" to bendy buses', johndoepolitics, 14 February 2008, https://www.youtube.com/watch?v=nwaZOE4v3nE (accessed August 2020).
58 'Study backs Thames island airport', BBC News, 19 October 2009.
59 Ibid., and Andrew Gimson, 'Interview: Daniel Moylan – "Boris will never surrender his vision of building a great new airport east of london"', ConservativeHome, 26 November 2014, http://www.conservativehome.com/highlights/2014/11/interview-daniel-moylan-boris-will-never-surrender-his-vision-of-building-a-great-new-airport-east-of-london.html (accessed August 2020).
60 'The Garden Bridge', Greater London Authority, 2018, https://www.london.gov.uk/sites/default/files/garden_bridge_review_1.pdf (accessed August 2020).

61 Sam Jones, 'Thames cable car plan to link Olympic venue in time for 2012 games', *The Guardian*, 5 July 2010.

62 Matthew Weaver, 'By the busload: £940m bill for Boris Johnson's mayoral "vanity projects"', *The Guardian*, 18 August 2017.

63 Rowan Moore, 'Boris Johnson's dire legacy for London', *The Guardian*, 10 April 2016.

64 The details about the campaign are provided on the Skyline Campaign website: http://www.skylinecampaign.org/about (accessed August 2020).

65 'London View Management Framework', Greater London Authority, 2012, https://www.london.gov.uk/what-we-do/planning/implementing-london-plan/planning-guidance/london-view-management (accessed August 2020).

66 Douglas Murphy, *Nincompoopolis: The Follies of Boris Johnson* (London: Watkins Publishing, 2017).

67 'London's skyscraper boom runs out of steam', *Financial Times*, 21 April 2010.

68 'Newsletter', November 2008, London Communications Agency archive.

69 'Boris Johnson: What's his track record', BBC News.

70 Niall Firth, '"Rabbit-hutch" Britain: UK's new homes are "smallest in Europe"', *Daily Mail*, 11 September 2008.

71 Laura Chan, 'London mayor pledges end to "hobbit homes"', *Building*, 8 July 2009.

72 Emily Twinch, 'Calls to overhaul failing London Delivery Board', *Inside Housing*, 10 August 2012.

73 'Mayor of London and London Assembly Elections: Results 2012', London Elects, https://www.londonelects.org.uk/im-voter/election-results/results-2012 (accessed August 2020).

74 'George Osborne booed at Paralympics medal ceremony – video', *The Guardian*, 4 September 2012.

75 'Mayor of London Boris Johnson's Speech – Our Greatest Team: Athletes' Parade Live', BBC One, 10 September 2012, https://www.youtube.com/watch?v=57gg2sinGK0 (accessed August 2020).

76 Tim Donovan, 'Is there an Olympic Games bounce for Boris?', BBC News, 31 July 2012.

77 See, for example: Chris Mason, 'Boris Johnson and the future PM question', BBC News, 26 March 2013.

78 Andrew Gimson, *Boris: The Making of the Prime Minister*.

79 Rafael Behr, 'Cheering on Boris is the polite Tory way of calling Cameron a loser', *New Statesman*, 25 July 2012.

80 'Boris Johnson: £250,000-a-year salary is "chicken feed"', BBC *HARDtalk*, 25 July 2019, https://www.youtube.com/watch?v=dnX024WuzFk (accessed August 2020).

81 Sonia Purnell, *Just Boris*, pp. 361–2.

82 'Newsletter', October 2011, London Communications Agency archive.

83 Julian Glover, 'The London method: a look back at Boris Johnson's stint as Mayor as he battles to become PM', *Evening Standard*, 10 July 2019.

84 Douglas Murphy, *Nincompoopolis: The Follies of Boris Johnson*.

85 'Mayor of London and London Assembly Elections: Results 2016', London Elects, https://www.londonelects.org.uk/im-voter/election-results/results-2016 (accessed August 2020).

86 George Eaton, 'How Sadiq Khan won the London mayoral election', *New Stateman*, 6 May 2016.

87 Dave Hill, *Zac versus Sadiq: The fight to become London Mayor* (London: Double Q, 2016).

88 Ibid., and Jill Lawless and Danica Kirka, 'London elects first Muslim mayor', *Times of Israel*, 7 May 2016.

89 Tanveer Mann, 'Britain First candidate turns his back during Sadiq Khan's speech', *Metro*, 7 May 2016.

90 'Sadiq's Manifesto', Labour in London, 2016, https://labourinlondon.org.uk/sadiq/2018/02/28/sadiqs-manifesto/ (accessed August 2020).

91 Dave Hill, *Zac versus Sadiq*, p. 84.

92 Ibid.

93 George Parker and Conor Sullivan, 'Sadiq Khan on London after Brexit: "Open is what we are"', *Financial Times*, 4 October 2016.

94 Fiona Jones, 'Sadiq Khan's bullish response to caller who say's he's failed as Mayor', LBC, 3 July 2020, and Sadiq Khan, 'The people must have another vote – to take back control of Brexit', *The Guardian*, 15 September 2018.

95 'London Is Open', Greater London Authority, https://www.london.gov.uk/what-we-do/arts-and-culture/london-open (accessed August 2020).

96 Dave Hill, 'How did Sadiq Khan do in 2018?', OnLondon, https://www.onlondon.co.uk/how-did-sadiq-khan-do-in-2018/ (accessed August 2020).

97 'Mayor's statements on the major fire at Grenfell Tower in Kensington', Greater London Authority, https://www.london.gov.uk/about-us/mayor-london/mayors-statements-major-fire-grenfell-tower-kensington (accessed August 2020).

98 'Mayor condemns Government for "most anti-London Budget in a generation"', Greater London Authority, 22 November 2017, https://www.london.gov.uk/press-releases/mayoral/mayor-condemns-most-anti-london-budget (accessed August 2020), and Darren Hunt, '"Obsessed getting on the TV!" Tory MP rips into Sadiq Khan over his record as London Mayor', 6 April 2018.

99 See, for example: Lucie Heath, 'Jenrick sends scathing letter blocking Khan from publishing London Plan', *Inside Housing*, 13 March 2020, and Dave Hill, 'Sadiq Khan accuses government of "punishing Londoners" and "bad faith" over TfL bailout', OnLondon, 21 May 2020, https://www.onlondon.co.uk/sadiq-khan-accuses-government-of-punishing-londoners-with-tfl-bailout-terms/ (accessed August 2020).

100 John Collingridge, 'London Mayor Sadiq Khan "knew about delay to Crossrail"', *The Times*, 25 November 2018.

101 Nicole Badstuber, 'Why fewer Londoners are taking the tube – a transport researcher explains', The Conversation, 15 May 2018, https://theconversation.com/why-fewer-londoners-are-taking-the-tube-a-transport-researcher-explains-94754 (accessed August 2020).

102 Adam Bienkov, 'Yes we Khan: The inside story of how Sadiq Khan defeated a dog-whistle campaign', politics.co.uk, https://www.politics.co.uk/comment-analysis/2016/05/10/yes-we-khan-inside-story-sadiq-khan-defeated-dog-whistle (accessed August 2020).

103 Mark Townsend, 'Donald Trump in new attack on Sadiq Khan with Katie Hopkins retweet', *The Guardian*, 20 July 2019.

104 'Sadiq Khan on course for Mayoral election victory according to latest poll from Queen Mary's Mile End Institute', Queen Mary University of London, 10 March 2020, https://www.qmul.ac.uk/media/news/2020/hss/sadiq-khan-on-course-for-mayoral-election-victory-according-to-latest-poll-from-queen-marys-mile-end-institute.html (accessed August 2020).

105 Kath Scanlon, Christine Whitehead and Fanny Blanc, 'The role of overseas investors in the London new-build residential market', LSE London, May 2017, https://www.london.gov.uk/moderngovmb/documents/s58640/08b2b%20LSE%20Overseas%20Investment%20report.pdf (accessed August 2020), and Charles Wright, 'Sadiq Khan climbs down on London Plan housing targets', OnLondon, 18 December 2019, https://www.onlondon.co.uk/sadiq-khan-climbs-down-on-london-plan-housing-targets/ (accessed August 2020).

106 Peter Apps, 'Fact check: did Boris Johnson "massively outbuild Labour" as London mayor', *Inside Housing*, 26 November 2019.

107 'Sadiq breaks own record for genuinely affordable home starts', Greater London Authority, 14 May 2020, https://www.london.gov.uk/press-releases/mayoral/affordable-home-stats-show-record-number-of-starts (accessed August 2020).

108 'London murder rate overtakes New York's', BBC News, 2 April 2018, and 'London violence: Mayor urges "targeted" stop and search', BBC News, 7 April 2018.

109 'Boris Johnson blames Sadiq Khan for London knife crime "scandal"', BBC News, 23 July 2018.

110 Dave Hill, 'Tory criticisms of Sadiq Khan over knife crime aren't working. Why', OnLondon

https://www.onlondon.co.uk/tory-criticisms-of-sadiq-khan-over-knife-crime-arent-working-why/ (accessed August 2020).

111 Connor Ibbetson, 'The London Mayoral Race: Sadiq leads the pack', YouGov, 11 March 2020, https://yougov.co.uk/topics/politics/articles-reports/2020/03/11/london-mayoral-race-sadiq-khan-leads (accessed August 2020).

112 'Oxford Street pedestrianisation plans ditched', BBC News, 8 June 2018.

113 Jack Blanchard, 'Sadiq Khan's next job', POLITICO, 28 February 2020, https://www.politico.eu/article/sadiq-khans-next-job-london-mayor-uk-labour-party/ (accessed August 2020).

7: AN EVOLVING MAYORALTY

1 Gerald Rhodes, *The Government of London: The Struggle For Reform* (London: Weidenfeld & Nicolson, 1970, pp. 197–9.

2 Ibid., pp. 186–9.

3 Ben Pimlott and Nirmala Rao, *Governing London*, pp. 64–5.

4 See, for example: Fred Siegel with Harry Siegel, *The Prince of the City: Giuliani, New York and the Genius of American Life* (San Francisco: Encounter Books, 2005), pp. 92–5.

5 Tony Travers, *The Politics of London*, p. 84.

6 Ibid., p. 87.

7 Ben Pimlott and Nirmala Rao, *Governing London*, p. 96.

8 Andrew Hosken, *Ken: The Ups and Downs of Ken Livingstone*, p. 322.

9 Hélène Mulholland and Hugh Muir, 'Johnson loses third deputy as Ian Clement quits over credit card misuse', *The Guardian*, 22 June 2009.

10 'Boris Johnson sacked me because he felt threatened, says Sir Ian Blair', *Evening Standard*, 9 November 2009.

11 Tony Travers, *The Politics of London*, pp. 88–9.

12 Robert Gordon Clark, 'Who is to blame for TfL needing a bailout? And what will happen next?', OnLondon, 1 June 2020, https://www.onlondon.co.uk/robert-gordon-clark-who-is-to-blame-for-tfl-needing-a-bailout-and-what-will-happen-next/ (accessed August 2020).

13 'The Mayor's Office for Policing and Crime (MOPAC)', Greater London Authority, https://www.london.gov.uk/what-we-do/mayors-office-policing-and-crime-mopac (accessed August 2020).

14 'Governance: How is the London Fire Brigade governed?', London Fire Brigade https://www.london-fire.gov.uk/about-us/governance-london-fire-commissioner/ (accessed August 2020).

15 Richard Brown, 'What housing and planning powers do London Mayors actually have?', OnLondon, 9 January 2020, https://www.onlondon.co.uk/richard-brown-what-housing-planning-powers-do-london-mayors-have/ (accessed August 2020).

16 Mark Sandford, 'The Greater London Authority', 05817, House of Commons Library, 7 June 2018.

8: TRANSPORT

1 T. C. Barker and M. Robbins, *A History of London Transport: Passenger Travel and the Development of the Metropolis*, vol. 2, (London: Allen and Unwin for the London Transport Executive, 1974).

2 Stephen Glaister (ed.), *Transport Options for London* (London: Greater London Group, 1991), p. 26.

3 For more on 'Fares Fair', see John Carvel, *Citizen Ken* (London: Chatto & Windus, Hogarth Press, 1984).

4 Louise Butcher, 'London Underground PPP: background', SN1307, House of Commons Library, 16 January 2012.

5 Government Office for London, 'Road Charging Options for London', (London: The Stationary Office, 2000).

6 'Roads Task Force – Technical Note 10: What is the capacity of the road network for private motorised traffic and how has this changed over time?', Transport for London, 2012.

7 Tony Travers and Peter Hendy, 'Bob Kiley obituary', *The Guardian*, 10 August 2016.

8 'TfL Finances: the End of the Line?', London Assembly, November 2018, https://www.london. gov.uk/sites/default/files/tfl_finances_-_final.pdf (accessed August 2020).

9 The bus services operating grant is paid to bus operators as a partial rebate on duty paid for fuel. From October 2013 it was paid direct to TfL rather than to bus operators, see Louise Butcher, 'Buses: grants and subsidies, SN1522, House of Commons Library, 4 December 2013.

10 'Costs, fares and revenue', BUS04, Department for Transport, June 2020, https://www.gov.uk/ government/statistical-data-sets/bus04-costs-fares-and-revenue (accessed August 2020).

11 'Transport for London Business Plan 2020/21 to 2024/25', Transport for London, p. 38.

12 'Roads Task Force – Technical Note 10', p. 14.

13 'London's Bus Network', London Assembly, 2017, https://www.london.gov.uk/about-us/ londonassembly/meetings/documents/s65233/Appendix%202%20-%20Bus%20Network%20 Report.pdf (accessed August 2020).

14 Tom Geoghegan,'Can a simple bus be so hated?', BBC News, 25 March 2008.

15 'Board Meeting – Open Session', Transport for London, 24 October 2007, http://content.tfl. gov.uk/Board-papers-October-2007.pdf (accessed August 2020) and 'Board meeting 23.9.08, Secretariat memorandum', London Travel Watch, 23 September 2008, https://web.archive.org/ web/20090304043549/http://www.londontravelwatch.org.uk/document/3526/get (accessed August 2020).

16 'New Bus for London Roll Out', Transport for London, 20 September 2012, http://content.tfl. gov.uk/Part-1-Item08-New-Bus-for-London-Rollout.pdf (accessed August 2020).

17 'Average age of the bus fleet used as Public Service Vehicles by metropolitan area status and country', BUS0605, Department for Transport, December 2019, https://assets.publishing. service.gov.uk/government/uploads/system/uploads/attachment_data/file/852521/bus0605. ods (accessed September 2020).

18 Stephen Glaister, Rosemary Scanlon and Tony Travers, *Getting Partnerships Going: PPPs in Transport* (London: Institute for Public Policy Research, 2000).

19 Louise Butcher, 'London Underground PPP: background', p. 17.

20 Ibid., p. 19.

21 Anthony King and Ivor Crewe, *The Blunders of Our Governments*, (London: Oneworld, 2013), pp. 201–21 and Stephen Glaister, 'Transport', in Anthony Seldon (ed.) *Blair's Britain 1997–2007*, (Cambridge: Cambridge University Press, 2007), pp. 241–73.

22 'Bob Kiley outlines proposals for London Regional Rail Authority', Transport for London, 13 March 2004, https://tfl.gov.uk/info-for/media/press-releases/2004/march/bob-kiley-outlines-proposals-for-london-regional-rail-authority (accessed August 2020) and 'Mayor of London calls for TfL to take charge of key infrastructure', Mayor of London, 26 March 2019, https://www.london.gov.uk/ press-releases/mayoral/mayor-calls-for-tfl-to-control-rail-infrastructure (accessed August 2020).

23 Gwyn Topham, 'Sadiq Khan pushes for tube-style service on London's railways', *The Guardian*, 26 March 2019.

24 Hansard, House of Commons debate, 9 October 1990, vol. 522, cc. 269–70WA.

25 See Jack Brown interview with Ken Livingstone in Chapter 5.

26 'Funding', Crossrail, https://www.crossrail.co.uk/about-us/funding# (accessed August 2020).

27 Tony Travers, 'A Levy on the National Non-Domestic Rate', in Stephen Glaister (ed.) *Transport Options for London*, pp. 117–

28 Caroline Wadham, 'Crossrail: "We do not plan to ask for any more money"', *Construction News*, 17 December 2019.

29 'Mayor hails finance agreement for North Line extension', Mayor of London, 5 December 2012, https://www.london.gov.uk/press-releases-4780 (accessed August 2020).

30 Katherine Smale, 'TfL projected spend on Northern Line Extension revealed', *New Civil Engineer*, 28 February 2019.

31 Government Office for London, 'Road Charging Options for London'.

32 Greater London Council, *Supplementary Licensing* (London: GLC, 1974).

33 Stephen, Glaister, 'The Smeed Report at 50: will road pricing always be 10 years away?' in John Walker (ed.), *Road Pricing: Technologies, Economics and Acceptability* (Stevenage: Institution of Engineering and Technology, 2018), pp. 17–36.

34 'Central London Congestion Charging Impacts Monitoring' annual reports, numbers one to six, Transport for London.

35 'Travel in London: Report 12', Transport for London, 2019, http://content.tfl.gov.uk/travel-in-london-report-12.pdf (accessed August 2020), Table 2.1, p. 33.

36 'Smoothing the Traffic Flow', Transport for London, April 2009, http://content.tfl.gov.uk/smoothing-traffic-flow-report.pdf (accessed August 2020).

37 'Roads Task Force', Transport for London, https://tfl.gov.uk/corporate/publications-and-reports/roads-task-force (accessed August 2020).

38 '£4bn plan to revamp London's roads announced', BBC News, 4 March 2014.

39 Chris Ames, 'Khan slams Boris over funding as Netflix hits TfL revenue', Transport Network, 12 January 2018, https://www.transport-network.co.uk/Khan-slams-Boris-over-funding-as-Netflix-hits-TfL-revenue/14734 (accessed August 2020).

40 'Transport for London Business Plan 2020/21 to 2024/25', p. 57.

41 'Annual Local Authority Road Maintenance Survey', Asphalt Industry Alliance, 24 March 2020, https://www.asphaltuk.org/wp-content/uploads/ALARM-survey-2020-FINAL.pdf (accessed August 2020).

42 'Average Traffic Speeds', Mayor of London. See also detailed analysis by David Bayliss, 'London's Road Traffic Problems and Their Causes' (Unpublished manuscript, 2017).

43 'Roads Task Force – Technical Note 10: What is the capacity of the road network for private motorised traffic and how has this changed over time?', Transport for London.

44 See, for example: 'Congestion Charging', Alliance of British Drivers, https://www.freedomfordrivers.org/congestion.htm (accessed September 2020).

45 'Proposed Cycle Superhighways Schemes' Transport for London, 4 February 2015, http://content.tfl.gov.uk/board-20150204-part-1-item-07a-propose-csh-scheme.pdf (accessed August 2020).

46 Ibid., see table in paragraph 5.53, p. 65.

47 'TfL 2015–16 Quarter 3 Performance Report (Oct – Dec 2015)', London Travel Watch, May 2016, https://www.londontravelwatch.org.uk/documents/get_lob?id=4188&age=&field=file (accessed August 2020), p. 5 and p. 28, and 'Transport for London Budget 2019/20', Transport for London, http://content.tfl.gov.uk/tfl-budget-2019-20.pdf (accessed August 2020), p. 29.

48 'Travel in London: Report 12', Transport for London, 2019, http://content.tfl.gov.uk/travel-in-london-report-12.pdf (accessed August 2020), Table 2.1, p. 33.

49 'Uber London Limited found to be not fit and proper to hold a private hire operator licence', Transport for London, 25 November 2019, https://tfl.gov.uk/info-for/media/press-releases/2019/november/uber-london-limited-found-to-be-not-fit-and-proper-to-hold-a-private-hire-operator-licence (accessed August 2020).

50 John Vidal, 'Blears reopens Thames Gateway bridge inquiry', *The Guardian*, 26 July 2007.

51 Peter Spence, 'Just four commuters use Boris' £60m Emirates Airline cable cars', *City A.M.*, 20 November 2013.

52 Transport for London Annual Report and Statement of Accounts 2018/19', Transport for London, 24 July 2019, p. 24.

53 'Silvertown Tunnel', Transport for London, https://tfl.gov.uk/travel-information/improvements-and-projects/silvertown-tunnel (accessed August 2020).

54 'Transport for London Annual Report and Statement of Accounts 2018/19', Transport for London, p. 25.

55 Joseph Davies, 'Ridden and rated: Ultimate guide to London's bike-sharing rental bicycles', Cyclist, 29 May 2020, https://www.cyclist.co.uk/reviews/4062/ridden-and-rated-ultimate-guide-to-london-s-bike-sharing-rental-bicycles (accessed September 2020).

NOTES

56 'Analysis of Cycling Potential 2016', Transport for London, March 2017, http://content.tfl.gov.uk/analysis-of-cycling-potential-2016.pdf (accessed August 2020).

57 'Transport for London Business Plan 2019/20 – 2023/24', Transport for London, p. 78.

58 'Mayor: Ultra-Low Emission Zone to expand up to North & South Circular', Mayor of London, 8 June 2018, https://www.london.gov.uk/press-releases/mayoral/ultra-low-emission-zone-to-expand (accessed August 2020).

59 'Fleet audit report', Transport for London, 31 March 2020, http://content.tfl.gov.uk/fleet-audit-report-31-march-2020.pdf (accessed September 2020).

60 'Travel in London: Report 12', Section 10.

61 'Transport for London Annual Report and Statement of Accounts' 2010/11 to 2018/19, Transport for London.

62 'Transport for London Business Plan 2009/10 – 2017/18', Transport for London.

63 Patrick McLoughlin letter to Boris Johnson, 2 March 2016, http://content.tfl.gov.uk/spending-review-2015-funding-agreement-letter-march-2016.pdf (accessed August 2020).

64 'Transport for London Business Plan 2019/20 – 2023/24', Transport for London.

65 Like all local authorities, under the Local Government Act 2003 TfL has powers to borrow but has to have regard to the Prudential Code and central government has reserve powers to make regulations.

66 'Information Memorandum £3,300,000 Medium Term Note Programme', Transport for London, 25 November 2004.

10: POLICING, CRIME AND PUBLIC SAFETY

1 'Financial sustainability of police forces in England and Wales 2018', National Audit Office, 11 September 2018, https://www.nao.org.uk/wp-content/uploads/2018/09/Financial-sustainability-of-police-forces-in-England-and-Wales-2018.pdf (accessed August 2020).

2 Andrew Sparrow, 'In summary: Boris Johnson's crime manifesto', The Guardian, 13 February 2008.

3 James Sturcke, Jenny Percival and Hélène Mulholland, 'Sir Ian Blair resigns as Met police commissioner', The Guardian, 2 October 2008.

4 Chloe Chaplain, 'Sir Bernard Hogan-Howe denies early retirement is due to friction with Sadiq Khan', Evening Standard, 29 September 2016.

5 Hélène Mulholland, 'Critics accuse Boris Johnson of using Ian Blair for political advantage', The Guardian, 3 October 2008.

6 Matthew Tempest, 'Livingstone launches re-election bid', The Guardian, 6 May 2004.

7 Andrew Sparrow, 'In summary: Boris Johnson's crime manifesto'.

8 While London regional breakdowns from the Crime Survey for England and Wales would tell us more about crime as experienced by a sample of London residents, such breakdowns are not publicly available from the Office for National Statistics. Recorded crime data at the London level is therefore the best available.

9 Gavin Hales, et al., 'What is driving serious violence: drugs', Crest Advisory, February 2020, https://b9cf6cd4-6aad-4419-a368-724e7d1352b9.usrfiles.com/ugd/b9cf6c_5aad01b7fa2743d8b5508fb85faf2aa4.pdf (accessed August 2020).

10 'Public Safety and Security in the 21st Century: The First Report of the Strategic Review of Policing in England and Wales', The Police Foundation, July 2020.

11 For a discussion on this see the commentary in 'Crime in England and Wales: Year Ending December 2019', Office for National Statistics, https://www.ons.gov.uk/peoplepopulationandcommunity/crimeandjustice/bulletins/crimeinenglandandwales/yearendingdecember2019 (accessed August 2020).

12 'Met hits Mayor's neighbourhood crime reduction target', Mayor of London, 23 March 2015, https://www.london.gov.uk/press-releases/mayoral/neighbourhood-crime (accessed August 2020).

13 'Metropolitan Police sex abuse case "failings put children at risk"', BBC News, 25 November 2016.

14 'A Safer City for All Londoners: Police and Crime Plan 2017–2021', Greater London Authority, March 2017, https://www.london.gov.uk/sites/default/files/mopac_police_and_crime_plan_2017-2021.pdf (accessed September 2020).

15 'Respecting others: tackling antisocial behaviour in London', London Assembly, https://www.london.gov.uk/sites/default/files/pcc_respecting_others_tackling_antisocial_behaviour_in_london_18012018.pdf (accessed September 2020).

16 Ibid.

17 Paul Waugh, 'Livingstone plans a £63-a-year council tax rise to fund more police and buses', *The Independent*, 17 December 2002.

18 Sam Jones and Matthew Taylor, 'Johnson puts crime at forefront of London mayoral battle', *The Guardian*, 14 February 2008.

19 For police funding figures see 'Financial sustainability of police forces in England and Wales 2018'.

20 'Police workforce England and Wales statistics', Home Office, 17 July 2013, https://www.gov.uk/government/collections/police-workforce-england-and-wales (accessed September 2020).

21 Ibid.

22 For a review of the evidence see Jacqui Karn, 'Policing and Crime Reduction: The evidence and its implications for practice', The Police Foundation, June 2013, http://www.police-foundation.org.uk/2017/wp-content/uploads/2017/06/police-foundation-police-effectiveness-report.pdf (accessed August 2020).

23 Andy Higgins, 'The Future of Neighbourhood Policing', The Police Foundation, May 2018, http://www.police-foundation.org.uk/2017/wp-content/uploads/2010/10/TPFJ6112-Neighbourhood-Policing-Report-WEB_2.pdf (accessed August 2020).

24 Ibid.

25 'Public Voice Dashboard', Mayor's Office for Policing and Crime', June 2020, https://www.london.gov.uk/what-we-do/mayors-office-policing-and-crime-mopac/data-and-statistics/public-voice-dashboard (accessed August 2020).

26 Ibid.

27 Ibid.

28 William Macpherson 'The Stephen Lawrence Inquiry', Cm 4662–1, February 1999, https://assets.publishing.service.gov.uk/government/uploads/system/uploads/attachment_data/file/277111/4262.pdf (accessed August 2020).

29 'Stop and search dashboard', Metropolitan Police, https://www.met.police.uk/sd/stats-and-data/met/stop-and-search-dashboard/ (accessed August 2020).

30 Ibid.

31 Gavin Hales, 'An examination of police workforce data on ethnicity, role, rank and gender 2007 to 2018', The Police Foundation, 21 January 2020, http://www.police-foundation.org.uk/2017/wp-content/uploads/2010/10/police_work_force_charts.pdf (accessed August 2020).

32 'Regional ethnic diversity', Home Office, 1 August 2018, https://www.ethnicity-facts-figures.service.gov.uk/uk-population-by-ethnicity/national-and-regional-populations/regional-ethnic-diversity/latest (accessed August 2020).

33 Gavin Hales, 'An examination of police workforce data on ethnicity, role, rank and gender 2007 to 2018'.

34 'My 30-year struggle with racism in the Metropolitan police', BBC News, 30 June 2020.

11: GETTING CONTROL OF THE MET

1 Archie Bland, 'Whatever happened to London's knife-crime epidemic', *The Independent*, 24 April 2014.

2 Vikram Dodd, 'Tories claim: we have seized control of Scotland Yard', *The Guardian*, 2 September 2009.

12: ECONOMY AND LIVING STANDARDS

1 With much thanks to Elizabeth Bamford for assistance.

2 Although it was eighteen months late and £1.5 billion over budget, 'Project Profile: Jubilee Line Extension (JLE)', OMEGA Centre, UCL, 2014, http://www.omegacentre.bartlett.ucl. ac.uk/wp-content/uploads/2014/12/UK_JLE_PROFILE.pdf (accessed August 2020).

3 'Labour Force Survey, ILO Unemployment Rate: London, 1992 to 2000', Office for National Statistics, https://www.ons.gov.uk/employmentandlabourmarket/peoplenotinwork/ unemployment/timeseries/ycni/lms (accessed August 2020).

4 Ibid.

5 'London Long Term Labour Market Projections', Greater London Authority, https://data. london.gov.uk/dataset/long-term-labour-market-projections (accessed September 2020).

6 Ben Gardiner et al., 'Spatially unbalanced growth in the British economy', *Journal of Economic Geography* (March 2013), pp. 889–928.

7 Robert M. Solow, 'We'd Better Watch Out', *New York Times Book Review*, 12 July 1987, p. 36.

8 London Planning Advisory Committee, *London: World City Moving Into the 21st Century*, (London: London Planning Advisory Committee, 1991).

9 Llewelyn Davies, *Four World Cities: A Comparative Study of London, Paris, New York and Tokyo*, (Llewelyn Davis Planning, 1996).

10 Greg Clark, *The Making of a World City: London 1991 to 2021* (Chichester: Wiley Blackwell, 2015).

11 'Creativity: London's Core Business', GLA Economics, 2002, https://www.london.gov.uk/sites/ default/files/create_inds_rep02.pdf (accessed August 2020).

12 'Regional gross value added (income approach)', Office for National Statistics, 2017, https:// www.ons.gov.uk/economy/grossvalueaddedgva/datasets/regionalgrossvalueaddedincome approach (accessed August 2020).

13 'Core Values: The Future of Central London', Centre for London, 26 February 2020, https:// www.centreforlondon.org/publication/central-london/ (accessed August 2020).

14 'Park Royal workforce skills analysis: Employer skills demand and training supply on London's largest industrial estate', SQW, May 2016, https://www.london.gov.uk/sites/default/ files/park_royal_workforce_skills_final_report-june2016.pdf (accessed August 2020).

15 'Convergence, Strategic Regeneration Framework: An Olympic legacy for the host boroughs', Olympic and Paralympic Legacy, October 2009, http://www.gamesmonitor.org.uk/files/ strategic-regeneration-framework-report.pdf (accessed August 2020).

16 'Relighting the torch: securing the Olympic legacy', London Assembly, 8 November 2017, https://www.london.gov.uk/about-us/london-assembly/london-assembly-publications/ relighting-torch-securing-olympic-legacy (accessed August 2020).

17 Michael Porter, *The Competitive Advantage of Nations* (London: Macmillan, 1990).

18 'The London Plan: Intend to Publish', Mayor of London, December 2019 https://www.london. gov.uk/sites/default/files/intend_to_publish_-_clean.pdf (accessed August 2020).

19 Ibid.

20 '2019 Global Cities Report', Kearney, 2019, 'Quality of living city ranking', Mercer, 2015 and 2019, and 'The Global Liveability Index', *The Economist* Intelligence Unit, 2015 and 2019.

21 'House price to residence-based earnings ratio', Office for National Statistics, 19 March 2020, https://www.ons.gov.uk/peoplepopulationandcommunity/housing/datasets/ ratioofhousepricetoresidencebasedearningslowerquartileandmedian (accessed August 2020).

22 'Percentage of total monthly household income spent on private rent, England 2012 to 2018', Office for National Statistics, 19 March 2020, https://www.ons.gov.uk/ peoplepopulationandcommunity/housing/datasets/percentageoftotalmonthlyhousehold incomespentonprivaterentengland2012to2018 (accessed September 2020).

23 'House price to residence-based earnings ratio', Office for National Statistics.

24 'London Stalling: Half a century of living standards in London' Trust for London, Resolution Foundation, 27 June 2018, https://www.resolutionfoundation.org/publications/london- stalling-half-a-century-of-living-standards-in-london/ (accessed August 2020).

25 Cassie Barton and Wendy Wilson, 'Overcrowded housing (England); House of Commons Library, 31 March 2020, https://commonslibrary.parliament.uk/research-briefings/sn01013/ (accessed August 2020) and 'IFS Green Budget 2018', Institute for Fiscal Studies, 16 October 2018, https://www.ifs.org.uk/green-budget/2018 (accessed August 2020).

26 'The London Plan, Policy 3.4 Optimising housing potential', Mayor of London, https://www.london.gov.uk/what-we-do/planning/london-plan/current-london-plan/london-plan-chapter-3/policy-34-optimising (accessed August 2020).

27 'London Plan Annual Monitoring Report 15, 2017/18', Mayor of London, October 2019, https://www.london.gov.uk/sites/default/files/amr_15_final.pdf (accessed August 2020).

28 'The Campaign for a Living Wage', Living Wage Foundation, https://www.livingwage.org.uk/ (accessed August 2020).

29 Ibid.

30 'Annual Population Survey', Nomis, 2020, https://www.nomisweb.co.uk/home/release_group.asp?g=16 (accessed August 2020).

31 This term was coined by William Cobbett in 1820; a 'wen' is a poisonous swelling.

13: THE LONDON DEVELOPMENT AGENCY AND LONDON 2012

1 'Budget Requirement and Precepts 2002–03', Greater London Authority, December 2001, https://www.london.gov.uk/moderngov/Data/London%20Assembly%20(FBQT)/20020116/Agenda/5%20GLA%20Draft%20consolidation%20PDF.pdf (accessed August 2020).

2 'A London Olympic Bid for 2012', House of Commons, Culture Media and Sport Committee, Third Report of Session 20012/03, http://www.gamesmonitor.org.uk/files/A%20London%20Olympic%20Bid%20for%202012%20-%20House%20of%20Commons%20Culture,%20Media%20and%20Sport%20Committee%202003.pdf (accessed August 2020).

3 'Say goodbye to The London Development Agency', *Evening Standard*, 3 November 2010.

4 Dave Hill, 'Boris Johnson: is the LDA his piggy bank', *The Guardian*, 9 September 2009.

5 'The London Development Agency's Annual Report 2011–12', London Development Agency, https://www.london.gov.uk/sites/default/files/lda_annual_report_11_12_final.pdf (accessed August 2020).

14: PLANNING AND DEVELOPMENT

1 'ULI Case Study: King's Cross – London, United Kingdom', Urban Land Institute Europe, 9 July 2014, https://europe.uli.org/uli-case-study-kings-cross-london-united-kingdom/ (accessed August 2020).

2 Jonathan Prynn and Mira Bar-Hillel, 'Riverside view will be ruined by towers, say campaigners', *Evening Standard*, 4 October 2010.

3 Dave Hill, 'The future of Denmark Street: rebirth opportunity or dystopian hell?', *The Guardian*, 20 December 2016.

4 'When and Where Did the Word Gentrification Originate', KQED, 18 May 2014, https://www.kqed.org/news/136343/gentrification-a-word-from-another-place-and-time (accessed September 2020).

5 'The Draft London Plan', Greater London Authority, December 2017, https://www.london.gov.uk/sites/default/files/new_london_plan_december_2017.pdf (accessed September 2020).

6 Ian Richard Gordon, Tony Travers, 'London: Planning the ungovernable city', *City, Culture and Society* (June 2010), vol. 1, issue 2, pp. 49–55.

7 'London Plan Overview and Introduction', Greater London Authority, https://www.london.gov.uk/what-we-do/planning/london-plan/current-london-plan/london-plan-overview-and-introduction/london (accessed September 2020).

8 'What powers does the Mayor have for planning applications?', Greater London Authority, https://www.london.gov.uk/what-we-do/planning/planning-applications-and-decisions/what-powers-does-mayor-have-planning-applications (accessed September 2020).

9 'Greater London Authority Act 2007', The National Archives, https://www.legislation.gov.uk/ukpga/2007/24/contents (accessed September 2020), and 'The Town and Country Planning (Mayor of London) Order 2008', The National Archives, https://www.legislation.gov.uk/uksi/2008/580/contents/made (accessed September 2020).

10 'Mayoral Community Infrastructure Levy', Greater London Authority, https://www.london.gov.uk/what-we-do/planning/implementing-london-plan/mayoral-community-infrastructure-levy (accessed September 2020).

11 'Great Fire of London: How Science Rebuilt a City', Science Museum, 28 August 2019, https://www.sciencemuseum.org.uk/objects-and-stories/great-fire-london-how-science-rebuilt-city (accessed August 2020).

12 Duncan Bowie, *Politics, Planning and Homes in a World City* (London: Routledge, 2010), p. 16.

13 Marcus Fairs, 'Interview: Renzo Piano on The Shard', *Dezeen*, 18 May 2012 and Will Dahlgreen, 'Londoners grow fond of the Shard', YouGov, 13 April 2014, https://yougov.co.uk/topics/politics/articles-reports/2014/04/13/londoners-grow-fond-shard (accessed August 2020).

14 'The Town and Country Planning (Mayor of London) Order 200, The National Archives, https://www.legislation.gov.uk/uksi/2000/1493/made (accessed September 2020).

15 Matt Weaver, 'Prescott approves disputed "shard of glass" tower', *The Guardian*, 20 November 2003.

16 Rowan Moore, 'The Shard: a symbol of towering ambition', *The Guardian*, 30 January 2011.

17 'Mayor backs London Olympic bid', BBC News, 1 November 2002.

18 Private interview.

19 Simon Parker, 'Interview: Ken Livingstone', *Prospect*, 29 April 2007.

20 Ibid.

21 Private interview.

22 Crispin Dowler, 'Boris reveals his plans to thaw frozen market', *Inside Housing*, 28 November 2008.

23 Nancy Holman, 'The changing nature of the London Plan', in Kath Scanlon and Ben Kochan (eds), *London: Coping With Austerity* (London: LSE, 2010), pp. 29–40, p. 37.

24 Ibid.

25 A striking exchange during a debate in the 2008 election campaign went roughly as follows. Johnson: 'I don't mind tall buildings as long as they are in the right place.' Livingstone: 'Well, you wouldn't want them in the *wrong* place, would you, Boris?'

26 Richard Waite, 'Islington Council attacks Boris over Mount Pleasant approval', *Architect's Journal*, 3 October 2014.

27 Dave Hill, 'How will Sadiq Khan's 35 per cent affordable housing threshold work?', OnLondon, 18 August 2017, https://www.onlondon.co.uk/how-will-sadiq-khans-35-affordable-housing-threshold-work/ (accessed September 2020).

28 Dave Hill, 'LSE report shows value of overseas housing investment, despite its flaws', OnLondon, 16 June 2017, https://www.onlondon.co.uk/lse-report-shows-value-of-overseas-housing-investment-despite-its-flaws/ (accessed August 2020).

29 'Draft London Plan – Consultation and Minor Suggested Changes', Mayor of London, https://www.london.gov.uk/what-we-do/planning/london-plan/new-london-plan/draft-london-plan-consultation-and-minor-suggested-changes (accessed August 2020).

30 'The Green Belt: A Place for Londoners?', London First, May 2018, https://www.londonfirst.co.uk/sites/default/files/documents/2018-05/Green-Belt.pdf (accessed September 2020).

31 Richard Brown, 'Is it time to review London's green belt', Centre for London, 6 August 2019, https://www.centreforlondon.org/blog/green-belt/ (accessed August 2020).

32 Robert Jenrick MP, 'Letter to the Mayor of London', Ministry of Housing, Communities and Local Government, 13 March 2020, https://www.london.gov.uk/sites/default/files/letter_to_the_mayor_of_london_13_march_2020.pdf (accessed August 2020).

16: HOUSING

1 'London mayoral election: Housing top concern, poll suggests', BBC News, 1 April 2016.

2   The Valuation Office Agency did not produce borough-level rents data before 2011, so it is not possible to produce a comparable map for the first decade of the mayoral period.

3   'Affordable Housing and Viability Supplementary Planning Guidance', Greater London Authority, https://www.london.gov.uk/what-we-do/planning/implementing-london-plan/london-plan-guidance-and-spgs/affordable-housing-and-viability-supplementary-planning-guidance-spg (accessed September 2020).

4   'Homes for Londoners – affordable homes programme 2017/21 – approval of programme budget', Greater London Authority, 2017.

5   'Housing in London 2019: The evidence base for the Mayor's Housing Strategy', Greater London Authority, 2019, https://data.london.gov.uk/dataset/housing-london (accessed September 2020).

6   Duncan Bowie, *Politics, Planning and Homes in a World City* (London: Routledge, 2010), p. 6.

7   Karen West et al., 'The Greater London Authority: problems of strategy integration', *Policy and Politics* (October 2003), vol. 31, issue 4, p. 485.

8   Ibid, p. 482.

9   Simon Parker, 'Interview: Ken Livingstone', *Prospect*, 29 April 2007.

10 'Ken Livingstone: London needs some more clusters of tall buildings', *The Independent*, 13 June 2001.

11 Richard Rogers, *Towards an Urban Renaissance: The Report of the Urban Task Force* (London: Urban Task Force, 1999).

12 Ken Livingstone speaking at Mayor's Question Time, 28 February 2001, cited in Yvonne Rydin et al., 'The Greater London Authority – a Case of Conflict of Culture? Evidence from the Planning and Environmental Policy Domains', *Environment and Planning C: Government and Policy* (February 2004), vol. 22, issue 1, p. 66.

13 Jerry White, 'The Greater London Council, 1965–1986', in Ben Kochan (ed.) *London Government 50 Years of Debate: The Contribution of LSE's Greater London Group* (London: LSE, 2008).

14 Peter Adams, 'Ken Livingstone Defends Housing Record as London Mayor', Property Notify, 14 June 2019, https://www.propertynotify.co.uk/news/ken-livingstone-defends-housing-record-as-london-mayor/ (accessed August 2020).

15 Adapted from Fanny Blanc, Kath Scanlon and Tim White, 'Living in a denser London: How residents see their homes', LSE London and LSE Cities, March 2020, https://www.lse.ac.uk/cities/Assets/Documents/2020-LSE-Density-Report-digital.pdf (accessed August 2020).

16 Duncan Bowie, *Politics, Planning and Homes in a World City*.

17 Fiona Hamilton, 'Boris Johnson to end London's hobbit habit with 50,000 new homes', *The Times*, 21 November 2008.

18 'No "Kosovo-style cleansing" of poor says Johnson', BBC News, 28 October 2010.

19 Matthew Carmona, 'The London Way: The Politics of London's Strategic Design', *Architectural Design* (January 2012), vol. 82, issue 1, p. 42.

20 Kath Scanlon et al., 'Housing zones as new housing acceleration tools', LSE Blogs, 7 March 2016, https://blogs.lse.ac.uk/lselondon/housing-zones-as-new-housing-acceleration-tools/ (accessed August 2020).

21 'Housing in London: 2019', Greater London Authority, September 2019, https://www.london.gov.uk/sites/default/files/housing_in_london_2019.pdf (accessed August 2020).

22 Loretta Lees and Hannah White, 'The social cleansing of London council estates: everyday experiences of "accumulative dispossession"', *Housing Studies* (November 2019), pp. 1–22.

23 'Housing in London: 2019', Greater London Authority, September 2019.

24 Nick Gallant et al., 'Can "Permission in Principle" for New Housing in England Increase Certainty, Reduce "Planning Risk", and Accelerate Housing Supply?', *Planning Theory and Practice* (October 2019), vol. 20, issue 5, pp. 673–88.

25 Simon Jeffrey, 'Delivering Change: How city partnerships make the most of public assets', Centre for Cities, June 2017, https://www.centreforcities.org/wp-content/uploads/2017/06/17-06-15-City-Assets.pdf (accessed August 2020).

26 '2004 London Housing Capacity Study', Mayor of London, July 2005, https://www.lbbd.gov. uk/sites/default/files/attachments/London-Housing-Capacity-Study-20041%2019.22.55.pdf (accessed September 2020).

27 'July 2020 update on the implementation of the Grenfell Tower Inquiry Phase 1 recommendations', Mayor of London, https://www.london.gov.uk/sites/default/files/mayor_ update_gti_recommendations_july_2020.pdf (accessed August 2020).

28 Kate Proctor, 'Sadiq Khan says London election will be vote on rent controls', *The Guardian*, 3 March 2020.

29 'Reforming private renting: The Mayor of London's blueprint', Greater London Authority, July 2019, https://www.london.gov.uk/sites/default/files/reforming_private_renting_-_the_ mayor_of_londons_blueprint.pdf (accessed August 2020).

30 'London Plan annual monitoring report 15, 2017/18', Greater London Authority, October 2019, https://www.london.gov.uk/sites/default/files/amr_15_final.pdf (accessed August 2020), p. 71.

31 Ibid.

18: CIVIC LEADERSHIP

1 Interview with City business figure, May 2020.

2 Livingstone, speech at Royal Opera House, 2007, 'Livingstone stands for third term', BBC News, 3 May 2007.

3 Interview with City business figure, May 2020.

4 Ibid.

5 See, for example: 'Johnson defends "pariah" bankers', BBC News, 5 October 2009.

6 Private interview.

7 Private interview.

8 Joe Murphy, '100 business leaders back Mayor contender Khan to be their "friend at City Hall"', *Evening Standard*, 1 April 2016.

9 Interview with former GLA official, May 2020.

10 Interview with former GLA official, May 2020.

11 Interview with City business figure, May 2020.

12 Ibid.

13 'Boris Johnson "shocked" by news of Bob Crow's death – video', *The Guardian*, 11 March 2014.

14 *Any Questions*, BBC Radio 4, 25 March 2011.

15 'Bob Crow calls to Boris Johnson during radio phone in show', BBC News, 4 February 2014.

16 Interviews with former TfL official and RMT official, June 2020.

17 Thomas Mackintosh, 'London Underground: More than 36,000 shifts lost to Tube strikes', BBC News, 10 September 2019.

18 Interview with former TfL official, June 2020.

19 Ibid.

20 Anna Mikhailova, 'Boris Johnson attacks "dubious" campaign to "photoshop" Britain's history', *Daily Telegraph*, 14 June 2020.

21 Private interview.

22 Peter Tatchell, 'Ken apologises (sort of)', *The Guardian*, 7 April 2008.

23 'Ken Livingstone stands by Hitler comments', BBC News, 30 April 2016.

24 Jonathan Freedland, 'I've backed Ken Livingstone for mayor before, but this time I just can't do it', *The Guardian*, 23 March 2012.

25 Nilima Marshall, 'London mayor Sadiq Khan: You do not commit these disgusting acts in my name', *The Independent* (Ireland), 5 June 2017.

26 Caroline Davies, 'Boris Johnson heckled in Clapham Junction over London riots', *The Guardian*, 9 August 2011.

27 'London Mayor Ken Livingstone wins appeal against suspension', Landmark Chambers, 19 October 2006, https://www.landmarkchambers.co.uk/resources/cases/london-mayor-ken-livingstone-wins-appeal-against-suspension/ (accessed September 2020).

28 'Mayor's aide: Police move in', *Evening Standard*, 28 January 2008.

29 'Ken Livingstone to quit Labour amid anti-Semitism row', BBC News, 21 May 2018.

30 'London Mayor Boris Johnson swears over "News International links" story', BBC News, 30 April 2012.

31 Ian Dunt, 'Boris shouts at journalists over phone-hacking "codswallop"', politics.co.uk, 18 July 2011, https://www.politics.co.uk/news/2011/07/18/boris-shouts-at-journalists-over-phone-hackin (accessed September 2020).

32 Interview with former GLA official, May 2020.

33 @realDonaldTrump, 3 June 2019.

34 Matthew Weaver, 'Timeline: Donald Trump's feud with Sadiq Khan', *The Guardian*, 16 June 2019.

35 Richard Spender, 'Livingstone compares poll tax riots to China massacre', *Daily Telegraph*, 10 April 2006.

36 'Boris Johnson rugby tackles schoolboy in Japan: His other sporting slips', BBC News, 15 October 2015.

20: CULTURE AND SOFT POWER

1 Richard Rogers and Mark Fisher, *A New London* (London: Penguin, 1991).

2 London Planning Advisory Committee, *London: World City Moving Into the 21st Century* (London: London Planning Advisory Committee, 1991).

3 'HLF Major Grants – The first 100, Heritage Lottery Fund, June 2015, https://www.heritagefund.org.uk/sites/default/files/media/research/hlf_major_grants_-_the_first_100.pdf (accessed August 2020).

4 'Creative Industries Mapping Document', Department for Culture, Media and Sport, 1998, https://assets.publishing.service.gov.uk/government/uploads/system/uploads/attachment_data/file/183544/2001part1-foreword2001.pdf (accessed August 2020).

5 Greater London Authority Act 1999, https://www.legislation.gov.uk/ukpga/1999/29/notes/division/5/10 (accessed August 2020), Sections 375 and 376.

6 Ken Livingstone, 'Festivals play their part in fighting racism', *The Guardian*, 6 June 2008.

7 See generally: https://creativeindustrieslondon.com (accessed August 2020).

8 'Creative London', report of the Mayor's Commission on the Creative Industries, London Development Agency, 2004.

9 'London Cultural Capital: Realising the potential of a world-class city', Greater London Authority, April 2004, https://www.haringey.gov.uk/sites/haringeygovuk/files/london_cultural_capital-realising_the_potential..._mol_2004_red-v1-2.pdf (accessed September 2020).

10 Matthew Carmona, Claudio de Magalhães, Leo Hammond (eds), *Public Space: The Management Dimension* (London: Routledge, 2008), p. 180.

11 Dave Hill, 'Veronica Wadley affair: gush, denial and gritted teeth', *The Guardian*, 11 June 2010.

12 'Cultural Metropolis: The Mayor's Priorities for Culture 2009 – 2012', Greater London Authority, 2008, http://www.welllondon.org.uk/files/969/culture-tradition/8.%20Cultural%20Metropolis%20-%20The%20Mayor's%20Priorities%20for%20Culture%20.pdf (accessed August 2020).

13 'Our Remarkable Year for London: London & Partners 2012–13 Review', London & Partners, https://files.londonandpartners.com/l-and-p/assets/our-annual-review-2012-13.pdf (accessed September 2020).

14 'Tech Nation: Powering the Digital Economy', Tech City UK, 2015, https://technation.io/wp-content/uploads/2018/04/Tech-Nation-Report-2015.pdf (accessed August 2020).

15 'Cultural Infrastructure Plan', Greater London Authority, 2019, https://www.london.gov.uk/sites/default/files/cultural_infrastructure_plan_online.pdf (accessed August 2020).

16 'What we do', Film London, https://filmlondon.org.uk/what-we-do (accessed August 2020).

17 Ibid.

18 Agenda and minutes from Barking and Dagenham Planning Committee meeting, 10 July 2020, https://modgov.lbbd.gov.uk/Internet/ieListDocuments.aspx?CId=176&MId=10048&Ver=4 (accessed September 2020).

19 'London & Partners' Business Plan 2018/19' and '2019/20', https://www.londonandpartners. com/about-us/our-business-strategy-and-economic-impact (accessed August 2020).

20 'Culture for all Londoners', Greater London Authority, 2018, https://www.london.gov.uk/sites/ default/files/2018_culture_strategy_1212_single.pdf (accessed August 2020).

21 Culture for all Londoners', Greater London Authority.

22 'Cultural Infrastructure Plan', Greater London Authority and 'Creative Supply Chains Study', Greater London Authority, 2019, https://www.london.gov.uk/sites/default/files/creative_ supply_chains_study_final_191011.pdf (accessed August 2020).

22: ARCHITECTURE AND DESIGN

1 Nancy Holman, 'The changing nature of the London Plan', in Kath Scanlon and Ben Kochan (eds), *London: Coping With Austerity* (London: LSE, 2010), pp. 29–40.

2 'The London Plan', Greater London Authority, February 2004, https://www.london.gov.uk/ sites/default/files/the_london_plan_2004.pdf (accessed August 2020).

3 Michèle Champenois, '*L'ouverture du Centre Culturel des Halles L'architecture bouche-trou*', *Le Monde*, 22 February 1983. https://www.london.gov.uk/file/259533/download?token=0SIzHSPs (accessed August 2020).

4 '"Appeal fund"' for Mandela statue', BBC News, 5 November 2004.

5 'The London Plan', Greater London Authority, February 2004, https://www.london.gov.uk/ sites/default/files/the_london_plan_2004.pdf (accessed August 2020).

6 Alastair Jamieson, 'The Prince of Wales on architecture: his 10 "monstrous carbuncles"', *Daily Telegraph*, 13 May 2009.

7 Rowan Moore and Mira Bar-Hillel, 'Is Heron best for London's skyline?', *Evening Standard*, 22 October 2001.

8 Deyan Sudjic, 'Dizzy heights', *The Observer*, 31 July 2005.

9 Rowan Moore, 'Boris Johnson's dire legacy for London', *The Observer*, 10 April 2016.

10 'London Housing Design Guide', London Development Agency, August 2010, https://www. london.gov.uk/sites/default/files/Interim%20London%20Housing%20Design%20Guide.pdf (accessed August 2020).

11 'The Emperor's New Housing', &\also think tank, https://www.hawkinsbrown.com/cms/ documents/Emporers-new-housing-PDF-reduce.pdf (accessed August 2020).

12 Rowan Moore, 'Boris Johnson's dire legacy for London'.

13 Kate Proctor, 'Sadiq Khan fails to build any social housing in year as Mayor', *Evening Standard*, 16 August 2017.

14 'The London Plan: Intend to Publish', Greater London Authority, December 2019, https://www. london.gov.uk/sites/default/files/intend_to_publish_-_clean.pdf (accessed September 2020).

15 'Sadiq Khan targets house building by relaxing planning laws', BBC News, 29 November 2017.

16 Andrew Woodcock, 'Sadiq Khan plans to move office as coronavirus leaves £500m black hole in London's finances', *The Independent*, 24 June 2020.

CONCLUSION: THE GLA AT TWENTY AND THE FUTURE OF LONDON GOVERNMENT

1 Christopher Hope, 'Exclusive: Rural communities could get their own directly elected mayors and historic county names', *Daily Telegraph*, 6 September 2020.

2 See, for example: David Maddox, 'Alex Salmond: London is "dark star of the economy"', *The Scotsman*, 4 March 2014, and Nazia Parveen, 'More than half UK investment in transport is in London, says study', *The Guardian*, 20 February 2017.

3 See, for example: Luke Raikes, Arianna Giovannini and Bianca Getzel, 'Divided and connected: Regional inequalities in the North, the UK and the developed world – State of the North 2019', IPPR North, 27 November 2019, https://www.ippr.org/research/publications/ state-of-the-north-2019 (accessed August 2020).

4 'Get Brexit Done, Unleash Britain's Potential: The Conservative and Unionist Party Manifesto

2019', Conservative Party, https://assets-global.website-files.com/5da42e2cae7ebd3f8bde353c/
5dda924905da587992a064ba_Conservative%202019%20Manifesto.pdf (accessed August 2020),
pp. 25–9.

5 See, for example: 'Executive Summary', 'London's Poverty Profile 2017', Trust for London/New
Policy Institute, October 2017, https://www.trustforlondon.org.uk/publications/londons-
poverty-profile-2017/ (accessed September 2020), p. 2.

6 For a fuller exposition of this issue see: Tony Travers, 'London within England: A City State?',
in Michael Kenny, Iain McLean and Akash Paun (eds), *Governing England: English Identity and
Institutions in a Changing United Kingdom* (Oxford: Oxford University Press, 2018), pp. 219–21.

7 'GDP monthly estimate, UK: June 2020', Office for National Statistics, https://www.ons.
gov.uk/economy/grossdomesticproductgdp/bulletins/gdpmonthlyestimateuk/june2020
(accessed September 2020).

8 Joanna Partridge, 'UK office workers slower to return to their desk after Covid', *The Guardian*,
5 August 2020.

9 'Transport use during the coronavirus (Covid-19) pandemic', Department for Transport, 3
June 2020, https://www.gov.uk/government/statistics/transport-use-during-the-coronavirus-
covid-19-pandemic (accessed August 2020).

10 Sarah Whitebloom, 'Covid-19 Insights from history, Oxford Science Blog, https://www.ox.ac.
uk/news/science-blog/covid-19-insights-history-0 (accessed August 2020).

11 Robert Jenrick MP, 'Letter to the Mayor of London', Ministry of Housing, Communities and
Local Government, 13 March 2020, https://www.london.gov.uk/sites/default/files/letter_to_
the_mayor_of_london_13_march_2020.pdf (accessed August 2020).

12 Jessica Clark, 'Housing secretary Robert Jenrick slams Sadiq Khan's London homes plan', *City
A.M.*, 13 March 2020.

13 'What has the impact been on TfL's finances? Coronavirus (Covid-19) FAQs', Greater London
Authority, https://www.london.gov.uk/coronavirus/coronavirus-covid-19-faqs/what-has-
impact-been-tfls-finances (accessed September 2020).

14 'Government grants Transport for London funding package', Department for Transport, 15
May 2020, https://www.gov.uk/government/news/government-grants-transport-for-london-
funding-package (accessed August 2020).

15 'Passenger Rail Performance 2019-20 Q4 Statistical Release', Office for Rail and Road,
https://dataportal.orr.gov.uk/statistics/performance/passenger-rail-performance/ (accessed
September 2020), p. 9, and Jim Pickard, Tanya Powley and Gill Plimmer, 'UK rail bailout hits
£3.5bn and set to rise further', *Financial Times*, 18 June 2020.

16 'London's transport agency needs a new funding model', *The Economist*, 1 August 2020.

17 John Elledge, 'Seven thoughts on TfL's bail out from national government', CityMetric, 15
May 2020, https://www.citymetric.com/transport/seven-thoughts-tfl-s-bail-out-national-
government-5111 (accessed August 2020).

18 'Planning for the Future', Ministry of Housing, Communities and Local Government,
6 August 2020, https://www.gov.uk/government/consultations/planning-for-the-future
(accessed August 2020).

19 Tom Welsh, 'The question can no longer be avoided: is it time to scrap the mayor of London?',
Daily Telegraph, 21 June 2020.

20 'Budget 2020: Delivering on our Promises to the British People', HC 121, HM Treasury, 11
March 2020, https://assets.publishing.service.gov.uk/government/uploads/system/uploads/
attachment_data/file/871799/Budget_2020_Web_Accessible_Complete.pdf (accessed August
2020). p. 48.

21 See comments by Gareth Bacon (assembly member and MP) in Michael Savage, 'Whitehall
"power grab" raises fears about who's really running London', *The Observer*, 16 August 2020.

INDEX